THE

RABBI

WHO

FOUND

MESSIAH

THE

THE STORY OF YITZHAK KADURI

RABBI

AND HIS PROPHECIES OF THE ENDTIME

WHO

FOUND

BY **CARL GALLUPS**

MESSIAH

WND Books

THE RABBI WHO FOUND MESSIAH

DEDICATION

My wife, Pam, was Valedictorian of our high school. From the fifth grade through our senior year, she never made less than an "A." We married shortly after our graduation and have been together happily ever since.

I am convinced nothing worthwhile that has come from my life and ministry could have been accomplished without her by my side. I am certain the Lord knew this when He brought her into my life years ago. Therefore, it is to Pam that this work is lovingly dedicated.

I also dedicate this book to the subsequent treasures resulting from my life's journey with my precious wife . . . my son Brandon, my daughter-in-law Hannah, and my grandson Parker.

And it shall come to pass in the last days, saith God, I will pour out of my Spirit upon all flesh: and your sons and your daughters shall prophesy, and your young men shall see visions, and your old men shall dream dreams: And on my servants and on my handmaidens I will pour out in those days of my Spirit; and they shall prophesy: And I will shew wonders in heaven above, and signs in the earth beneath; blood, and fire, and vapour of smoke: The sun shall be turned into darkness, and the moon into blood, before the great and notable day of the Lord come: And it shall come to pass, that whosoever shall call on the name of the Lord shall be saved.

—Acts 2:17–21, from Joel 2:28–32

RABBI YITZHAK KADURI

(Yitzhak also spelled Yitzchak; Kaduri also spelled Kadouri,
Kadourie, and Kedourie)

Ca. 1898–January 28, 2006

Estimated age at time of death: 106–116 years old

CONTENTS

ACKNOWLEDGMENTS

I wish to first acknowledge you, the reader, for not only reading this book, but also for taking a moment to read this particular section. Without the following people assisting and encouraging me along the way, this book might not have become a reality.

All of these people have played a significant part in my life and, most recently, in my writing endeavors. For this reason, I wish to recognize them here and express my thanks.

My father and mother—Bill and Holly Gallups.

My father- and mother-in-law—Nelson and Marlene Blount.

The entire church family of Hickory Hammock Baptist Church in Milton, Florida. We have been serving our Lord together since 1987. They are a magnificent church family.

To the Hickory Hammock Baptist Church staff whose efforts made it possible for me to have the time to write this book: Dr. Greg Robards, Senior Associate Pastor; Rev. Jim Rinehart, Associate Pastor and Worship Minister; Mrs. Amie Morrell, Senior Administrative Assistant; and Mrs. Joanne Parker, Administrative Assistant.

Mike Shoesmith, Executive Editor of the *PPSIMMONS*

News and Ministry sites.

Jeff Kuhner, *The Kuhner Report*, WRKO in Boston, Massachusetts.

Dr. Grace Vuoto, Editor of Politics and Culture for the *World Tribune*.

Dr. Mark Foley, President, University of Mobile, Mobile, Alabama.

Dr. Chuck Kelley, President, New Orleans Baptist Theological Seminary, New Orleans, Louisiana.

Greg Burnley, Captain (Ret.), Florida Highway Patrol.

Donna Tucker, Lee and Darlene Parker, and all the wonderful people of the Santa Rosa County Chamber of Commerce, Santa Rosa County, Florida.

I have had a long relationship (since 2002) with the following people at 1330 WEBY—Northwest Florida's Talk Radio. They have been of great encouragement and assistance to me: Mike Bates, Owner/Manager; Mike Mashburn, Host of *Open Mic*; Dave Daughtry, Host of *Morning Folks*; Mallory Bardwell, Programmer/Producer; Anthony Daughtery, Programmer/Producer; Joey Wallace, Programmer/Producer; and Barbara Baker, Secretary.

Several congregations of people, besides the church where I pastor, have encouraged me and supported me in my writing endeavors. They are dearly appreciated for their prayers and support.

Dr. Dennis Brunet and Midway Baptist Church, Midway, Florida. Dr. Brunet offered much valuable counsel upon the undertaking of this project.

Rev. Tim Bullington and The Church on the Hill, Dundee, Florida.

Dr. Fred Lackey and West Side Baptist Church, Jasper, Alabama.

Rev. Brad Lowery and New Prospect Baptist Church, Lawrenceburg, Tennessee.

Dr. Rick Kelley and First Baptist Church of Monticello, Florida.

Rev. Larry Harkness and Saragossa Baptist Church, Nauvoo, Alabama.

And lastly, and most particularly, to all the wonderful staff at WND Books. They have been excruciatingly patient, professional, and ever helpful. To them I am deeply grateful. My special thanks are extended to: Aryana Hendrawan, Renee Chavez, Michael Thompson, George Escobar (WND Films), Elizabeth Farah, and to Joseph Farah for inspiring the topic and the research.

FOREWORD

I first encountered Carl Gallups when I read his best-selling book *The Magic Man in the Sky*. I was enthralled by the book, and when I finished reading it, I wanted to shout, "Wow!" He clearly demonstrated that he could use both Scripture and logic to prove the existence of God and to destroy the so-called scientific foundation of the theory of evolution.

I got in touch with him immediately to compliment him on his outstanding achievement and to invite him to appear on my television program. That's when we got personally acquainted, and I had the joy of experiencing firsthand his zeal for the Lord and his love of the Word of God.

Carl is a master communicator, both orally and in writing. And he has a gift for being able to provide biblical interpretations to contemporary national and international issues.

This book is completely different from his first one. It reads more like a mystery novel. Carl was in the field of law enforcement for ten years before he entered the ministry, and his training as an investigator clearly shows up in this book as he applies investigative techniques to analyze one of the most explosive events in the modern history of Orthodox Judaism.

So, get ready to be captivated by the story of an event that recently shook the foundations of Orthodox Judaism. You will be fascinated by the event, and you will be mesmerized by Carl's insightful analysis of it.

—Dr. David R. Reagan
Founder, Lamb & Lion Ministries
Host, Christ in Prophecy television program

PROLOGUE

Jesus Christ is Lord. He is the soon-coming Messiah. Those are the preeminent proclamations of the New Testament and the Christian world.

Mahdi will come with a company of his chosen ones. Jesus will come with the Mahdi. That is what the Muslim religion declares.

Mashiach ben David *will ultimately appear and rule and reign from Jerusalem, thus establishing Israel as first among the nations.* This is the messianic hope and the claim of the Jewish world.

So, why would a 108-year-old Jewish rabbi, reportedly one of the most famous in the entirety of Jewish history, claim something different than what a rabbinical Orthodox Jew might expect? Why would this venerated, aged rabbi upset the religious applecart in such dramatic fashion and thus jeopardize all of his life's work and his eternal legacy? Read on. What you will discover may very well astound you.

[The elderly Rabbi Kaduri] had his own consulting rooms in the Old City, where he taught clients how to predict the future by divining secret texts hidden in the Psalms, or how to summon angels to help overcome personal problems.

He refused money for these services, and worked as a bookbinder to keep body and soul together. The Jerusalem writer Haim Be'er recalled: "His appearance was striking; he radiated a great deal of human warmth. [Whenever he] passed by, people would whisper, 'There goes a truly righteous individual.'"[1]

—Lawrence Joffe

ADORED BY MILLIONS

I have seen the Messiah! And I know who He is—I know His name.
I know where He is. I know when He is coming. Furthermore, you will
know these things as well—one year after my death.

—Rabbi Yitzhak Kaduri

The above is not an exact quote from the venerated late
Rabbi Yitzhak Kaduri; however, it paraphrases a collection of documented declarations he made in the final
years and even the final days of his life. Rabbi Kaduri's
controversial kabbalistic (Jewish mystic) prophecies—as well as
his deep connections to the powerful politics of both nineteenth-
century Palestine and modern-day Israel—make him one of the

most intriguing characters of our time.

Kaduri's fascinating life spanned the years of three centuries, beginning on an unknown date in the late 1800s, and ending with his death in January 2006. He lived in the land of his ancestors before it was once again proclaimed to be Israel. He was there when the nation claimed and then gained its independence.[1] And he lived to see many of the horrors of Jewish persecution— including the rise of the Muslim Brotherhood, the reign of Hitler, the atrocities of World War II, and every war launched against Israel until the early years of the twenty-first century.

Rabbi Kaduri was something of a Jewish male version of Mother Teresa. He was known not only for his astounding prophecies but also for his tender displays of ministry, mercy, and a life of simplicity. Millions adored him.

I became interested in his story about a year after his death, when *Israel Today*[2] ran a news piece, in several languages, stating that Rabbi Kaduri had hand-scribbled a note declaring that the name of the *true Messiah* would be revealed. The catch was that the note could not be opened and inspected until one year *after* his death. Until that revealing, the note was to be kept under lock and key.[3]

Reportedly, his instructions were followed to the letter.

On the day of the unveiling, the contents of the scrawled note stunned the world—that is, the few parts of the world that were willing to *print* and reveal its message. And that was the problem. The words were too shocking, particularly to the Judeo-Christian community. The note's cryptic message was embarrassing and blasphemous to many, uplifting and too-good-to-be-true to others. Some people were even enraged.

Mere months after *Israel Today* ran the in-depth exposé on the note and the events leading up to the rabbi's revelation, the web article was apparently pulled. Some claimed the story was purposely scrubbed. If that was the case, it was simply too late to hide the affair. The note was out, and the message reverberated throughout synagogues, churches, and Internet chat rooms the world over.

However, *Israel Today* has assured me, in writing, that the article was not *scrubbed*—there was nothing nefarious about its disappearance.

In an official statement concerning the renowned Rabbi Yitzhak Kaduri story, *Israel Today*'s Mr. Ryan Jones wrote:

> We did a revamp of our website earlier this year, and simply have not gotten around to putting all of our older content back online.
>
> It [the original story] will be put back online soon. We absolutely stand by the original article.[4]

In further clarification of the matter, Mr. Jones explained that the Internet story on Rabbi Kaduri was the cover story for *Israel Today*'s print magazine. The original Internet article was restored on May 30, 2013, and can now, once again, be found on the *Israel Today* Internet site.[5]

Today, because of the continually unfolding events connected to the rabbi's cryptic message, and the undeniably prophetic times in which we live, the note's significance continues to resonate. Three of the world's largest monotheistic religions—Judaism, Islam, and Christianity—believe a Messiah, of some type, is to appear relatively soon. Each of these faith systems is looking for its own version or understanding of this Messiah. Accordingly, Kaduri's message captured the imagination of the world's *Messiah seekers*—and continues to reverberate around the world. To this day, the note still has life. Millions, in anxious anticipation, are watching the political and sometimes seemingly prophetic events of the world, *especially* as they may relate to Kaduri's note and his end-of-life pronouncements.

One of the most stunning of these pronouncements was that the Messiah would not appear until the occurence of a particular individual's death. That individual just happened to be, at the time of Kaduri's statement, one of the most popular and controversial political and military figures in Israel. Once again, the ancient rabbi had shocked the world.

So, who is this renowned individual? Read on. Following is the story of the Rabbi Yitzhak Kaduri and the death note that shook, and still shakes, the Judeo-Christian world. It is a story that is not finished—and perhaps will not be finished . . . until the coming of the *Messiah*.

THE YOUNG RABBI AND HIS VISION

rabbi
noun:

1: master, teacher—used by Jews as a term of address
2: a Jew qualified to expound and apply the halacha and other Jewish law
3: a Jew trained and ordained for professional religious leadership; *specifically*: the official leader of a Jewish congregation
         —Merriam-Webster Dictionary

ome say the old rabbi was 108. Others say he was older.[1] But everyone who knew the man claimed the rabbi had received a glorious vision from *HaShem*.[2] And supposedly, that sacred vision from the Holy One of Israel had revealed to the ancient little Jewish sage the name of the *true Messiah*.

Many believed the old Jew was simply delusional, too aged

to know what he was saying, and perhaps a bit senile as well. A number of people at the time claimed the old man had plainly said that *Jesus* was the name of the *true* Messiah, and that soon He would reveal Himself to Israel and to the world. But how could *that* be? A Jewish rabbi would never say such a thing. Or would he? And if so, how *could* he? The story simply did not make sense.

Up until the very last, he had been an inspirational leader—a teacher of Israel. But to some, his visions were becoming more difficult to understand. Still others said the old rabbi never wrote the note he was supposed to have written. *It wasn't even his handwriting*, they claimed. *It was a mere hoax*, numerous people insisted. Whatever the case, there it was, in black and white.

A vision, a dream, a note, a cryptic message, a Yom Kippur announcement, mysterious and occultic *Pulsa Denura* (lashings of fire) death curses, a prophecy of impending death laid upon the soul of a revered Israeli warrior and statesman, vehement denials, and incessant spinning of information. What was happening? Had the beloved old rabbi gone mad? Perhaps . . . but doubtful. Regardless, the intrigue continues to this day.

***

Could it really be that the Messiah of Yahweh would appear in the *flesh*, or even in a vision or a dream, and reveal Himself to a Jewish rabbi as the one and true Messiah? Is that actually a plausibility? Why would Messiah do such an incredible thing in the first place? Furthermore, what if that rabbi had been deeply involved in wickedness of some sort, maybe even in strange and unbiblical customs? What if he had devoted himself to teaching *against* Christianity or had actually struck out against Christians?

Before we embark on the remarkable journey of Rabbi Yitzhak Kaduri, let us journey back in time for a moment and remember the account, as recorded in the New Testament, of another venerated rabbi, a teacher of the Law, and a leader among the Jews. Our story begins where it must, in downtown Jerusalem, in the heart of ancient Judaism . . . almost two thousand years ago. The New Testament book of Acts records the narrative. It is primarily a story about Jews, Jewish leaders, Jewish authorities, early Jewish converts to Christianity, and a celebrated Jewish rabbi.

CIRCA AD 34

He was a young man, full of the power of God, grace, and wisdom. He had only moments earlier been personally presented, along with six other men newly chosen by the congregation of believers, to the apostles of the first distinctly Christian church the world had ever known. His name was Stephen.

The apostles—Peter, James, and John, revered shepherds of the fledgling flock of God—laid hands on Stephen and his partners in ministry, and prayed over them. These freshly selected men were then charged with the immediate task of settling a dispute among the Grecian Jews and the Hebraic Jews.

The contentious dispute involved the daily distribution of food. It seemed some of the Grecian widows were complaining that they were being overlooked in the meal distribution process in favor of the Hebrew widows.

The task appeared simple enough—mundane, even. A few logistical details to work out, but not overly difficult. However, it was in the supremacy of Stephen's simple performance of that duty that the Lord of the universe began to move in his life in an extraordinary way. Stephen had been faithful with the one talent newly bestowed upon him; now God would confer upon him a myriad of spiritual gifts.

God anointed Stephen with a special endowment of miraculous power, equipping him for the ministry to which he had been called and ordained. He began to preach and teach with a spiritual authority that was striking and deeply convicting. People were healed when Stephen prayed for them. And through his divinely inspired messages, often delivered in and around Solomon's colonnade in the Temple courts, a large number of priests were converted to a belief in Jesus Christ as Messiah.

News of Stephen's persuasive powers reverberated throughout the Sanhedrin, the Jews' supreme council. Synagogue after synagogue began to speak out against the young Christian preacher. Soon Stephen was invited to speak before various groups of Jews, not because they wanted to hear his message, but because they desired to humiliate him publicly.

But they could not prevail against his persuasive presentations. Instead, his preaching grew more powerful. More priests were saved and began to declare, without shame, that Jesus Christ was Messiah.

Jewish anger continued to boil. It seemed this *Jesus* thing was not really dead after all. Sure, there had been a cross—there had been a crucifixion. There had even been a burial, with the tomb sealed and guarded by a Roman cohort of soldiers. But there had also been an alleged resurrection—and now a *church*! These followers of Jesus were multiplying like mice—in spite of Jesus's earthly absence. Stephen, a faithful Jew, had now become a very sharp thorn in the side of Rabbinic Judaism. He needed to be eliminated—quickly.

It was settled. The trap was set.

"We have heard Stephen speak words of blasphemy against Moses and against God!" his accusers cried out, with great displays of Hebraic drama, to an audience of Jewish elders from the heart of Jerusalem.

"Well then, we have no choice but to hear this matter before the Sanhedrin," the elders agreed, with a collective wink. And the order was given: "Arrest Stephen, and bring him before the Sanhedrin." The Sanhedrin's power was given by the full authority of Rome.

Stephen was seized by evil men, with murder in their hearts, and dragged before the Jewish ruling council, where council-friendly witnesses continued to heap up their charges against him: "This fellow never stops speaking against this holy place and against the Law! We have heard him preach that Jesus of Nazareth is the real Christ, the Messiah of Israel, and that this same Jesus will destroy this temple *and* the customs and laws of Moses!"

Stephen's accusers hurled one twisted distortion of truth after another onto the raptly listening ears of the men who had already decided to condemn him to death. Presently the high priest asked Stephen, "Are these charges true?"

Stephen's face shone with a glow like that of an angel—so much so that his appearance startled those who looked upon him.

Full of the Holy Spirit of God, he began, "My fathers and brothers, please hear me!" And he preached on, with unmitigated power, as the chosen "listeners" listened, waiting for just the right moment. Stephen finally delivered to them the words they needed:

"You stubborn men! You are cursed with uncircumcised hearts and ears! You are just like your fathers who were before you. You are forever resisting the power and persuasion of the Holy Spirit of God! Was there ever a prophet who lived among us that your fathers did not persecute? They even killed those who prophesied of the Coming One! Now, you have betrayed and killed that very One who was to come!" He was filled with passion—a passion that inflamed his antagonistic listeners.

Stephen paused and caught his breath. Then, pointing his finger directly at the high priest and those of his inner council, he shouted, "*You* delivered Jesus the Christ into the hands of Gentiles to be crucified! *You* murdered him! *You* who have the Law of God, put into action by angels—but you have not obeyed that same law!"

In one accord, the councilmen rushed upon Stephen. They seized him, yet again, and dragged him violently through the streets of Jerusalem to the edge of the city boundaries. And there they murdered him—stoned him to death—with the full and onlooking approval of a respected teacher of the Law, a Pharisee of Pharisees, a *rabbi*. This man was *Saul*.[3]

Saul was now inflamed with passion and zeal. Stephen's stoning was a delight to him. The Christian movement—that pagan *cult*—must be destroyed. But to destroy the sect would require that its people be eliminated—all of them. Accordingly, Saul sought out the proper legal paperwork and embarked upon his duty with fervor. Then he went from house to house, seeking to destroy the church of Jesus—the one they called *the Messiah* (Acts 6–8).

CIRCA AD 35

Some months later, Saul went back to the high priest and asked for letters of authority to the synagogues of Damascus. He had heard the Christian sect was beginning to take hold there at an alarming rate. Saul was enraged. How could his fellow Jews so quickly succumb to this blasphemous outrage?

The Sanhedrin court gave him the authority he needed. Saul was to arrest all he could find who dared admit to being followers of Jesus, and bring these followers of *the Way* back to Jerusalem, in chains. He set out on his mission with alacrity.

Along the road to Damascus, Rabbi Saul, the *teacher of the Law,* was suddenly struck down. A light from heaven—like a lightning bolt out of a clear blue sky—flashed, enveloping him in a shroud of brilliance. Its explosive sound was deafening; its radiance dazzling and blinding. Saul fell to the ground as though dead, his eyes clenched tightly, burning with pain. Wrenching in anguish, he groaned and tried his best to whimper a command to his cohorts. But he could not. His traveling companions stood speechless as they witnessed the spectacle before them.

Then Saul heard a voice—a godlike voice—resonating with power and authority, yet mixed with a depth of love he had never before felt. "Saul, my dear Saul—why do you persecute Me?"

Saul's companions did not hear those words; they heard only a rumbling. The message was meant for *Saul's ears only.*

"Lord? *Adonai,*" Saul responded, "who are You?"

The voice from heaven answered, "I am *Jesus,* the One you are persecuting. Now, get up and go into the city, and you will be told what you must do."

With that command, a young, up-and-coming leader of the Jews—a Pharisee of great standing and a rabbi respected among his people—became a disciple of Jesus, the Christ of God. And within days, Saul was preaching in the Jewish synagogues that Jesus was the Christ and that he had received this marvelous information in a *revelation* from heaven.

Saul was soundly reviled and rejected (Acts 9). *He has gone mad,* his enemies said. Though Saul's experience was real, his message was ridiculed—and would be for decade upon decade.

***

It would not be until fourteen years later (see Gal. 2:1) that Paul, formerly called Saul, would go back to the elders at the church in Jerusalem to finally convince them that he no longer desired their destruction. His new message was: *I have had a revelation. I have spoken to the Messiah. I know who He is, and I know the signs that must accompany His return. He has given me a mission to fulfill, and I will embark upon this holy task even if it means the slandering of my name and my reputation among the Jews—even if it means my death.*

Ultimately, the revelation *would* cost Paul his life. A despotic and narcissistic Roman emperor by the name of Nero would lop off Paul's head in his insatiable thirst for Christian blood.

THE MESSIANIC DREAM OF A RABBI

I ask you again, *could* the Messiah of God reveal Himself to a Jewish rabbi? *Would* He reveal Himself to a mere Hebrew sage, *even* if that leader were engaged in wickedness, murder, and other outrages against humanity? Would He actually place His hand of revelation and anointing upon a man who spent his life attempting to destroy the work of those who first claimed the Messiah? Would the Lord then use that same man to strengthen, and even build up, the very ones he used to attack?

Of course He would. And according to the Bible, He did. Additionally, in Acts 18, we read of a ruler of the synagogue— another respected Jewish rabbi—named Crispus, who had a *revelation* of the true Messiah through the preaching of Paul. This leader then acknowledged Jesus Christ as Savior and the Messiah of God.

Yes, God has spoken time and time again to unbelieving people—some of whom had done wicked things in their lives prior to encountering the living God. God spoke through a burning bush to a Hebrew man who had committed murder and then ran to the far side of the desert to hide from his family and from God (Exod. 3–4). He also spoke—and made a donkey speak!—to the money-hungry prophet Balaam (Num. 22:22–35). God speaks when He *wants* to speak and to *whom* He wishes to speak, and He does it in the manner in which He alone wishes to do it—for *He is God.*

One of the most touching examples of a messianic revelation given to an elderly Jewish holy man is that of the experience of Simeon. His story is recorded in the gospel of Luke, chapter 2. Joseph and Mary had arrived at the temple in Jerusalem to present the infant Jesus for His ritualistic dedication, as was prescribed in the Hebrew Scriptures. There, the man Simeon, described as one who had received a revelation from the Holy Spirit of God that he would literally lay his eyes upon the long-awaited Messiah before his own death, approaches the young parents. The account records that Simeon took Jesus in his arms and proclaimed, "Lord, now lettest thou thy servant depart in peace, according to thy word: for mine eyes have seen thy salvation, which thou hast prepared before the face of all people; a light to lighten the Gentiles, and the glory of thy people Israel" (Luke 2:29–32).

To many of Simeon's day, it may have appeared improbable that the Lord of heaven would have made such a promise to an old man, much less fulfill the incredulous revelation. But the Lord always fulfills His word. He always keeps His promises. He never disappoints. Simeon had seen the Messiah.

So is God able to speak to a Jewish rabbi in a vision and reveal to him that Jesus is the Christ? Yes, He is able; there can be no doubt. That question is forever settled. Still, there is another question that follows the first—and it is perhaps the more important of the two: *How do we know that God has actually spoken to someone?*

What if a purported vision was simply the effect of a bad meal? Or, what if the person was merely the victim of a nightmare? Or worse yet, what if he was being purposely deceptive, *claiming* he had received a vision from God when he really had not? Ah . . . these are the questions of questions. The veracity of a claimed vision can sometimes be difficult to discern.

Let us now turn our attention to the purported visions and the acclaimed prophecies of the late Rabbi Yitzhak Kaduri.

2

THE OLD RABBI AND HIS VISIONS

AD 2003-2006

Jews must come to the land of Israel to receive our righteous Mashiach (Messiah), who has begun his influence and will reveal himself in the future.[1]

— *Rabbi Yitzhak Kaduri, October 2005*

"I have a word from *HaShem*. This revelation will also involve the fulfillment of several prophecies—some ancient, some relatively modern. I will explain."

The teacher made this pronouncement with the trembling voice of a man well past one hundred years of age. But his voice was not frail. It resonated with an authoritative strength. An eerie hush fell over the synagogue as the elderly rabbi slowly, with the help of two attendants, ascended the small flight of steps to the teacher's seat.

It had been rumored that the revered old rabbi had received an especially holy revelation that he planned to disclose to the anxiously gathered assembly. A few congregants nervously cleared their throats as the deeply loved man of God prepared to speak. The date was Thursday, October 13, 2005—Yom Kippur (the Day of Atonement), the holiest day on the Jewish calendar.

It had been on this hallowed day during the deep ages of Israel's past, in the times of the great Temple rituals, that the kohen gadol (high priest) had entered the Holy of Holies, or Most Holy Place, located at the center of the Temple. It was important in those days that the high priest had been purified, spiritually and physically, when he entered behind the veil of the Holy of Holies. To ensure his purity, many rituals of legalistic exactness were tediously performed to guarantee that he did not carry any ritual defilement into the Holy of Holies, lest the judgment of Adonai fall upon him and the people.

Yom Kippur had become an even more somber holiday among the people since the destruction of the Temple, in AD 70. The day was now observed with much personal sacrifice and a laser focus on the Word of God, especially the Law. The Torah calls the day Yom HaKippurim. Its book of Leviticus strictly prohibits work and affliction of the soul on the tenth day of the seventh month, the Hebrew month known as *Tishrei*. On the evening before Yom Kippur, a twenty-five-hour period of fasting and prayer began.

A prominent and required part of one's Yom Kippur duty was synagogue attendance. Rabbi Yitzhak Kaduri's congregation had been faithful. The place was packed to standing room only. The Jewish men were devotedly adorned in their *kittels* and *tallits*.[2] The women were festooned in white apparel, symbolizing the purity of their lives once their sins were wiped away through the faithful performances of this day's sacred rituals. In keeping with the deepest devotion to the rituals of the day, not a person in attendance wore an item made of gold, for to do so on this day was a sacrilege—an unholy reminder of the sins associated with the golden calf that had been shamefully constructed by the Jews' ancient ancestors in the wilderness journey.

It was late afternoon, just before sunset, and the hour of the gathering for *Mincha*. As he took his seat, Rabbi Kaduri fell into a trance-like state. Mumbling lightly to himself, he shielded his eyes and bowed his head in apparent meditation.

For forty-five grueling minutes he remained in this condition. Several of his students, fearing the rabbi was suffering some sort of illness or spiritual attack, tried to communicate with the aged man. He remained in the trance, without uttering a word to those around him. He did not acknowledge their presence, even in the slightest manner. No one said another word to the rabbi. No one left the room. Then, the old rabbi lifted his head and muttered, "I have met the Messiah."

A collective gasp rippled through the crowd. Rabbi Kaduri gently and reverently raised his right hand, signaling for silence. The crowd hushed obediently. Kaduri continued, "I have met the Messiah . . . He has appeared to me in a vision. He has attached his soul to a particular person in Israel. I will spend this day teaching you how to recognize the Messiah, for He shall appear soon. You must be ready for His coming. Many events of awe will take place before His coming . . . but they will happen quickly."

The old rabbi looked over his congregation. He clearly had their attention. Not a soul stirred. All eyes were fixed on their beloved teacher. "I must tell you something disturbing," he somberly continued. "I have no specific information to give you on the following matter other than what I am about to share with you now . . . The Messiah has revealed to me that He will not present

Himself until after the death of our prime minister, Ariel Sharon.”

Many congregants began to stealthily wipe tears from their eyes. Others gasped, their hands over their mouths. This indeed was an especially holy word brought from their adored rabbi. Everyone in attendance was aware—this was a pivotal day . . . perhaps like none other. Would the controversial prime minister be struck with a curse? Would he die soon? Was Messiah’s appearance actually just around the corner? Normalcy of Jewish life had now vanished. The long-awaited Messiah was on His way. *The teacher* had spoken.

The scroll of Psalm 145 was opened, and the congregation recited the ancient prayer in unison. On this day, the Mincha, which had been delivered in the same manner for ages past, suddenly held a particularly holy message for its recipients—a message that promised a *revelation* to those longing for a touch from God. The hearts of Rabbi Kaduri’s congregation were particularly warmed as they spoke the ancient words together:

> I will extol thee, my God, O king; and I will bless thy name for ever and ever. Every day will I bless thee; and I will praise thy name for ever and ever. Great is the LORD, and greatly to be praised; and his greatness is unsearchable. One generation shall praise thy works to another, and shall declare thy mighty acts. I will speak of the glorious honour of thy majesty, and of thy wondrous works. And men shall speak of the might of thy terrible acts: and I will declare thy greatness. They shall abundantly utter the memory of thy great goodness, and shall sing of thy righteousness. The LORD is gracious, and full of compassion; slow to anger, and of great mercy. The LORD is good to all: and his tender mercies are over all his works. All thy works shall praise thee, O LORD; and thy saints shall bless thee. They shall speak of the glory of thy kingdom, and talk of thy power; to make known to the sons of men his mighty acts, and the glorious majesty of his kingdom. Thy kingdom is an everlasting kingdom, and thy dominion

endureth throughout all generations. The LORD upholdeth all that fall, and raiseth up all those that be bowed down. The eyes of all wait upon thee; and thou givest them their meat in due season. Thou openest thine hand, and satisfiest the desire of every living thing. The LORD is righteous in all his ways, and holy in all his works. The LORD is nigh unto all them that call upon him, to all that call upon him in truth. He will fulfil the desire of them that fear him: he also will hear their cry, and will save them. The LORD preserveth all them that love him: but all the wicked will he destroy. My mouth shall speak the praise of the LORD: and let all flesh bless his holy name for ever and ever. (Ps. 145)

Upon completion, the congregants declared their agreement in a chorus of solemn *Amens*. The ancient rabbi lifted his right hand over the congregation and with a tremulous voice recited the *blessing*, the same one priests and rabbis had pronounced over God's people since time immemorial:

"'The LORD bless you and keep you; the LORD make His face shine upon you and be gracious to you; the LORD lift up His countenance upon you, and give you peace.' Amen" (Num. 6:24–26 NKJV).

The worshippers rose to their feet and silently filed out of the synagogue. They spoke not a word aloud—only uttering hushed whispers.

But the people would not stay silent for long. What they had heard was too marvelous. The news was monumental—eternal. The truthfulness of it could not be in doubt—this was the word of their rabbi, and the man was revered throughout Israel. The teacher of Israel had received a holy vision. Soon the whole world would know. How could they not?[3]

And so, it is here that our story begins.

***

The Baghdad-born Rabbi Yitzhak Kaduri gained worldwide notoriety for issuing numerous apocalyptic warnings and striking endtime prophecies, and for claiming that in November 2003, he had met the long-awaited Jewish Messiah in a vision. Following is a brief time line and synopsis of significant events, as well as declarations and predictions made by Rabbi Kaduri. It is from this time line that this amazing account of the man unfolds.

TIME LINE OF IMPORTANT VISIONS AND EVENTS

1990: In a meeting with famed Rabbi Menachem Mendel Schneerson, the rabbi of Lubavitch,[4] words of blessing are pronounced over Rabbi Kaduri. Among them are this blessing: *"You will not pass from this world until you meet the Messiah."*

November 2003: Rabbi Yitzhak Kaduri, more than one hundred years old, claims he has met the Messiah in a mystical vision and knows His name. He begins to share bits and pieces of his purported revelation.

December 12, 2004: The *Yediot Aharonot*, Israel's most widely circulated newspaper, reports a prediction by Rabbi Kaduri of "great tragedies." The rabbi further declares these catastrophes will be fulfilled where Jews are going *to the East*. He also announces to the Israeli press that "the *Mashiach* [Messiah] is already in Israel."[5]

September 2005: Kaduri again says, "The Messiah is already [here] in Israel," adding, "Whatever people are sure will not happen, is liable to happen, and whatever we are certain will happen may disappoint us. But in the end, there will be peace throughout the world."[6] Also during this month, Kaduri allegedly writes his mysterious *Messiah note*, with orders that it not be opened until one year after his death. The note is said to contain the identity of the *true Messiah.*[7]

October 2005: On Yom Kippur, Rabbi Kaduri delivers a sermon in his synagogue, teaching how to recognize the Messiah. Following is an excerpt of an extensive report on this matter, posted by WND.com.[8]

> About his encounter with the Messiah Kaduri claimed is alive in Israel today, he reportedly told close relatives: "He [the Messiah] is not saying, 'I am the Messiah, give me the leadership.' Rather the nation is pushing him to lead them, after they find [in my words] signs showing that he has the status of Messiah."
>
> Kaduri was also quoted as saying the imminent arrival of the Messiah will "save Jerusalem from Islam and Christianity that wish to take Jerusalem from the Jewish Nation—but they will not succeed, and they will fight each other."
>
> . . .
>
> "It is hard for many good people in society to understand the person of the Messiah," Kaduri wrote before his death. "The leadership and order of a Messiah of flesh and blood is hard to accept for many in the nation. As leader, the Messiah will not hold any office, but will be among the people and use the media to communicate. His reign will be pure and without personal or political desire. During his dominion, only righteousness and truth will reign."

In another controversial part of his Yom Kippur revelation, Kaduri also mentions the Messiah will appear to Israel *after* Ariel Sharon's death. (Sharon is a renowned Israeli diplomat and retired general who served as Israel's eleventh prime minister.) Just a little more than two months later, Kaduri's followers will hold their collective breath as a dramatic turn of events appears to indicate his prophecy might be nearing fulfillment.

January 4, 2006: Ariel Sharon suffers a massive stroke and lapses into a coma.

January 28, 2006: Twenty-four days after Sharon's medical calamity, Rabbi Kaduri dies after a brief bout with pneumonia. He is surrounded by loved ones at the time of his death.

January–April 2007: Rabbi Kaduri's final wishes are carried out. A handwritten note, reportedly penned by Kaduri and sealed for the past year, is opened. The contents of this note, said to contain a cryptic message revealing the name of the soon-to-come Messiah, shake the religious world to the core. The announcement of the note's contents is reported on Kaduri's own website (kaduri.net), on *News First Class* (written entirely in Hebrew), and in *Israel Today*.

January 2013: Doctors proclaim that Ariel Sharon is beginning to exhibit brain wave activity.[9] Some now speculate that he may be in the early stages of waking up.

THE VARIOUS REVELATIONS

As discussed earlier, Rabbi Kaduri purportedly shared two clues about the soon-to-come Messiah (*Mashiach* in Hebrew). The first was that He would soon appear on earth, but only *after* the death of Ariel Sharon. As the time line shows, Sharon has been in a coma for the last several years. But on January 28, 2013, Fox News reported that tests showed "robust activity" in Sharon's brain in response to pictures of his family and recordings of his son's voice.[10]

Sharon's miraculous brain wave activity was medically recorded and subsequently reported to the world almost exactly *seven years* from the date he initially lapsed into the vegetative state. Numerous people see a striking symbolism in the undeniably and biblically significant number *seven*, since it is the number of *completion*.

The second and probably the most shocking clue about the Messiah was that He had revealed His *name* to the rabbi. Kaduri claimed to have left this name for the world to see in a cryptic riddle of a message.

Shortly after the unveiling of the revelation, *Israel Today* published what soon became a highly controversial article concerning Rabbi Kaduri's death note. Following is a brief excerpt from that story and a statement from Kaduri's son, David, who was in his eighties at the time of his father's passing.

> *Israel Today* was given access to many of the rabbi's manuscripts, written in his own hand for the exclusive use of his students. Most striking were the cross-like symbols painted by Kaduri all over the pages. In the Jewish tradition, one does not use crosses. In fact, even the use of a plus sign is discouraged because it might be mistaken for a cross.
>
> But there they were, scribbled in the rabbi's own hand. When we asked what those symbols meant, Rabbi David Kaduri said they were "signs of the angel." Pressed further about the meaning of the "signs of the angel," he said he had no idea. Rabbi David Kaduri went on to explain that only his father had had a spiritual relationship with God and had met the Messiah in his dreams.[11]

Numerous followers of the story have asked several obvious and interesting questions. For example, if the use of a cross or a "cross-like" symbol is forbidden or highly discouraged in Judaism because of its obvious connection to Jesus and Christianity, why would one of the most celebrated teachers of Judaism make such liberal and unexplained use of the forbidden and offensive symbol? Furthermore, why would Kaduri's elderly son, David, say they were "signs of the angels," as though that explanation would suffice? If the crosses truly were revealed to Rabbi Kaduri by angels, would those revelations not necessarily lend powerful credence to the *heavenly* symbolism of a cross? One can certainly understand the younger Kaduri's trepidation in attempting an answer to his father's use of such symbols.

In October 2005, *Israel National News (INN)* published an online *Arutz Sheva* article concerning the growing Rabbi Kaduri phenomenon and the recent predictions he had made. The article began with the tantalizing headline teaser: "On Thursday night, Rabbi Yitzhak Kaduri said, 'Jews must come to the land of Israel to receive our righteous Mashiach (Messiah), who has begun his influence and will reveal himself in the future.'"[12]

The article then told of the surprising encounter the Yom Kippur prayer attendees had experienced with the elderly and revered Kaduri, recounted in creative fashion at the beginning of this chapter. And finally, the article reported that Kaduri often spoke of the *Gog and Magog* war, that cataclysmic, multinational war believed by many Bible students to be a literal endtimes event.[12] Gog and Magog are spoken of in a prophetic and end-times nature in both the Old and the New Testaments:

> Son of man, set thy face against Gog, the land of Magog, the chief prince of Meshech and Tubal, and prophesy against him, and say, Thus saith the LORD God; behold, I am against thee, O Gog, the chief prince of Meshech and Tubal: and I will turn thee back, and put hooks into thy jaws, and I will bring thee forth, and all thine army, horses and horsemen, all of them clothed with all sorts of armour, even a great company with bucklers and shields, all of them handling swords. (Ezek. 38:2–4)

> And when the thousand years are expired, Satan shall be loosed out of his prison, and shall go out to deceive the

nations which are in the four quarters of the earth, Gog and Magog, to gather them together to battle: the number of whom is as the sand of the sea. And they went up on the breadth of the earth, and compassed the camp of the saints about, and the beloved city: and fire came down from God out of heaven, and devoured them. (Rev. 20:7–9)

According to the *Arutz Sheva* article, this monumental war is predicted to fall on Hoshana Rabba, the seventh day of the Jewish holiday of Sukkoth, just after the conclusion of the seventh, or *shemittah* (agricultural sabbatical) year.[13]

The article posted on September 24, 2001, went on to say that Channel One Israel TV broadcasted a news report on what Torah and Kabbalah mystics were claiming in the aftermath of the Islamic terrorist World Trade Center attack in New York City, and the Pentagon attack in Washington, D.C. They, Kaduri included, saw a striking connection between the Gog and Magog war and the events of September 11, 2001.

Speaking from the room adjacent to where Rabbi Yitzhak Kaduri receives visitors, *Arutz Sheva* Hebrew radio show-host Yehoshua Meiri, a close confid[a]nt of the Kabbalist, explained to the cameras Rabbi Kaduri's understanding of the events based on the calculations of the Vilna Gaon [an eighteenth-century Kabbalist]: "On Hashanah Rabba, the actual war of Gog and Magog will commence and will last for some seven years," said Meiri.

The article continues:

Precise to the minute, 13 days later on October 7th as the sun was setting and the Jewish holiday of Hoshana Rabba was ushered in, US and British forces began an aerial bombing campaign targeting Taliban forces and Al-Qaida. That year was the Hoshana Rabba just after the shemittah year of 5761.

According to the calculation, a 7-year count from that Hoshana Rabba is the date of a major revelation associated with Mashiach. Those close to Rabbi Kaduri say in his name that the 5th year of this redemption process is now beginning.

They explain that the above-mentioned "attaching" of a righteous soul to a person of Israel makes the recipient a candidate for Mashiach, but not yet the actual Mashiach. This person gets an additional soul which finds expression in the adding of a letter to his name, without changing its pronunciation.

The elder Rabbi Kaduri says that the letter added to this person's name is "vav" and the secret of his power is a Star of David hidden in his attire.[14]

It is interesting to note that Rabbi Kaduri supposedly suggested that a seven-year countdown from October 2001, at the time of Hoshana Rabba, would lead to a *major revelation associated with Mashiach.* A seven-year countdown beginning October 2001 falls in October 2008. Of course this date corresponds exactly with the epicenter of the tumultuous 2008 presidential election campaigns in the United States. One month later, Barack Hussein Obama was elected president. A year after that, on October 9, 2009, the Norwegian Nobel Committee announced Barack Obama as the winner of the Nobel Peace Prize. The committee specifically cited Obama's promotion of nuclear nonproliferation.[15] The committee also lauded Obama for the "new climate" he had created in international relations, especially in reaching out to the Muslim world.[16]

Shortly after Obama's election, *Newsweek* magazine ran a cover story titled "The Second Coming." The flattering story written by Evan Thomas ascribes messianic, even God-like attributes to the president. Nation of Islam leader Louis Farrakhan, another powerful Chicago-based political figure associated with the Reverend Jeremiah Wright and other longtime associates of

Democratic Party presidential candidate Barack Obama, left no doubt about what he thought of Obama.

In February of that same year, addressing a large crowd behind a podium with a Nation of Islam Saviours' Day 2008 sign, Farrakhan proclaimed, "You are the instruments that God is going to use to bring about universal change, and that is why Barack has captured the youth. And he has involved young people in a political process that they didn't care anything about. That's a sign. When the Messiah speaks, the youth will hear, and *the Messiah is absolutely speaking.*

"Brothers and sisters," he continued, "Barack Obama to me, is a *herald of the Messiah.* Barack *Obama is like the trumpet that alerts you something new, something better is on the way.*

"A black man with a white mother became a saviour to us," Farrakhan went on, referring to Fard Muhammad, founder of the Nation of Islam. "A black man with a white mother could turn out to be one who can lift America from her fall." Fard Muhammad, like Obama, had a black father and a white mother.

"Would God allow Barack to be president of a country that has been so racist, so evil in its treatment of Hispanics, Native Americans, blacks?" asked Farrahkhan. "Would God do something like that? Yeah. Of course he would. That's to show you that the stone that the builders rejected has become the headstone of the corner. This is a sign to you. It's the time of our rise. It's the time that we should take our place. The future is all about you."[17]

As if that were not enough, who can forget the messianic-style message delivered by Obama himself on January 7, 2008, at a campaign rally in Lebanon, New Hampshire, at Dartmouth College, just before the New Hampshire primary? There Obama declared, "A light will shine through that window, a beam of light will come down upon you, you will experience an epiphany, and you will suddenly realize that you must go to the polls and vote [for Obama]."[18] Predictably, websites were constructed, seemingly overnight, proclaiming either seriously, or tongue in cheek, that Barack Obama was indeed the new Messiah—or at least the forerunner of a soon-coming Messiah.[19]

As time moved along, the messianic-connected infatuation with Obama only grew more fervent. In fact, Hollywood actor Jamie Foxx stunned the entire religious world with his overtly blasphemous assessment of Barack Obama. At the taping of the November 2012 BET Soul Train Awards, and during the show, live onstage, Foxx proclaimed, "It's like church over here. It's like church in here. First of all, give an honor to God and our Lord and Savior Barack Obama."[20]

For the first time in United States history, a popular actor and public figure had openly declared a sitting president to be both *God* and our *Lord and Savior.*

But not everyone felt that way. Just weeks after the awards show, WND posted a column by the Reverend Jesse Lee Peterson, a conservative black minister and founder of BOND (Brotherhood Organization of a New Destiny). It was titled "How Obama Replaced Christ Among Blacks." In the article, after recounting Foxx's remark, Peterson proclaimed, "President Barack Obama is the most divisive man to ever occupy the White House—period! Yet, 95 percent of black Americans worship him as if he's the messiah. Why?"[21]

***

To a large number of those faithfully following the unraveling events, Rabbi Kaduri's prophecies were now being further and dramatically bolstered—on the evening news and in the Internet blogosphere. Something very *messianic* was indeed in the air and reverberating throughout the world and in the headlines of renowned news sources. A *major revelation associated with the Messiah*, just as Kaduri had predicted,[22] was seemingly making an appearance in the exact month and year Kaduri proclaimed it would. In the minds of his devoted followers, Kaduri's astounding and cryptic prophecies continued to possess life . . . even several years after his passing.

3

THE LAST OF A LOST GENERATION

[Israel has lost] one of its biggest figures ever.[1]

—Israeli president Moshe Katsav

That January day was a dismal one—no matter how one looked at it. That day was a day of mourning, and the weather dutifully matched the somber occasion. The sky had settled in to be heavily overcast. The clouds were low and gray. The edgy air over Jerusalem possessed a moist coolness that cut to the bone. A steady breeze further chilled the gloomy Sunday. The not-too-distant mountains surrounding

Jerusalem were visible—but just barely. A thick haze hung over them like a thin veil of sorrow, as though heaven itself were appropriately responding to this bleak event.[2]

But the physically uncomfortable nature of the day did not stop the multitudes from coming. More than a dozen planes, packed to capacity with faithful followers from France, had recently arrived at the airport. And the grieving multitudes came. They came in innumerable taxis, and they came in stuffed and cramped busloads—shuttled from faraway central parking areas. They came on foot, on bicycle, some on crutches or with canes, others clutching babies in their arms. Wrapped in warm clothing, shawls, and heavy jackets, by the hundreds of thousands—well over three hundred thousand by some estimates—*they came.*

Their beloved Rabbi Yitzhak Kaduri had died just days before. And now, practically every taxi and bus in Jerusalem had a picture of the adored rabbi dangling from its rearview mirror—a citywide show of respect and admiration. Downtown Jerusalem was a madhouse. Horns honked. Sirens blared relentlessly. Some folks shouted; others stood on street corners, wailing openly in heartfelt grief. Little children plodded submissively along under the watchful eyes of their parents and older siblings. Mourners prayed aloud along the way or muttered kabbalistic blessings for the dear one who had departed. Many dabbed tears from the corners of their eyes. The outpouring of grief was uninhibited—and the service had not even begun.

Police and military personnel, their presence overwhelming and ominous, had barricaded the inner and largest streets of Jerusalem. Most were simply doing their jobs, but some had also been followers of the old rabbi—occasionally, even a few of them quickly brushed back a tear. There was nothing of which to be ashamed in the matter; the nation was in mourning. A tear and a trembling lip were appropriate—and admired. A revered *righteous one* was no longer in their midst. His spirit had flown.

The funeral was scheduled to begin at noon. But in spite of the currently late hour, the throngs continued to come. It was now 11:50 a.m., and young Josiah was fearful that he would not be able to get close enough to have one final glimpse of his dear teacher's body. He had, only moments ago, piled off of a packed-to-standing-room-only city bus, having shuttled from a designated parking lot miles away, on the other side of the ancient and biblical city. Even *he* had not anticipated the vast numbers in the still-blossoming crowd. Everywhere he looked, the masses persisted in descending upon the place.

Josiah continued to inch his way through the thickening crowds, careful not to appear too insistent or rude as he moved forward. He was incessantly bumped—and he occasionally and accidentally bumped back. But no one complained. It was to be expected. "Excuse me . . . excuse me . . . *Shalom* . . . Blessings be upon you," he found himself muttering, almost in robot fashion.

In time, he stood just outside the rabbi's yeshiva—the institute of learning where Yitzhak Kaduri had dispensed his immense wisdom and knowledge to multiplied thousands through the almost seventy years of his teaching endeavors. Josiah was now in a position that, if *HaShem* blessed him that day, he might just get one last touch, one last, close glimpse. He pulled his collar up around his neck—he was chilled to the bone, but he would endure it with a sense of dignity and duty. It was the least he could give to *the teacher*, this one who claimed to have seen the *Mashiach*—and to even know His *name*.

Josiah turned and looked at the gathering crowd around him and behind him. It was an ocean of black garb for as far as he could see. This would be one of the largest funerals in the modern history of Israel.[3] Not even a past political leader's death had occasioned such a multitudinous gathering. Josiah knew that somehow he was now a part of history.

"He is the last of a lost generation," an unknown old man muttered to Josiah, as he waited for the service to begin.

"Excuse me, sir, what did you say?" Josiah asked respectfully, struggling to speak the words. He had not been paying attention to any one person—he had been too overwhelmed with grief and the sheer size of the crowd around him to notice a singular old man standing right beside him—looking at him.

"I said, *this one is the last*—the very last of a lost and great generation," the man repeated. "There will be none like him to follow. This is it."

Josiah nodded in agreement. A lump swelled in his throat. He knew the stranger's words were true. He had not been the first to utter such a pronouncement.

"Are you one of his students?" the man asked, grinning slightly.

Josiah attempted to answer, but the knot in his throat prevented speech. He nodded again, pulling his collar up closer to his neck. The wind was getting colder.

The man smiled knowingly. "You were blessed to be so," he said.

The old man *understood*. Josiah smiled and briefly touched the man's shoulder in a display of gratitude. Then he turned to look behind him again.

Many thousands of people were now standing side by side. A feather could not be passed between most of them. Men and boys stood on rooftops. Others were perched on various monuments and low-lying structures. Elevated porticos of ancient buildings were packed to overflowing. Verandas appeared strained under the weight of too many people crammed atop them. The press of the crowd was near-strangulating. Josiah caught himself holding his breath, suddenly claustrophobic. He was not the only one.

Sirens continued to wail through the streets as ambulances hurriedly carted off the stricken. He gasped for air as his lungs rebelled. He had to remain calm.

Josiah turned back to speak to the old man who had spoken to him just moments ago—and the man was gone! It was as though he had never been there!

How could the elderly gentleman have exited such a mass of people? It would have been impossible. *Was he an angel?* Josiah wondered. Had he been rewarded with a heavenly visitation on the occasion of his beloved rabbi's funeral? He would contemplate more upon the possibility later, but the matter was too overwhelming for his consideration right now. He scanned the crowd around him once more, looking for the old man. He was nowhere to be seen. *How odd.*

The rabbi's body lay in state, wrapped head to toe in a shroud and shawl, on the wood paneled floor of the funeral platform. His head was enshrined in two semicircles of small candles, each contained in a little round tin. A circle of elders surrounded the lovingly prepared body. They chanted, prayed, and read scripture—at once, and aloud—their bodies gently rocking back and forth. A microphone stand was strategically located within the circle. This would be from where the chosen dignitaries would address the mourners.

The cheap sound system screeched and rumbled as Rabbi Obadiah Yosef and the Shas Council of Torah Sages issued a statement mourning the loss of Rabbi Kaduri. After a few quick adjustments were made, Shas chairman Eli Yishai announced, "All the people of Israel today are one family in mourning. Today, the man whom all of Israel had been praying for went heavenward."

In paying his respects, chief Sephardi Rabbi Shlomo Amar said, "Rabbi Kaduri wished that each and every one of you would accept upon himself or herself one good deed—this day. Show one act of kindness to your fellow Jew and child of *HaShem*.

"Rabbi Kaduri was sacrificed for all of us," he continued. "We must repent." A rumble of murmuring agreement went through the crowd.

Rabbi Reuven Elbaz, another chosen orator, spoke with heart-piercing lamentations of Kaduri's righteousness. "He was our spiritual light tower," he cried. "We are lost without him." Rabbi Elbaz wept openly as he left the dais.

Rabbi Ya'acov Hilel, head of the Ahavat Shalom Yeshiva and a respected teacher of Kabbalah, was next to speak. "Rabbi Kaduri was not just a Jewish mystic," he said. "He was a role model for the pursuit of truth. He had mastered anger, never argued, nor was he ever jealous or hateful. He had nothing but love for the Jewish people."

The depth of Kaduri's popularity among all walks of the Jewish people was apparent in the crowd. Their overwhelming presence was a testimony of trust and honor. Observed from a distance, the prevailing colors of the masses that had packed Jerusalem's streets were black and dirge blue. But interspersed were colors and styles that revealed other religious affiliations as well. Secular men had hastily pinned throwaway yarmulkes to their heads. And some women were dressed in pants.

Rabbi David Batzri moved to the microphone to pay his tribute to Kaduri. After two pitiful and mournful attempts to speak, he gave up trying for a moment, overcome with near-hysterical crying. Finally, after collecting himself, he continued. "I simply cannot believe that Rabbi Kaduri is no longer among the living," he wailed. "I was certain the Mashiach would come in his lifetime!" Some in the crowd wept aloud with him as his shoulders heaved under the soul-piercing burden of the moment.

Oddly, to many, Rabbi Kaduri had passed away on a Saturday night. This delicate matter had to be addressed. The city was already abuzz with the undeniable fact. Saturday was an inauspicious time to pass from this life, according to Jewish mysticism. Kabbalists teach that Saturday night is the time at which the souls that are given a reprieve from *Gehinnom* (Hell) during the Sabbath must return to Gehinnom. However, passing away on Sabbath eve, according to Kabbalah, is a positive sign since the soul makes the transition into the Sabbath immediately.

Rabbi Batzri regained his composure for a moment and attempted to explain away this obvious embarrassment that was looming over the somber occasion. "Perhaps through his merits Rabbi Kaduri saved all those souls that were on their way back to Gehinnom," he explained. "Perhaps this is why it was ordained that Rabbi Kaduri pass from among the living on this day." The believers were now satisfied.

President Moshe Katsav delivered the eulogy for the elderly rabbi. Then, at last, the final words were spoken and the closing prayers were offered. The service had lasted an hour and a half. The congregation of hundreds of thousands called out together, "Amen"; then Rabbi Kaduri's body was lovingly and reverently placed upon a litter, to be carried ceremoniously by appointed pallbearers. He was gently lifted from the floor, and the procession began its journey through the streets, beginning at David Street, headed toward the cemetery. Miraculously, the throngs followed. The procession would take place on foot.

As the pallet came close to Josiah, he nudged forward with the clutch of people around him. The hundreds that were closest to the body let out a wailing lament, all at once, spiced with hands uplifted to the heavens. The grief was suffocating . . . and intoxicating.

As the body passed Josiah, he reached out . . . and touched Rabbi Kaduri—one last time. *HaShem* had answered his prayer! Unable to control himself, Josiah let out a moan of anguish, mixing his broken-hearted dirge with the crowd's. His *teacher* was gone, and Josiah wept bitterly.

He never again saw the old man who had spoken to him.

***

When Rabbi Yitzhak Kaduri died in January 2006, an estimated quarter of a million people or more attended his funeral.[4] In fact, half of Jerusalem had to be blocked off to enable the massive procession of mourners to accompany his body to Har Hamenuhot, the city's largest cemetery.[5] Practically every major media source in Israel had followed the ebb and flow of Kaduri's medical condition during his two-week hospitalization at Bikur Holim, so it is no surprise that when he died, foreign television, radio stations, and newspapers made time and space to devote attention to his funeral.

What was so alluring about Kaduri that there should be such a massive reaction to his life and subsequent death? He never wrote a book for mass publication, nor did he hold the specific position as designated rabbi of any community. He never led a named movement. Neither was he famously hailed as an accomplished orator.

Kaduri was indubitably most renowned for his prophecies, especially those having to do with the *endtimes* and the coming of the longed-for Jewish Messiah. In the final years of his life, the elderly rabbi's thoughts were almost wholly centered on this Messiah's coming. The Messiah, Kaduri claimed, would be the One who would finally and ultimately redeem Israel.

As we have already learned, Kaduri alleged that he had met the soon-coming Messiah in a vision, and knew his true identity. You will recall that Kaduri then handwrote the Messiah's identity, as well as other pertinent disclosures, in a note, to be opened and divulged one year after his death.

Sadly, once the note's cryptic message was revealed, many of his devoted Jewish followers were shocked beyond description and immediately began dismissing the note as either a forgery or the mistaken and irrational ramblings of a very old man. Worse, only a handful of Jewish news sources reported on the unveiling. The most monumental event of Kaduri's life was largely ignored.

Interestingly, the rabbi's rise in fame seems to have coincided with the rise of mystical religion. The rabbi himself studied and practiced a system of Jewish mysticism called *Kabbalah*. In fact, his tombstone reads, "Head and Elder of the Kabbalists."[6] When the content of his note was revealed, numerous Christians regarded the

Kaduri's headstone

message in the negative and biblically questionable light of his deep involvement with Kabbalah. To better understand the particular concern of conservative Christianity, let us take a quick look at the ancient art of Jewish mysticism known as Kabbalah.

UNDERSTANDING KABBALAH[7]

Kabbalah is the largely Jewish practice of ancient mystic spirituality. The word itself means, "to receive." There are those who believe, in a more general sense of the word, that if anyone claims to have received *any* form of spiritual knowledge, he or she is practicing Kabbalah, having *received* a word or message *from God*. It is claimed that even when a Christian, for example, finds a hidden message or meaning in the Scriptures, or when some deep truth or mysterious insight is given, it is *Kabbalah*, because it has been *received*. At its shallowest level, Kabbalah's premise is that there are secret messages hidden in the biblical text, and that they can be discovered by examining the shapes of Hebrew letters, or by using gematria, the assigning of numeric values to words, to see how they relate to words with identical values.

Another aspect of Kabbalah, as some define it, is the search for *hidden* messages through word associations not normally discerned within the plain biblical text. For example, one might examine the genealogy from Adam to Noah, found in Genesis 5, to look for a hidden message in the names of the descendants. Many have undertaken this very endeavor. Numerous Bible students have reported on the amazing message that appears to be revealed when the Hebrew words are given their English equivalents. There seems to be a cryptic message regarding, of all things, *the coming Messiah.* The following chart demonstrates the associations between the words by listing the names of the Patriarchs on the left and their Hebrew meanings on the right.

GENEALOGY OF ADAM FROM GENESIS 5

HEBREW NAME	HEBREW MEANING
ADAM	MAN
SETH	APPOINTED
ENOSH	MORTAL
CAINAN	SORROW
MAHALALEL	BLESSED ELOHIM
YARED	SHALL COME DOWN
ENOCH	TEACHING
METHUSELAH	HIS DEATH SHALL BRING
LAMECH	DESPAIRING
NOAH	COMFORT

The apparent message of the revelation would read something like this: "Man is appointed to a life of mortal sorrow. But the blessed Lord Himself shall come down, teaching the way to life. His death shall bring comfort to those who are in despair."

***

The word associations are undeniably interesting. There certainly appears to be a reference to *Jesus the Messiah* discovered in the connection of the words. Many would claim these kinds of word associations—*looking for hidden meanings*—are a form of *Christian Kabbalah*, or as the Christianized version of the mystic art is spelled, *Cabala*. A number of conservative Christians, however, object to the attachment of kabbalistic definitions to the Hebrew word-discovery process. They would insist that the practice is nothing more than simple word association from the clear and present text of Scripture as revealed to the searcher by the Holy Spirit. It is no secret, they would claim, that most Hebrew names have a *meaning* attached to them. To simply discern the meaning of the various names and then to observe the association of those meanings, they say, has nothing to do with Kabbalah.

Dr. Chuck Missler is a renowned and highly respected conservative Christian Bible teacher and preacher. Missler, a Naval Academy graduate and former branch chief of the Department of Guided Missiles, has also had an incredible thirty-year executive career, serving on the board of directors of twelve public companies, and as CEO of six of them. He was a weekly Bible study teacher at Calvary Chapel in Costa Mesa, California, since the early 1990s. He currently heads the Koinonia House ministry in Coeur d'Alene, Idaho.

Dr. Missler often uses the same illustration we just observed, the Adam–Noah genealogy, in his Bible teachings. Certainly, few in the Christian world would accuse Dr. Missler of practicing Kabbalah. A 2013 report by WND explains his teaching on this subject:

> He explained there is a message in the sequence of the names Adam, Seth, Enosh, Kenan, Mahalalel, Jared, Enoch, Methuselah, Lamech and Noah.
>
> According to the associated letters in Hebrew alphabet, the names together say: "Man appointed mortal sorrow. Blessed God shall come down teaching that His death shall bring the despairing comfort."
>
> A miracle, he said.
>
> "There's no other way to convince me that the complete Gospel message from the New Testament would have been included in the Old Testament by a bunch of Jewish rabbis," he said.
>
> He described it as a supernatural document.
>
> "Do you get the feeling God knows what he's doing? Get the feeling he's in control of every detail?" he asked.
>
> "The more you study your Bible you'll see these connections."[8]

Yet, kabbalists would argue that the revelation had been *received* through the Spirit, and thus a mysterious *hidden* message had been revealed—therefore, *Kabbalah* was involved. They would also argue, then, that Rabbi Kaduri left a purely kabbalistic message, similar to the word association chart, in his encrypted death note—revealing the name of the supposed Messiah by coding in the first letters of his name within a plain text. The person wishing to *receive* the name of the Messiah had to first decode the message.

It is believed that Christian Kabbalah first appeared during the late fifteenth century, the Kabbalah theory having gained consideration among various Christian scholars. Emanating from the scholarly considerations, Kabbalah theory established a foundation among the common Christian community, until it became an authentic kabbalistic movement. Some prominent Christians of the time, believing they discerned similarities between the basics of the Kabbalah and the basics of Christian belief, began fervently seeking supporting evidences for the foundations of Christian beliefs in the Kabbalah. The newly appeared movement started printing kabbalist literature in various languages. Some claim that the kabbalistic Christian movement preceded the first Jewish printed kabbalist writings.[9]

Others actually argue, quite fervently, that the apostle Paul was a practicing kabbalist. Paul was a Pharisee, a teacher, and, therefore, a rabbi who consistently spoke of the deep *mysteries* of God and the necessity of spiritual illumination for those mysteries to be discerned (see, for example, Rom. 16:25; 1 Cor. 2:7; Eph. 1:9, 3:3). Paul also dispensed prayer cloths for healing (Acts 19:11–12), a practice many claim to be similar to Kaduri's dispensing of amulets for blessings and healing. One can clearly understand why there is much confusion, and even dissension, over the issue of defining *Kabbalah* within the modern religious community.

Even though Kabbalah originally developed entirely within the realm of Jewish thought, certain kabbalistic practices have been adopted by other mystical religions, including the New Age movement and overtly occultic groups. The more mystical form of Kabbalah seeks to define the nature of the universe, the reasons for our existence, and other intricate matters of ontology. Kabbalists most often use classical Jewish sources, and even Scripture, to exhibit and elucidate its mysterious teachings. These obscure tidbits of revelation and wisdom are thus held by followers in Judaism to define the inner meaning of both the Hebrew Bible and traditional rabbinic literature.[10] Millions of people, both Jew and Gentile, study Kabbalah. It is a major, and relatively modern, spiritual phenomenon that is literally sweeping the planet. Major publishing houses print a plethora of books on Kabbalah, aimed at general audiences. Merely entering the word *Kabbalah* into an Internet search engine reveals thousands of sites catering to the modern thirst for the ancient Jewish mysticism.

Kabbalah practice is largely condemned by most of the conservative Christian community, and even a large portion of the Jewish community, because of its deep ties to magic, incantations, and even supposed conversations with the spirit world. Even so, Kabbalah has gained new popularity worldwide, even among celebrities, and especially from the entertainment industry. Madonna, Britney Spears, and several others have reportedly engraved Hebrew letters from the world of Kabbalah on their bodies. Some have even complemented their given names with a Jewish name. Madonna, for example, added the name *Esther* to her birth name. "I wanted to attach myself to the energy of a different name," she said in an interview.[11]

A 2004 *New York Times* article described Madonna's incongruous infatuation with Kabbalah:

> She wears a Jewish star, says she attends synagogue, performs with a version of the prayer accessory known as tefillin and with Hebrew letters flashing across a screen, and has let it be known that she won't have concerts on the Jewish Sabbath. . . .

Madonna is just the latest in a great tradition of stars who have been beguiled by Judaism. . . . In the case of Madonna, who was born Roman Catholic, her fascination with Jewish images flows mostly out of her attraction to something that she calls cabala but that many dismiss as a distillation of New Age notions about the genuine cabala.

In cabala, Hebrew letters are said to have enormous power, with some writers believing that God created the universe out of the energy in words and that words contain the secrets of creation. According to one of her cabala advisers, Michael Berg, the Hebrew letters Madonna displays, lamed, aleph, vov—roughly equivalent to L, A, V—form one of the 72 names of God and denote a diminishing of the ego to connect with joy and fulfillment. But an observant Jew would never flash a name of God across the screen in so frivolous a forum as a rock concert, nor imprint the letters as tattoos, as Madonna sometimes does, since tattoos are regarded as pagan.[12]

Obviously, one can now understand the confusion existing in a large part of the Christian community over Rabbi Kaduri's kabbalistic encrypted note purported to contain the name of the real Messiah. Some saw nothing wrong with the old rabbi leaving a message as a word association. Others, however, were not as understanding. Even though the revelation of the name was striking, in the minds of some, it smacked of the purely mystical, if not the *magical*, realm. If, in fact, God had plainly revealed the Messiah to Rabbi Kaduri, why did Kaduri not then plainly reveal the message to the world? Why would he leave the Messiah's name in a kabbalistic and cryptic death note? For this reason alone, some in the Christian world have dismissed the note altogether. *How*, they asked, *could a man reported to have spoken with demons, a practice expressly forbidden by God's Word, be the one through whom God would reveal His Messiah to the Jewish world?*

A few weeks after Rabbi Kaduri's death, the *Jerusalem Post* published an article titled "Judaism: The Magic of the Late Rabbi Yitzhak Kaduri." The article contained a quote from another rabbi who is identified as one of Israel's greatest Jewish mystics.

> Rabbi Mordechai Sharabi, one of the greatest Jewish mystics of the previous generation, purportedly said that Kaduri was the only person capable of writing amulets that have the power to bring success, heal, improve fertility or change reality for the better in some other way. In Kabbalistic thought it is believed that amulets tap the powers of demons and spirits and use them to perform miracles. In order to harness these supernatural powers, it is normally necessary to force these demons or spirits to take an oath. This is considered incredibly dangerous since the demons and spirits, once released from the oath, seek retribution. Asked once if he forces an oath on demons when he writes his amulets, Kaduri replied, "God forbid! It is forbidden to force them to take an oath. I only ask nicely. If they want to listen to me, they listen. Most of the time they respect me because I am so old."[13]

So, who was this elderly kabbalistic rabbi who claimed to have personally met the Messiah and to have received from Him personal illumination concerning His appearance and the timing of His return? Who was this one who could bring three hundred thousand people together in the streets of Jerusalem, some even endangering their lives to be there? What do we really know about him? And why would the Messiah appear to this man—if, in fact, the event actually happened? If the Messiah did not appear to the ancient rabbi, why in the world would he purposely leave such a dubious legacy, only to tarnish his name—*forever*?

Rabbi Yitzhak Kaduri was a distinctly unique and controversial figure indeed. And in death . . . he had only become more controversial.

4

KADURI'S JOURNEY:
OUT OF BAGHDAD

[They] have turned Rabbi Kaduri into a circus, just to make money.[1]
—*Rabbi Baruch Abuhatzeira, also known as the Baba Baruch*

"You have so much promise, my young Yitzhak!" the wise old Kabbalah sage uttered with delight. His grin stretched with pride from ear to ear. Rabbi Yosef Chaim, one of the most influential Sephardi rabbis of the nineteenth century, foresaw wonderful possibilities for his young student, Yitzhak Diba.

Yitzhak knew Rabbi Chaim was considered a *righteous one* among the people. A master teacher of the Torah and the deep mysteries of Kabbalah, he had endeavored to do the will of God for ages. The rabbi was a man of piety, prayer, and kindly speech toward others. He never spoke a word of vulgarity or expressed evil designs upon anyone. God recognized such men. Yes . . . Rabbi Chaim was *one* who could easily be used as a channel for pronouncing God's blessings upon others. And now, Rabbi Chaim was about to lay hands upon him!

"On this very special day, I bless you in the name of Adonai." Rabbi Chaim placed his hand gently upon the head of his young pupil. "It is the will of *HaShem* that you, Yitzhak, shall be a conduit of blessing to many multitudes within your lifetime. Thousands will stream to your door—seeking the blessing and the power that only you shall possess.

"You shall live to be a very old man—older than any of those around you. You will see many things . . . blessings, curses, triumphs, and horrors. But *HaShem* will use you to guide many—especially in times of trouble. May *HaShem* grant unto you *braha vehatzlaha* [blessings and success]."

The young Yitzhak held his breath. This was no small thing, no ordinary blessing. Rabbi Chaim was in a trance-like state of prayer and in connection with the power of special blessing apparently flowing from the throne of God. The blessings were being transferred through the spirit and hand of his rabbi—to him!

"*HaShem* of all blessings has revealed something else to me . . . " Rabbi Chaim paused. Then a low guttural sound emanated from somewhere deep within his chest. "What?" the old rabbi asked of no one. "What is *this* that I see?"

The rabbi was now going to prophesy over Yitzhak! The young Kabbalah student was ecstatic. He shut his eyes tight and listened intently for his mentor's next words. He could scarcely breathe.

"You shall live to see the coming of *Mashiach*—in your lifetime! Mashiach shall come to *you*! You, Yitzhak, will receive a vision—

when the time is right, when the times have been fulfilled . . . Mashiach shall reveal Himself to you, and you will be used to announce His arrival to restore His people, Israel!"

The old man lowered his head as if in continued prayer—muttering softly. Yitzhak had seen these types of blessings before. But never before had he heard such a blessing, such wonderful things pronounced over . . . anyone! Wide-eyed with wonder, he looked around the room, half expecting to see God Himself. He heard only the soft breeze blowing through the window and the far-off sounds of children playing. *How can this be?* Yitzhak wondered. *Am I really the one to announce the arrival of Mashiach? When will Mashiach confirm this astounding prophecy? When will the vision be revealed to me?*

Isaac (Yitzhak) would soon change his last name to *Kaduri* and would eventually become a living legend—adored by millions. But the thirteen-year-old Baghdadi lad could not have dreamed of that improbable stature at this moment in time.[2]

***

Before we launch into Kaduri's history, it is important at this point that I discuss with you a term you will see again in this book: *rabbinical Judaism.*

What does that term mean? Aren't all Jews followers of the rabbis? The answer is no. In fact, the next time you read the Gospels, notice who Jesus, or Yeshua, repeatedly chastised and held up for harsh criticism. It was the "Pharisees." But who were they? They were the rabbinical Jews of their time, which meant that the authority they gave to the traditional, oral teachings of the rabbis was equal to—and sometimes, higher than—that which they gave to the Torah, or the Holy Scripture. That was Jesus's beef with them. He criticized them because they were *adding to* the Word of God. There have always been some Jews who were, as Christians might say, *sola scriptura*—Scripture only. But when the Temple was destroyed in AD 70, the Pharisees, who added the traditions of men to God's Word, emerged as the dominant force in Judaism. Today, we call that tradition *Orthodox Judaism*.

Yitzhak Kaduri Z"L[3] eventually became the most celebrated *Mizrahi Haredi* rabbi and kabbalist of modern times. The *Mizrahi* are Jews descended from the Jewish communities of the Babylonian era in the Middle East. The *Haredi* sect of Judaism is the most conservative form of Orthodox Judaism, often referred to, by those outside the Hebrew faith, as *ultra-Orthodox*.

Kaduri was born in Baghdad, in what is now modern-day Iraq. At the time of his birth, that area of the world was a part of the Ottoman Turkish province. Kaduri's father was Katchouri Diba ben Aziza, a rabbi and a trader in exotic spices.

While still in his teens, Kaduri developed an attraction to the practice of Kabbalah and thus immersed himself in the ancient studies while most of his young friends were playing the games of children. Soon young Kaduri became a student of renowned Kabbalist Rabbi Yosef Chaim of Baghdad, and studied at the Zilka Yeshivah in Baghdad. A *yeshiva* is an educational institution that focuses on the study of traditional religious texts, primarily the Talmud (the collection of ancient rabbinic writings constituting the basis of religious authority in Orthodox Judaism) and the Torah (the first five books of the Old Testament). A yeshiva is similar in function to a seminary.

Kaduri claimed that Rabbi Yosef Chaim blessed him, at age thirteen (some report the age of the blessing to be sixteen), and revealed to him that he would live to see the revelation of the Messiah.[4] Some say this is where Kaduri's burden to have a Messianic revelation may have first been instilled. Many years into the future, yet another prominent rabbi would once again pronounce the numinous destiny upon him by declaring that Kaduri would meet the Messiah sometime before he died.

During the course of the First World War, the Ottoman Empire was forcibly enlisting the Jews of Baghdad into the army. The word on the street was that the Ottomans were going to raid the Jewish yeshiva in Baghdad. A call went out for young scholars who would be willing to go into hiding within the city to preserve the Torah and other sacred writings. The volunteer scholars were to be hidden inside the walls that surrounded the neighborhood. They were to remain in hiding for the duration of the war. Rabbi Kaduri was one of four young men that volunteered. He successfully completed the mission and was hailed as a hero.[5]

In 1923, after Rabbi Chaim's death, Yitzhak Kaduri set out from Baghdad and migrated to the British Mandate of Palestine. This move was undertaken on the advice of the elders of Baghdad who hoped he might *ebb the incursion of Zionism* in the post–World War I state. It was here that he changed his last name from Diba, of his father's family, to Kaduri.

This name change is an interesting consideration. Yitzhak's first name is a Hebrew name, and when translated to English, it becomes *Isaac.* The name Isaac means "He laughs." Yitzhak's original surname was *Diba*. This name in Hebrew means "slander." So, young Kaduri's original name meant "He laughs at slander." Changing the name Diba to Kaduri was an important move for young Yitzhak because it bespoke his intention to dedicate himself fully to the practice of Kabbalah. The word *Kaduri* means "ball" or "sphere." The imagery of a sphere, now associated with the name by which he would be forever known, was no accidental choice on Kaduri's part.

In an article devoted to the deeper understanding of the practice of Kabbalah, we find this description that sheds much light on Yitzhak's name change from Diba to Kaduri:

The building blocks of the Kabbalah terminology are the ten spheres. These are ten sources or "lights" through which God communicates with his world. They are also 10 different ways of revealing god, one per level.

In the Kabbalah terminology, numbers are more than just mere mathematical symbols. They have qualitative characteristics and meaning. The special meaning of the number 10 results from the fact that it constitutes our mathematical basis.

Common belief has it that the use of the basis 10 results from the fact that we have 10 fingers. God wanted the humane system to be decimal. The spheres are unique and some contradict others. The basic division of spheres is called right, left and middle, or in accordance with their leadership, mercy, judgment and grace. The sphere system maintains tensions between opposite forces and the cabalist seeks mediation between, namely bringing them to the middle ground, thus establishing harmony. This will yield positive effects and vitality for the world.[6]

The particular Orthodox sect, of which Kaduri was now a strict adherent, believed that Israel could not become a truly restored nation again until Messiah physically returned and then literally established the nation-state of Israel Himself. The sect was a strict opponent of the current political attempts of his day, called *Zionism*. Zionism sought to firmly reestablish the modern-day nation of Israel. Some see Kaduri's journey as a contemporary mirroring of that of the biblical Abraham. Abraham set out initially from Ur of the Chaldees—the current nation of Iraq.

Upon his arrival in Palestine, Kaduri attached himself to the Shoshanim LeDavid Yeshiva for kabbalists from Iraq. He later absorbed himself in regular study of the Talmud and rabbinical law in the Porat Yosef Yeshiva in Jerusalem's Old City.

Rabbi Kaduri and his young family moved to the Old City (Jerusalem) in 1934. The Porat Yosef Yeshivah, where he was studying, granted him an apartment, along with the assignment

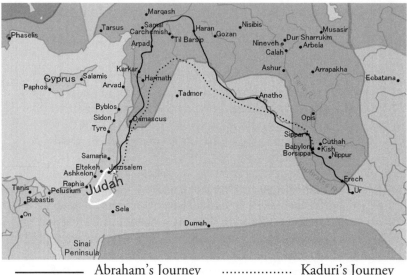

——————— Abraham's Journey   ·············· Kaduri's Journey
(exact route unknown)

of binding the yeshiva's books and constructing copies of rare manuscripts in the yeshiva's library. Kaduri applied himself to this undertaking with such vigor that until his dying day, he would be known by many as Rabbi Kaduri *The Book Binder*. The original books remained in the yeshiva's library, while the copies were deposited in Rabbi Kaduri's personal library. Reportedly, Kaduri would study each book intently before binding it, and commit the text, or large sections of it, to memory. He allegedly had a photographic memory, had mastered the Talmud, and could recite vast portions of it by heart.

During the tumultuous years of the 1930s and 1940s, the muftis (Muslim legal experts) of Jerusalem and the Muslim Brotherhood of Egypt collaborated with Adolf Hitler in Germany, seeking to bring about the Final Solution for the Jewish problem. Kaduri's life would take a dramatic turn when, during the massive Arab-Israeli hostilities that led up to the 1948 war, the Porat Yosef

Yeshivah was necessarily transformed into a stronghold against recurrent outbreaks of aggression. As the troubles between the Jordanians and the embryonic Jewish state began to increase, Kaduri began smuggling many of the yeshiva's antique and priceless texts out of the Old City of Jerusalem and into the New City.

When the Jewish quarter of the Old City fell to the invading Jordanian army during the 1948 Arab-Israeli War, the Jordanians set ablaze the yeshiva and all the surrounding homes and apartments. The inferno destroyed all the books and manuscripts that Rabbi Kaduri was not able to smuggle out of the quickly burning section of Jerusalem.

A little over forty years later, the leading kabbalist, Rabbi Efraim Hakohen, died. Rabbi Yitzhak Kaduri was soon appointed the new head of the Kabbalah group. During his leadership, Kaduri produced several books and articles that he allowed only his students to read. He never published a single piece of his written work for public consumption. He also spoke out heavily against the practice of Kabbalah for profit (the dissemination of advice or charms), a popular practice of his day.

Kaduri learned, from the great kabbalists of previous generations, the secrets of *amulets*. Amulets are usually necklaces, with writings of blessing or charms inscribed upon them, believed by many to bring healing and success. It is reported that over the years, many thousands of people pilgrimaged to seek Kaduri's advice, blessings, and amulets, which he would create specifically for the individual in need and dispense without charge. These articles of blessing were widely sought by those in financial need, couples with fertility problems, the sick and diseased—even those seeking a spouse. Countless people attributed personal miracles and blessings to Rabbi Kaduri.[7]

Rabbi Kaduri's rise to celebrity status, though, began when his son, Rabbi David Kaduri, who ran a poultry store in the

Bukharim Market, determined to establish a reputable yeshiva under his father's name and teachings. The new institute for Jewish and Kabbalah studies was named Nachalat Yitzhak Yeshiva and was located adjacent to the family home in the Bukharim neighborhood of Jerusalem.[8]

There was outrage, in some circles, over Kaduri's liberal dispensing of amulets and special blessings. According to the UK's *Guardian*:

> If dispensing blessings was one of Kaduri's stocks-in-trade, so was sending curses. In 1991 he sought out the name of Saddam Hussein's mother, so that he could send efficacious pulsa denura—Aramaic for "lashings of fire"—against this enemy of the Jews. Kaduri was also implicated in the death curse on Yitzhak Rabin, which was eerily pronounced just a month before the Labour premier's assassination in November 1995. Although he was never proved to be a signatory, in the eyes of secular detractors guilt by association was good enough.
>
> Conventionally Orthodox Jews, too, lampooned Kaduri's folk customs as foolish and alien to normative Judaism. They enjoyed pointing out that his supposedly divine amulets were marked "Made in Taiwan."
>
> . . .
>
> Even former Sephardi chief rabbi Ovadiah Yosef questioned the credentials of a man who had never written a single religious article, let alone a book. Kaduri, in turn, criticised show-business and other celebrities who claimed to have taken up Judaism's mystical tradition. When Madonna made a midnight visit to the grave of a sage while visiting Israel in 2004, he asserted: "It is forbidden to teach Kabbalah to a non-Jew."[9]

According to the rabbi's son, David, the elder Kaduri was involved in the exorcising of at least twenty *dybbuks*. A dybbuk is said to be a lost soul that has strayed into the body of an unfortunate living person to torment him or her. However, according to sources close to the ancient mystic, Kaduri never dabbled in the most dangerous types of Kabbalah. Those practices would have included forcing oaths upon demons. Kabbalists believe that it is possible, at least in theory, to use holy names to ensnare demons and to harness their powers. But those who do so risk a dark and deeply spiritual retribution.[10]

Kaduri eventually became widely known and revered as a serious prophet among his many followers. His fame increased all the more near the end of his life. In late 2004, Kaduri predicted "great tragedies in the world." This statement was made two weeks before the 2004 Indian Ocean earthquake and tsunami. News reporter Baruch Gordon, of *Arutz Sheva*, connected these events with Rabbi Kaduri's prophecy.[11]

The last twenty years of Kaduri's life, however, were blemished, many thought, by the notorious manner in which some political figures used him to promote different political parties.

A POLITICAL PAWN?

Kaduri's reputation as supernatural mystic had begun during and after the Yom Kippur War of 1973. Families of soldiers missing in action sought out Kaduri to ask him to use his powers to determine whether their loved ones were dead or alive.[12] However, Rabbi Kaduri attained celebrity status and popular political fame during the 1996 Knesset elections. Reports say he probably swung the crucial balance of 29,000 voters who ensured that Likud party leader Benjamin Netanyahu was elected prime minister of Israel. He did so by distributing thousands of "magic" amulets to his devotees, who were then obliged to vote for Netanyahu in the prime ministerial poll and for the Orthodox Shas party in the simultaneous party elections. Kaduri bolstered Netanyahu's platform of "restoring Jewish values" by publicly endorsing him before polling day.[13]

Kaduri was flown by helicopter to multiple political rallies in support of the Israeli Shas Party. At these rallies, he would distribute the amulets he had produced, in his name, for supporters of that party. The *Jerusalem Post* reported on the event:

> At the time, Shas was at an electoral low point. Shas managed to distribute 100,000 amulets before chairman of the Elections Committee Theodore Or prohibited their use. Soon after Ophir Paz-Pines drafted a bill ratified by the Knesset that anchored Or's prohibition in legislation. But the amulets did the trick: Shas mustered 10 mandates.
>
> In the 2003 elections Kaduri's grandson Yossi, who had demanded and been refused a realistic spot on the Shas list, attempted to use his grandfather to rekindle the electoral success of 1996 with his own political party called Ahavat Yisrael. But the party failed to gain the minimum votes needed to enter the Knesset.
>
> Kaduri's son David claims his father passed on to him the secrets of amulet writing. However, others claim that Kaduri's metaphysical powers cannot be inherited.[14]

LIVE CAMERAS AND OPEN MICROPHONES

In October 1997, Benjamin Netanyahu, then in his first term as prime minister of Israel, came to visit Kaduri at his synagogue. In a conversation between the two, Netanyahu reportedly whispered in Kaduri's ear, "The left has forgotten what it is to be a Jew" and that they were willing to "place our security in Arab hands."[15] Apparently, neither Netanyahu nor Kaduri realized that the television cameras were rolling and the microphones were still open. The incident was considered a disconcerting action on the part of the prime minister. The report of it reverberated through the press. Even so, the UK's *Guardian* reported, in fairness to the rabbi, that Kaduri never asked to be Netanyahu's confidant.[16]

Undaunted by his critics, Kaduri pronounced with holy

authority over Netanyahu in March 1997, "May the Almighty keep and protect the prime minister; may he live long, defeat all his enemies and win the next elections."[17]

Many people, especially his grandson Yossi Kaduri, saw the sage as a senile victim of mischievous associates and people with political aspirations.[18] Others, however, saw the elderly Kaduri as somewhat of a victim of his own popularity. There was quite an expression of outrage over the perceived exploitation of the rabbi. Following Rabbi Kaduri's death, the *Guardian*'s obituary stated:

> Shas politicians exploited his reputation, while others literally cashed in on his name. Kaduri was once delivered by helicopter to bless a sausage factory in a development town. Apparatchiks then collected monetary pledges from townsfolk who believed they could purchase heaven's favour via this holy conduit.
>
> To David Levy, Israel's Moroccan-born former foreign minister, the Kaduri roadshow was "surrealistic," an abuse of innocent faith which was "dragging us back to the dark ages [and] leading us towards an abyss, blindness and near civil war." Even fellow mystics, like "Baba Baruch" Abu-Hatzeira, criticised those who "have turned Rabbi Kaduri into a circus, just to make money."
>
> Small, bent and wizened, invariably draped in the white robes of an oriental Jewish Kabbalist (or purveyor of Jewish mysticism), Kaduri was little known in political circles until May 1996. But images of his benignly smiling face, which dangled from the rear-view mirrors of taxis scuttling between Tel Aviv and Jerusalem, indicated his popularity.[19]

Rabbi Kaduri was also popular for his efforts at achieving global peace. In fact, his persistent interventions for world peace resulted in a well-publicized personal friendship with King Hussein of Jordan. So deep was their friendship that the king even arranged for a special road to be constructed that would allow the rabbi to visit the shrine of Aaron, the ancient father of the Hebrew high priestly line. Often, the king would accompany Kaduri to the site after the rabbi was greeted at the airport and then flown to Aaron's shrine in King Hussein's private helicopter.[20]

In spite of the rabbi's high-profile friendships, practically every historical resource of Kaduri's life recounts that he generally led a minimalist life of scarcity and simplicity. He consumed very little food, seldom communicated in small talk, and was known to pray each month at the grave sites of *tzaddikim* (a title given to personalities considered *righteous* in Jewish tradition) in Israel. The only luxury he still allowed himself in his twilight years was an occasional foreign cigarette, which he smoked through a cigarette holder.

When asked about his lifelong cigarette habit, Kaduri quipped, "Smoke is good for angels."[21]

5

WORLD PEACE OR
WORLD DISASTERS?

In the future, the Holy One, Blessed be He, will bring about great disasters in the countries of the world to sweeten the judgments of the Land of Israel.[1]

—*Rabbi Yitzhak Kaduri, 2005*

Toward the end of his life, Rabbi Kaduri was the recipient of yet another messianic prophecy spoken over him—the same as that declared when he was only thirteen.

In a 1990 meeting with Rabbi Menachem Mendel Schneerson, the Rabbi of Lubavitch, Schneerson spoke words of blessing to Kaduri, including, as previously mentioned, the prophecy that Kaduri would not pass from this world until he

met the Messiah.[2] Schneerson's prophecy was reportedly fulfilled when Kaduri had a mystical vision on 9 Cheshvan 5764
(November 4, 2003), during which, Kaduri claims, he actually
spoke with the Messiah, and the Messiah revealed His name.
"Kaduri later noted to his disciples that the revealed name of the
Messiah was subsequently hidden among his writings"[3]—to be
revealed at a later date.

In 2005, Kaduri made headlines again with the dramatic
announcement that disasters were soon to fall upon the world.
He called for all the Jews worldwide to come to Israel as quickly
as possible. He is quoted in an Israel National News article titled
"Kabbalist Urges Jews to Israel Ahead of Upcoming Disasters":

> This declaration I find fitting to issue for all of the Jews of
> the world to hear. It is incumbent upon them to return to
> the Land of Israel due to terrible natural disasters which
> threaten the world.
>
> In the future, the Holy One, Blessed be He, will bring
> about great disasters in the countries of the world to sweeten
> the judgements of the Land of Israel.
>
> I am ordering the publication of this declaration as a
> warning, so that Jews in the countries of the world will be
> aware of the impending danger and will come to the Land
> of Israel for the building of the Temple and revelation of our
> righteous *Mashiach* (Messiah).[4]

The same publication reported that earlier in the year, Kaduri
had predicted great world tragedies. As we discussed in chapter
3, the article pointed out that Kaduri's predictions fell just two
weeks before the massively destructive tsunami in Southeast
Asia. Rabbi Kaduri was quoted in the *Yediot Acharonot* (daily
newspaper) as saying:

We are now in the fourth year of what could be the seven-year Redemption period, according to the calculation of the Vilna Gaon.[5] [However] in the coming three years, uncertainty about the future will hang over our heads, unless we work and strive that the Mashiach be revealed.

The Mashiach is already in Israel. Whatever people are sure will not happen, is liable to happen, and whatever we are certain will happen may disappoint us. But in the end, there will be peace throughout the world.

Great tragedies in the world are foreseen, that's the thing of the Jews going to the East. But our enemies will not prevail over us in the Land of Israel, "fear and trembling will fall upon them," in the power of Torah.[6]

The INN report further states that in the week prior to the interview, Rabbi Kaduri had said, "What can save the world from calamities is real repentance by Jews, who must increase acts of kindness towards one another . . . The cry of the many poor in Israel and the expulsion of Jews from their homes shakes the world . . . It's not for naught that this place was hit, where many of our compatriots went to look for this-worldly lusts."

Rabbi Kaduri reportedly told his students that the current Israeli government would be "the last one of the 'old era.' He is on record as saying that Sharon will be the last prime minister in Israel, and that the new government will already have leadership of the Messianic era."[7]

Of course, there have been prime ministers since Sharon's lapse into a vegetative state. However, many of the loyal adherents to Kaduri's prophecies note that Sharon was never voted out of office, nor did he resign. He is still living, and therefore, they claim, is still technically Israel's prime minister.

Just before Yom Kippur, the Day of Judgment, in October 2005, Rabbi Kaduri's grandson, Rabbi Yosef Kaduri, held a private but officially witnessed meeting with his grandfather. The meeting was accompanied and documented by reporter Baruch Gordon from Israel's *Arutz-7*. Gordon has admitted close ties with the Kaduri enclave.[8]

"Not many Jews are coming from overseas," said Kaduri's grandson during the session. "Why should they come?"

Rabbi Kaduri responded, "Because of impending danger . . . be extremely protective of your lives."[9]

The elder Rabbi Kaduri went on to speak of the "struggle between the oceans." He declared that the large oceans would "strike the world," and that this "striking" should be a "warning to the Jews living in America." Kaduri said the American Jews should *take note* of the devastating hurricanes Katrina, Rita, and Wilma, some of the strongest and costliest hurricanes of all time—all of which struck America's Gulf Coast in 2005, just before this particular meeting. The portents to follow would only be of "greater catastrophic proportions," he warned.[10]

In January 2006, Rabbi Kaduri was hospitalized with pneumonia. He was taken to the Bikur Holim hospital in Jerusalem, where he died around 10 p.m. on January 28. Dr. Yosef Kleiman, the rabbi's personal doctor for the previous fifteen years, said Kaduri's wife,[11] children, and grandchildren were by his side when he passed away.[12]

Shas leader Eli Yishai mandated party activists to honor a suspension of political activity for the next seven days, an initial period of mourning as prescribed by Jewish custom. "I call on the whole of the house of Israel, as I've called on all Shas activists, to prepare and arrive at the funeral of Rabbi Kaduri," said Yishai.[13]

Once again, his immense following would hold their collective breath, for Rabbi Kaduri had given a strange and seemingly ominous deathbed instruction. *There is yet another prophetic unveiling to come*, the old rabbi had promised. However, as we have already seen, the unveiling of the elderly sage's last revelation was not to occur until one year after his death. This was his last request. It was his last prophecy. And this would be the last piece of the complex puzzle of his nearly ninety-year legacy. His power and the shroud of his mystery would continue to live.

And then . . . the time came to open *the note.*

6

THE MYSTIFYING DEATH
MESSAGE, *UNSEALED*

He will lift the people and prove that his word and law are valid.[1]
—*Rabbi Kaduri, concerning his vision of Mashiach*

"This cannot be! May *HaShem* forbid it! The atrocity which I hold in my hand is an obvious forgery! Some trick of the devil or a *son of the devil*!" The rabbi paced the floor, clutching, and at times waving, the cryptic message. "It is not even written in the authentic hand of our dear teacher! This appears to be some type of a trick that, perhaps, one of those arrogant and so-called

Messianic Jews would thrust upon us!" The man's brow furrowed deeply; his face contorted into a mask of rage. His breathing became more labored as he pondered the magnitude of that which he held. He formed his right hand into a fist and slammed it down upon his desk. The sound thundered from his office and resonated down the hall. "I will not allow it! I will not *stand* for it! I cannot be convinced—I *will not* be convinced—that these are the words of our late rabbi (may *HaShem* bless his soul). They simply cannot be his words! Rabbi Kaduri would never have placed this burden upon his people!" The holy man paused to take a breath. He was visibly shaken to the core of his being.

"What does this mean?" he asked, his voice raising an octave. "That our beloved rabbi is a *Christian*?" As he said the word *Christian*, it was with disdain. "He *wouldn't*!" he said, with an intonation of deep sorrow. "Of all people . . . *he* wouldn't!"

All in the room concurred.

"We *must* meet—first thing in the morning. We must formulate our story . . . um . . . our *position* in this matter. We must be united when we speak to the media. There *will* be press on this matter. There will be no way around it."

This was the mandate of the elderly and ranking rabbi. The others knew the seriousness of the matter. They would be at the meeting. The *position* must be formulated.

"I suppose the Christians will now be dancing in the streets! This must be stopped, and it must be stopped now!" He plopped down into the chair behind his desk and buried his face in his hands. Almost imperceptibly, he began to weep.

The others in the room slowly filed out in deference to the rabbi's justified sorrow. This was going to get ugly. This note *could* change everything.[2]

***

On April 30, 2007, *Israel Today* published the article that rocked the Judeo-Christian world.[3] The article, which bore the startling headline: "Rabbi Reveals Name of the Messiah," attested to the widely reported fact that just before Kaduri's death, he had shocked his followers by telling them that he had personally met the Messiah. As outlined earlier, Kaduri had also delivered a synagogue message instructing his pupils on how to recognize the soon-coming Messiah. He had further floored the listening audience by proclaiming that the Messiah would not appear to Israel until after Ariel Sharon was dead. The *Israel Today* article proclaimed that other known rabbis had predicted the same message concerning the linking of Messiah's arrival with the death of Ariel Sharon.

Kaduri's grandson, Rabbi Yosef Kaduri attested that his grandfather spoke many times during his last days about the coming of the Messiah and the redemption that would be made available through Him. The elder Kaduri's cryptic portrayals of the Messiah were published on his own website, Kaduri.net. Following are some of those portrayals, as indicated in the *Israel Today* article:

> It is hard for many good people in society to understand the person of the Messiah. The leadership and order of a Messiah of flesh and blood is hard to accept for many in the nation. As leader, the Messiah will not hold any office, but will be among the people and use the media to communicate. His reign will be pure and without personal or political desire. During his dominion, only righteousness and truth will reign.
>
> Will all believe in the Messiah right away? No, in the beginning some of us will believe in him and some not. It will be easier for non-religious people to follow the Messiah than for Orthodox people.
>
> The revelation of the Messiah will be fulfilled in two stages: First, he will actively confirm his position as Messiah

without knowing himself that he is the Messiah. Then he will reveal himself to some Jews, not necessarily to wise Torah scholars. It can be even simple people. Only then he will reveal himself to the whole nation. The people will wonder and say: "What, that's the Messiah?" Many have known his name but have not believed that he is the Messiah.

Of course, many have noticed the distinct allusions to the New Testament Messiah, Jesus Christ, in Kaduri's website utterances.

THE UNSEALING

When Kaduri's mystery note was finally brought forth and opened, written in Kaduri's alleged, scribbled, Hebrew handwriting was this message (translated to English):

> Concerning the *letter abbreviation* (or secret coding) of the Messiah's name, He will lift the people and prove that his word and law are valid.
>
> This I have signed in the month of mercy,
>
> *Yitzhak Kaduri*

It was discerned by his closest circle that in these words the old rabbi had left a cryptic message of the revelation of the Messiah, which they were to unlock. The key to unlocking the message was determined to be the first portion of the sentence: *Concerning the letter abbreviation of the Messiah's name.* This seemingly clear clue led them to understand that they were to take the first letter of each of the remaining Hebrew words in the note and combine them to form the long-awaited messianic revelation. The message's remaining words were: *Yarim Ha'Am Veyokhiakh Shedvaro Vetorato Omdim.*

Translated to English:

"He will lift the people and prove that his word and law are valid."

As they read Kaduri's words—from right to left, as is done in the Hebrew language—a startling revelation unfolded before their eyes. The first Hebrew letter from each of the remaining six Hebrew words in the message, when joined together, spelled *Yehoshua*, or *Yeshua*. Translated to English, these words unarguably represent the name *Jesus*.

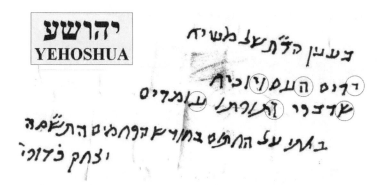

A BRIEF WORD STUDY

Yehoshua and *Yeshua* are, in effect, the same name, derived from the same Hebrew root of the word *salvation*. An example of the name's usage in this manner can be found in the Hebrew texts of Zechariah 6:11 and Ezra 3:2. Whereas Ezra wrote, "Yeshua son of Yozadak," Zechariah wrote, "Yehoshua son of Yohozadak," adding the holy abbreviation of God's name, *ho*, to the father's name, Yozadak, and to the name Yeshua. (Some researchers claim that the inserting of the divine abbreviation *ho* into the name *Yeshua* points to the *God-Man* nature of the true Messiah, who would be both God and man at the same time.)

Following are the English versions of these two verses, along with explanations based on *Strong's Exhaustive Concordance.*

> Then stood up Jeshua the son of Jozadak, and his brethren the priests . . . (Ezra 3:2)

YESHUA – Strong's Hebrew Dictionary **#3442**: Yeshua = *He will save* . . . the same as #3091
Then take silver and gold, and make crowns, and set them upon the head of Joshua the son of Josedech, the high priest. (Zech. 6:11)

YEHOSHUA – Strong's Hebrew Dictionary **#3091**: Yehoshua = *Jehovah saved* . . . the same as Yeshua.

Yeshua was a familiar alternate form of the name יְהוֹשׁוּעַ (*Yehoshua,* or Joshua) in later books of the Hebrew Bible. It was also commonly used among Jews of the Second Temple period. The name corresponds to the Romanized, Greek spelling, *Iesous,* from which comes the English spelling *Jesus.*[4] I will do a much more in-depth analysis of these names in a subsequent chapter. But for now, for the purpose of revealing the *message* of the note, the preceding information is linguistically accurate.

***

Certainly, many would have soon recalled the words on Kaduri's website—placed there, reportedly, by his own utterances: *Many have known his name but have not believed that he is the Messiah.* Amazingly, this declaration fits perfectly with the historical fact that many millions, perhaps billions, have known the name of Jesus and His claim as Savior, Messiah, and Lord—yet have not believed. Kaduri's note seemed to point perfectly to *Jesus Christ* as Messiah.

Other Christian students of the Old Testament saw shades of the writings of the ancient prophet Isaiah in the Kaduri revelation. The haunting words of Isaiah 53 now sounded with a louder and clearer ring:

> Who hath believed our report? and to whom is the arm of the LORD revealed?
>
> For he shall grow up before him as a tender plant, and as a root out of a dry ground: he hath no form nor comeliness; and when we shall see him, there is no beauty that we should desire him.
>
> He is despised and rejected of men; a man of sorrows, and acquainted with grief: and we hid as it were our faces from him; he was despised, and we esteemed him not.
>
> Surely he hath borne our griefs, and carried our sorrows: yet we did esteem him stricken, smitten of God, and afflicted.
>
> But he was wounded for our transgressions, he was bruised for our iniquities: the chastisement of our peace was upon him; and with his stripes we are healed.
>
> All we like sheep have gone astray; we have turned every one to his own way; and the LORD hath laid on him the iniquity of us all.
>
> He was oppressed, and he was afflicted, yet he opened not his mouth: he is brought as a lamb to the slaughter, and as a sheep before her shearers is dumb, so he openeth not his mouth. (vv. 1–7)

Rabbi Kaduri's alleged revelation shook Judaism to the core. *How can this be?* they wondered. How could perhaps the most celebrated rabbi in Jewish history have left such a seemingly blasphemous message to the Jewish world? Did the Jews now have another Rabbi Saul on their hands? Had their most beloved rabbi become a traitor to the Jewish faith and tradition? The ramifications were overwhelming.

The wheels of politics, power, religion, and wealth began to spin. In the minds of many people of great influence, some who stood to lose everything by Kaduri's revelation, this madness had to be stopped.

7

ISLAM, JESUS, MAHDI, AND THE ANTICHRIST

I fervently believe, and have meticulously demonstrated, that a scriptural case for an Islamic Antichrist can be made.
—*Joel Richardson,* New York Times *best-selling author and Middle East prophecy expert*

According to the *Israel Today* article we have been discussing, when the name Yehoshua appeared in Kaduri's message, ultra-Orthodox Jews from his Nahalat Yitzhak Yeshiva in Jerusalem argued that their master could not possibly have left the *exact solution* for decoding the Messiah's name. This so-called revelation was unthinkable! There had to be some sort of mistake, at the very least. It was a hoax or even a forgery, at the worst.

The supposed revelation received negligible coverage in the Israeli media. Only the Hebrew websites *News First Class* and *Kaduri.net* mentioned the Messiah note in the earliest days of its unveiling. Both sites insisted the note was authentic. The Hebrew daily *Ma'ariv* ran a story on the note but quickly described the cryptic message as a forgery. For the first time in a long time, the Israeli press ignored the prophetic utterances of their revered prophet and sage. His words were not the words they wanted to hear. Apparently they collectively decided to disregard this one last amazing prophetic utterance from their revered old sage.

Aviel Schneider, the author of the *Israel Today* story, said he was urged not to publish the story by the rabbi's yeshiva, where officials said it was "impossible" that the note was actually written by Kaduri.[1]

Jewish readers responded on blogs and web forums with skepticism: "So this means Rabbi Kaduri was a Christian?" and "The Christians are dancing and celebrating" were among the comments.[2] The *Israel Today* news article declared:

> *Israel Today* spoke to two of Kaduri's followers in Jerusalem who admitted that the note was authentic, but confusing for his followers as well. "We have no idea how the Rabbi got to this name of the Messiah," one of them said.
>
> Yet others completely deny any possibility that the note is authentic. Kaduri's son, Rabbi David Kaduri, said that at the time the note was written (September 2005), his father's physical condition made it impossible for him to write.[3]

Further, *Israel Today* attests, when the eighty-year-old son of the late Rabbi Yitzhak Kaduri was shown the note bearing the name *Yeshua*, he said, "It's not his writing." Reportedly, during a nighttime meeting in the Nahalat Yitzhak Yeshiva in Jerusalem, books with the elder Kaduri's handwriting from eighty years in the past were presented to *Israel Today* reporters in an attempt to prove that the Messiah note was not authentic. The reporters then told Rabbi David Kaduri that his father's own official website (www.kaduri.net) had mentioned the Messiah note. Rabbi David was reported to be shocked. "Oh no!" he said. "That's blasphemy."

Aviel Schneider, the author of the *Israel Today* story, said the worldwide reaction to the news of Kaduri's note was "crazy." He said he had never received so many e-mails and calls from around the globe. He also said that the rabbi's yeshiva urged him not to publish the story because it was "impossible" that the note was actually written by Kaduri.[4]

David Kaduri did confirm, according to the *Israel Today* article, that in the last year of his life, his father had talked and dreamed almost exclusively about the Messiah and his coming. "My father has met the Messiah in a vision," he said, "and told us that he would come soon." As reported in the original *Israel Today* piece, Orthodox Jews from the Nahalat Yitzhak Yeshiva told the publication a few weeks after the story that the account of the secret note of Rabbi Kaduri should never have come out. They claimed that the good name of Kaduri had been severely damaged by the report.

UNDERSTANDING THE JEWISH SKEPTICISM

As it stands today, the Judeo-Christian world remains hotly divided over the interpretation of the Kaduri note and the supposed messianic prophecy it contains. Many of the exact details surrounding the note—its initial delivery, its sealing and protection, the witnesses, the handling of the note in the interim, and its ultimate unveiling—are still unclear and perhaps, some have accused, have been purposely obscured. And of course, one can understand the Jewish world's confusion in the matter. For those who come from a distinctly Christian worldview and believe that ample evidence exists from history, the Bible, and extrabiblical sources to prove that Jesus Christ is, indeed, the Messiah, a revelation of this nature is indescribably exciting. But to announce to a Jew that perhaps one of his most revered rabbis has just declared *Jesus Christ* to be the true Messiah would be tantamount to the Catholic pope, Dr. Billy Graham, or some famous evangelical Christian pastor announcing that it had been lately revealed to him in a vision that the *Mahdi* (Islamic messiah) is the true and soon-coming Messiah.

NO ROOM IN THE INN

In case the reader thinks that perhaps I am being a bit over-dramatic in my comparison, let me remind you of a seldom-mentioned but very important fact: rabbinical Judaism rejects the notion of Jesus Christ as Messiah, *in full*. There is no room whatsoever for the person of Jesus Christ of Nazareth in their religious discussion. The same attitude of *Crucify Him!* that existed in Jesus's day among the Jews still exists to this day. Proverbially speaking, *there is still no room in the inn for Jesus*. In fact, Orthodox Judaism teaches that Jesus was a false prophet and an impostor—an absolute fraud—and to worship Jesus is nothing short of idolatry and abject heresy. There is an inherent loathing among the Orthodox Jews for all things Christian, New Testament, and Jesus-centric. The repulsion to the notion of Jesus Christ as Messiah goes deep and to the heart of practically every follower of rabbinical Judaism.

To further highlight my position, let me remind you that even the Muslims actually *revere* Jesus—deeply. They do not acknowledge Jesus as *God with us*, or Savior, or Lord, as the Christian does, but they *do* revere Him. The Muslim faith teaches that Jesus was the last and greatest prophet to the Jews. (Muhammad, they claim, was the last and greatest prophet, *period*.) Islam claims that Jesus was sent from Allah to the Jewish world to convince them to turn to Allah and away from their *false* God. Furthermore, and as a surprise to many Christians, Islam teaches that *Jesus will return* to establish Islam as the true religion of the world. The Islamic version of Jesus is exceptionally important to the Muslim world.

Following is some of what the Islamic authoritative teachings (the ahadith) say about the return of Jesus, taken from Christopher Logan's web article titled "Islam 101" (emphasis in original).[5]

Book 37, Number 4310:

Narrated AbuHurayrah:

The Prophet (peace_be_upon_him) said: There is no prophet between me and him, that is, Jesus (peace_be_upon_him). He will descent (to the earth). When you see him, recognise him: a man of medium height, reddish fair, wearing two light yellow garments, looking as if drops were falling down from his head though it will not be wet. *He will fight the people for the cause of Islam. He will break the cross, kill swine, and abolish jizyah. Allah will perish all religions except Islam.* He will destroy the Antichrist and will live on the earth for forty years and then he will die. The Muslims will pray over him.

Volume 4, Book 55, Number 657:

Narrated Abu Huraira:

Allah's Apostle said, "By Him in Whose Hands my soul is, surely (Jesus,) the son of Mary will soon descend amongst you and will judge mankind justly (as a Just Ruler); *he will break the Cross* and kill the pigs and there will be no Jizya (i.e. taxation taken from non Muslims). Money will be in abundance so that nobody will accept it, and a single prostration to Allah (in prayer) will be better than the whole world and whatever is in it." Abu Huraira added *"If you wish, you can recite (this verse of the Holy Book): —'And there is none Of the people of the Scriptures (Jews and Christians) But must believe in him (i.e Jesus as an Apostle of Allah and a human being) Before his death. And on the Day of Judgment He will be a witness Against them."* (4.159) (See Fateh Al Bari, Page 302 Vol 7)

Volume 4, Book 55, Number 658:

Narrated Abu Huraira:

Allah's Apostle said *"How will you be when the son of Mary (i.e. Jesus) descends amongst you and he will judge people by the Law of the Quran and not by the law of Gospel*[?"] (Fateh-ul Bari page 304 and 305 Vol 7)

For a more contemporary example of this Islamic teaching, I refer you to the 2006 statements made by then-president of Iran, Mahmoud Ahmadinejad. As documented in a WND article dated December 19, 2006, the Muslim Ahmadinejad believes wholeheartedly in the Islamic teachings of Jesus's return:

In a greeting to the world's Christians for the coming new year, Iranian President Mahmoud Ahmadinejad said he expects both Jesus and the Shiite messianic figure, Imam Mahdi, to return and "wipe away oppression."

He sees his main mission, as he recounted in a Nov. 16, 2005, speech in Tehran, as to "pave the path for the glorious reappearance of Imam Mahdi, may Allah hasten his reappearance."

With Iran's continued development of nuclear technology in defiance of the West, some analysts fear Ahmadinejad's intent is to trigger the kind of global conflagration he envisions will set the stage for the end of the world.

Ahmadinejad hosted a conference last week examining whether the Nazi genocide took place, drawing Holocaust deniers from around the world. The Iranian president has described the Holocaust as a "myth" and called for Israel to be wiped off the map.

"The Zionist regime will be wiped out soon the same way the Soviet Union was, and humanity will achieve freedom," he said.[6]

I emphasize this point and include these Islamic teachings in order that the reader might realize the full significance of Rabbi Kaduri's supposed revelation upon the Jewish psyche. For the rabbinical Jew to even begin to fathom that *Jesus Christ of the Christians* or *Jesus the Prophet of the Muslims* could somehow be the *real Messiah* is absolutely unthinkable! The statement is beyond the realm of anything acceptable. The very thought of it would be anathema to the Orthodox Jewish mind. Jesus is not even a historical figure to be seriously acknowledged, as far as the rabbinical Jew is concerned.

Confronted with the purported and shocking revelation from the venerated Rabbi Kaduri, rabbinical Jews had only a few choices. They could deny the report flatly and declare the whole thing to be a hoax. Or, they could say the note existed but had been wrongly interpreted. Or, perhaps they could claim the note was real, but that the elderly rabbi had lost his mind. Alternatively, an Orthodox Jew could take the interpretation at its face value—and give serious consideration to the possibility that their celebrated rabbi did, in fact, have a vision from God that pointed to Jesus Christ as Messiah.

As difficult as the last choice might be, unbelievably, some

Jews have made this choice and have turned to Jesus Christ as Savior and Lord—as a direct result of Kaduri's prophecies and death note. (I will expound upon that phenomenon later.) Additionally, we must not neglect the effect of the prophecy upon those in the Christian community who emphasize that the Antichrist must come *before* the true Messiah returns. To some, Kaduri's prophecy seemed to line up not only with the possibility of a *false Yeshua*, or an antichrist figure, but also, perhaps, with the coming of the Islamic Mahdi. Of course, many see the Mahdi as none other than the Antichrist about whom much prophecy is given in the New Testament. The following is an example of that line of thinking, taken from a prophecy blog on which the various posters were talking about the Rabbi Kaduri Messiah prophecies and the possible interpretations:

> This guy [Kaduri] actually foretells the coming of the anti-christ. He was a Kabbalist Jew which is forbidden in Judaism and the version of the "Christ" he gives is biblically different from the actual Christ. He says that Jesus is here on Earth now and when he comes he will abolish the cross and tell Christians they are wrong. In Islam he is called the Mahdi. Do some more research and you'll realize this prophecy isn't what it seems. People stop at the name "Yeshua" without testing the Spirit. God Bless.[7]

I asked Joel Richardson, a *New York Times* best-selling author and expert on prophecy and the Middle East, to comment on the possibility of an Islamic Antichrist as is represented in the Muslim Mahdi figure. His thought-provoking insight follows:

> Recently, and for the first time ever, a comprehensive study by the Pew Research firm was conducted concerning Muslim beliefs about the Mahdi. The study included tens of thousands of Muslims in more than twenty-three countries. The

Islamic participants were asked if they believed the Mahdi's emergence was imminent and that it would occur within their lifetimes. The results conclusively prove that which I have been warning about all along. Overwhelmingly, the Muslim world is expecting the soon appearance of the Mahdi.

When one considers how loose Sunni Muslim traditions are concerning the Mahdi, it is not difficult to imagine a significant leader gaining a reputation and developing a massive grassroots following, all the while never even claiming to be the Mahdi. In fact, throughout Islamic history, several significant Mahdi claimants have arisen and gathered a significant following. They have all been Sunni Muslims.

I have often demonstrated the frightening world of the Islamic apocalyptic views, comparing them with the biblical prophecies concerning the coming of the Antichrist. I believe I have shown, in my several books, beyond any doubt that in the Islamic doctrine of the Mahdi, the world should be very concerned.

I fervently believe, and have meticulously demonstrated, that a scriptural case for an Islamic antichrist can be made. As always, it is time for the Christian world to wake up and fall to their knees in prayer. The hour is far later than most think.[8]

However, let us not forget another previously documented and shocking feature of Rabbi Kaduri's prophecy of the coming of the Messiah. According to the elderly rabbi, before Messiah arrived, another monumental event had to first occur . . .

The death of Ariel Sharon.

8

THE LION OF GOD, THE KING OF ISRAEL, AND THE BUTCHER OF BEIRUT

I begin with the basic conviction that Jews and Arabs can live together. I have repeated that at every opportunity, not for journalists and not for popular consumption, but because I have never believed differently or thought differently, from my childhood on . . . I know that we are both inhabitants of the land, and although the state is Jewish, that does not mean that Arabs should not be full citizens in every sense of the word.[1]
—*Ariel Sharon, 1989*

She nestled her two children close to her in the shadows, in the cool dankness of their makeshift hiding-crypt. They were in the cowshed, just behind their house, in a hidden and cramped cellar. She didn't know the current hour, but it was deep into the night.

The cellar was located under a false bottom and through a trapdoor buried deep under a pile of hay and behind a stack of heavy wooden crates. But she knew the entrance, knew it well, and could find it blindfolded and within minutes. To the untrained, stumbling around in the dark, it might take half an hour, but her own little family had come here before, in practice drills.

However, tonight was not a drill—this was the real thing. Tonight may prove to be a matter of life or death. Vera Scheinerman would do her best to make certain that the outcome was *life*.

The dreaded Arabs were expected to launch an attack on their tiny village at any moment. The village elders had, only moments ago, received warning of the impending attack from a frantic scout. Vera's husband, Samuel, had joined the rest of the village men outside. Most of the men had secreted their families away as well.

The men of the village were heavily armed and had taken up strategic positions around the settlement. They had often trained for such a moment as this. Ample ammunition and weapons had been distributed to every able-bodied man.

The young mother trembled with a fiercely protective lioness's anxiety as she clutched her three-year-old daughter's hand and held her one-year-old son in her lap. "You must be my little *Lion of God*, Arik," she softly cooed to the little boy, running her fingers tenderly through his soft hair and silently praying that she would have many more such opportunities to express her love to him.

The baby did not know what was happening, but he could feel the fear—and it sent chills through his tiny little body. One day, when he became a man, he would still recall the terror of this singular moment.

The little girl, Dita, snuggled up closer to her mother and began to whimper. "There, there, Dita. All will be well," the mother comforted. "We are in the hands of *HaShem*. Look to Him for your strength. Pray. All will be well. Just you wait and see."

Vera was a good mother. She was a strong mother. And from

this point forward, her equally strong hatred for the terrifying Arabs would be passed to her children. She would see to it. The matter was settled.

Vera's marriage had been one of a powerful love; those who knew the young couple had never doubted their affection for one another. But their lives after marriage had been—and would continue to be—largely made up of political and religious turmoil, racial strife, and life-and-death decisions.

But they would also raise a child who would one day become a national hero and a living legend.

Tonight, this legend-of-a-man-to-be was only a frightened little boy, held in her lap. But in the not-too-distant future, he would be not only the son of Samuel and Vera Scheinerman, but the son of the brand-new nation of Israel. Practically every citizen of the future and mighty Israel would claim Samuel and Vera's boy as their own. Some would actually claim him as the nation's savior.

But for now, that magnanimous event was still years away.

***

Samuel and Vera had married in 1922. Vera was a medical student; Samuel was an agronomy student and head of the Zionist party in the city of Tbilisi, Georgia. Samuel longed for the day when *the People* could return to the land of their ancient ancestors, and that land would once again become the mighty and independent nation of Israel—the long-promised prophecy of *HaShem*. In later years, Samuel would pass on his love of the Zionist dream to his children, especially to his son.

Shortly after their marriage, the newlyweds came under vicious attacks by the activists of the Communist Revolution Movement in Georgia. Samuel and Vera fled, beginning what would turn out to be a long and arduous journey, mostly aboard a rickety and leaky ship, to the land of ancient Israel. They were poor, half-starved, and deeply frightened—but they were on a pilgrimage, an *aliyah*. Soon, they would be in the land of their fathers.

Upon arrival in their new homeland, Samuel enrolled in the Mikve Israel agricultural school. After graduating, the young couple joined a brand-new settlement called Ein Chai. Later, the name of the community would be changed to Kfar Malal.

Samuel's one presenting personality flaw caused a good deal of grief for the couple, and the family they would soon bring forth. Samuel liked to run things—he was a control freak. He incessantly called for order among the small population of his community.

Over the years, his overpowering personality gained him respect, mixed with a measure of fear, but there was little love for the man. Most in the small community looked upon Samuel as a man of arrogance; they would describe him, in hushed whispers and behind closed doors, as "overly aggressive" and "bitter."

The small village of Kfar Malal belonged to the *labor movement*—a socialist society despised by Samuel and Vera Scheinerman. The Scheinermans refused to cooperate with the communal makeup of the community's leadership, even fencing off their house—the only family to venture such an act of noncommunal independence. The move was viewed as a village outrage.

But it was to this man and this woman that young Ariel would be born. He came into the world in 1928, two years after his sister, Dita, and immediately became known by the endearing nickname Arik.

In late summer of 1929, deep in the night, the community of Kfar Malal was stunned when it received a frantic warning that nearby Arabs were planning a brutal attack on the diminutive Jewish settlement. Providentially, the evening scare proved to be a false alarm. But from that time on, Vera Scheinerman made it her life's purpose to instill a deep and abiding fear of the Arab people into the hearts and minds of her two little children. The Arabs were the enemy. They were cruel, vicious, never to be negotiated with, always to be destroyed—lest they first destroy you. Little Arik heard the lesson over and over again. He never forgot it. It was taught with fire and passion from his mother's insistent heart.

In the ensuing years, the Scheinerman family's relationship with the village grew even more strained. Vera and Samuel began to view themselves as superior in both their education and cultural upbringing.

Edginess concerning their attitude filtered throughout the community. The story was often angrily repeated among the villagers of how little Arik had once fallen and cut his chin, laying it open on the sharp rock over which he had stumbled. Rather than take Arik to the local community doctor, Vera had scooped him up and walked over two miles to the community of Kfar Saba. When news of that insult reached her community, the family began to feel the strain of the slowly smoldering anger. Arik bore the brunt of much of the angst.

Chubby little Arik began to be teased by his peers. The village boys nicknamed him the "bull" and tormented him without mercy. Consequently, Ariel "Arik" Sharon né Scheinerman adopted, full-fledged, his parents' disdain for the socialist community life. He became fiercely independent and headstrong.

One day, his father gave him a large stick and personally instructed the lad in its proper and brutal use as a weapon. He then instructed Arik to guard the fields and family orchards. Arik took the responsibility to heart and was seldom seen in the village without wielding his battering stick. By the time Arik was six, he had become known as "the bull who carried a big stick."

Arik's only real loyalty in life became loyalty to the dream of his father—*Zionism*. Arik, too, longed for the day when Israel would be restored, independent, free, and strong. Beyond strong, he desired for Israel to be mighty—able to defend itself entirely. Little did he know at the time that he would grow to become the driving force in making Israel that very thing—the mighty nation that it is today.

At fourteen, Arik became an instructor in the military youth movement, the Gadna. There he distinguished himself with his individualistic bravery and initiative. In time, he began sending his troops out on dangerous and previously forbidden night missions to actively patrol in the neighboring and unfriendly Palestinian Arab communities. His mother's earlier training came to life in his militaristic approach to his newfound passion in life.

Just a few years later, young Ariel Sharon formally joined the Hagana, a military organization that later became the official army of the newly formed State of Israel. And the rest, as they say, is history.[2]

***

What were the mysterious connections between Rabbi Kaduri, Ariel Sharon, and the rabbi's reported visions of Mashiach? Sharon was Israel's eleventh prime minister when Rabbi Kaduri made the ominous prediction that linked the coming of the Messiah with the prime minister's future and numinously envisioned death.

Oddly enough, according to ynetnews.com, Kaduri's name was tied to a blessing for *opponents* of Sharon's planned 2005 disengagement from Gaza, though Kaduri's son later said his father believed that "Gaza belongs to Palestine." Kaduri then surprised many followers when he personally offered his *support* for prime minister Ariel Sharon's Gaza pullout in 2005. "If we give them a small thing and there will be peace with them, we can leave Gush

Katif. We can trust Sharon, he is okay. It can cede territories in Gaza," the rabbi reportedly told an ultra-Orthodox newspaper. Then Kaduri added: "I have no faith in the Arabs, but we must have a little quiet. Sharon's government isn't so bad."[3]

While still in office, and just weeks after Kaduri's kabbalistic messianic pronouncement, Sharon suffered a massive stroke, on January 4, 2006, and lapsed into a coma. This shocking turn of events began within months of Sharon's assistance in the construction of the mechanism that eventually turned the Gaza Strip over to the Palestinian Arabs.

Twenty-four days later, Rabbi Yitzhak Kaduri died, on January 28, 2006.

To many, it appeared as though one biblical portent after another had fallen. Perhaps, just as Kaduri had predicted, the coming of Mashiach *was* soon to follow.

TIME LINE OF FOUR AMAZINGLY CONNECTED EVENTS

October 12, 2005: Israel withdraws from Gaza under the "Road Map" for peace agreement brokered by Prime Minister Ariel Sharon, United States President George W. Bush, the European Union, Russia, and Palestinian leader Mahmoud Abbas.

October 2005: Rabbi Kaduri predicts that the Messiah will soon appear—but only after Ariel Sharon dies.

January 4, 2006: Ariel Sharon suffers his second stroke and lapses into a coma. His first stroke had come a mere twenty-four hours after police announced on December 17, 2005, that they had found evidence of a $3 million bribe paid to Sharon's sons, Gilad and Omri, as part of a 1999 Israeli election fund scandal that also involved their father. Sharon was not charged with a crime, but his son Omri, a Knesset member at the time of the scandal, was eventually charged and in 2006, was sentenced to nine months in prison.

January 28, 2006: Rabbi Kaduri dies.

Four momentous national events had occurred within a little more than four months. The correlations were too much for some to simply overlook.

ARIEL SHARON—THE LION OF GOD

To better understand the alleged mystical associations between Sharon, Kaduri, and the messianic prophecies, it is first imperative to understand something about the striking life and history of the man Ariel Sharon.

Born Ariel Scheinerman (Scheinermann in some sources) on February 26, 1928, Sharon grew up in a family of Lithuanian-Russian immigrants in then–British-ruled Palestine.[4] (Rabbi Yitzhak Kaduri would have already been in his thirties by this time, and making a name for himself as a kabbalistic scholar and rabbi in the territory of the land of Palestine.) He later became the protégé of David Ben-Gurion, Israel's first prime minister, who gave the young Ariel the Hebraic name *Sharon*.[5] Like many Israelis, Sharon Hebraized his name in the early years of the newly formed nation of Israel.

Sharon's Hebrew first name, Ariel, is made up of two Hebrew words, *Aryeh* (Lion) and *El* (God).[6] The two Hebrew words together mean *Lion of God*. The last name *Sharon* (pronounced Sha-ROAN or Sha-RON) is a biblical name and is found in the Old Testament books of 1 Chronicles, Song of Solomon, and Isaiah—all describing a beautiful and fertile region of land in

Israel. The Hebrew word *Sharon* is derived from a root Hebrew word that means "prosperous or pleasant"—thus the biblical description of the land as the *Valley of Sharon.*

Interestingly, one of Sharon's greatest personal interests in life was farming, especially raising sheep. In 1972, he purchased a ranch in the northern Negev desert near Sderot. The ranch is named *Havat Shikmim*, Hebrew for *Sycamore Ranch.* Sharon's second wife and the mother of his two sons, Lily, is buried in Havat Shikmim.

Ownership of the ranch was eventually turned over to Sharon's sons, Omri and Gilad, to avoid the appearance of a conflict of interest when Sharon became agriculture minister and industry, trade, and labor minister.

ARIEL SHARON—THE KING OF ISRAEL

In his long and storied political career, Sharon served as minister of defense; minister of industry, trade and labor; minister of housing and construction; minister of energy and water resources; minister of agriculture; minister of foreign affairs; and finally as Israel's eleventh prime minister. However, he is equally known for his lengthy military career. Sharon was a commander in the Israeli Army from its inception in 1948. Consequently, he fought or led in every one of Israel's wars: 1948, 1956, 1967, 1973, 1982, and right up to the second intifada of 2000, which catapulted him into the office of prime minister in 2001. His lengthy and illustrious military career and his obvious and tenacious political prowess earned him an additional nickname—"the Bulldozer." During his military career, Sharon was repeatedly acknowledged as the greatest field commander and military strategist in Israel's history.[7] After his assault upon the Sinai region in the Six-Day War and his strategic surrounding of the Egyptian Third Army in the Yom Kippur War, the Israeli public nicknamed him "the King of Israel."[8]

ARIEL SHARON—THE BUTCHER OF BEIRUT[9]

The Sabra and Shatila massacre occurred between September 16 and 18, during the 1982 Lebanon War, while Ariel Sharon was defense minister of Israel. Various reports put the number of casualties in that battle between 800 and 3,500. Palestinian civilians in the Sabra and Shatila refugee camps were killed by the Phalange—a Lebanese Maronite Christian paramilitary organization. The security chief of the Phalange militia, Elie Hobeika, was the ground commander of the militiamen who entered the Palestinian camps. The Phalange had been sent into the camps to clear out Palestine Liberation Organization (PLO) fighters while Israeli forces surrounded the camps. The Israelis' intent was to block the camp exits and to provide logistical support. The horrendous loss of life in those few days led some to label Sharon "the Butcher of Beirut."[10]

The Kahan Commission was established by the Israeli government on September 28, 1982, to investigate the events of Sabra and Shatila. The commission formulated several striking conclusions concerning that fateful massacre, including that defense minister Ariel Sharon was *personally responsible* "for ignoring the danger of bloodshed and revenge" and "not taking appropriate measures to prevent bloodshed." Sharon's negligence in protecting the civilian population of Beirut that had come under Israeli control, the commission alleged, amounted to "non-fulfillment of a duty,"[11] an official indictment with which the defense minister was charged.

In early 1983, the Kahan Commission recommended the removal of Ariel Sharon from his post as minister of defense. The commission issued the following statement:

We have found . . . that the Minister of Defense [Ariel Sharon] bears personal responsibility. In our opinion, it is fitting that the Minister of Defense draw the appropriate personal conclusions arising out of the defects revealed with regard to the manner in which he discharged the duties of his office—and if necessary, that the Prime Minister consider whether he should exercise his authority . . . to . . . remove [him] from office."[12]

Sharon, at the outset, refused to resign as defense minister. Additionally, Prime Minister Menachem Begin refused to terminate Sharon. After a grenade was tossed into a dispersing crowd at an Israeli Peace Now march, killing one and injuring ten others, a compromise was reached. Ariel Sharon finally agreed to step down from his position as defense minister but stayed in the cabinet as a *minister without portfolio*—a figurehead position with no direct governmental authority.[13]

ARIEL SHARON'S RISE TO POWER—AGAIN

When Yitzhak Rabin became chief of staff in 1964, Sharon once again began his politically prosperous rise. He eventually occupied the positions of infantry school commander and head of the army training branch. He ultimately achieved the rank of major general.

During the now-historic 1967 Six-Day War, Ariel Sharon commanded the most powerful armored division on the Sinai front. In just a short while leading up to the war, it had been discovered by Israeli intelligence that Egypt, Jordan, and Syria were planning a coalition attack against Israel. Israel took preemptive measures, launching massive strikes against Egypt's airfields. In a domino effect, beginning with Egypt's humiliating defeat, the Arab coalition came tumbling down. Within six days, Israel had decisively won the war.

Following the massive and lightning-fast victory, Israeli forces seized from Egypt control of the Gaza Strip and the Sinai Peninsula. They also took from Jordan the West Bank and East Jerusalem, and from Syria the Golan Heights. All of these areas had been launchpads for Israel's enemies. Israel was determined that the strategically vulnerable locations would never again be used in this manner.

In 1969, Sharon was appointed head of the Israeli Defense Force's (IDF) Southern Command. After the war, Sharon went into reserve status.

Four years later, his services were required one more time. Israel was at war yet again.

ARIEL SHARON'S YOM KIPPUR

The war began when a coalition of Arab nations launched a joint surprise attack on Israel on Yom Kippur, the holiest day in Judaism. Egyptian and Syrian forces crossed ceasefire lines and entered the Israeli-held Sinai Peninsula in the south and the Golan Heights in the north. The United States and the Soviet Union initiated massive efforts to resupply their respective allies during the war. The involvement of these two nuclear super-powers almost led to a conflict between the two military giants.

At the start of the Yom Kippur War on October 6, 1973, Sharon was called back to active duty, along with his assigned reserve armored division. It is reported that on his farm, before Sharon left for the front line, the reserve commander, Zeev Amit, said to him, "How are we going to get out of this?"

Sharon replied, "You don't know? We will cross the Suez Canal and the war will end over there."

Sharon arrived at the front, to his fourth war, in a civilian car.[14]

Under cover of darkness, Sharon's forces moved to a point

on the Suez Canal. His division managed to encircle the Suez, cutting off and encircling the Third Army. Many Israelis regarded this move as the turning point of the war on the Sinai front. Thus, Sharon was broadly acclaimed accountable for Israel's 1973 ground victory in the Sinai. Once again, Sharon was an Israeli hero.

KADURI'S YOM KIPPUR

Thirty-two years after Sharon's Yom Kippur war, on Yom Kippur 2005, centenarian Rabbi Yitzhak Kaduri stepped to the teaching dais of his synagogue and proclaimed to his anxiously awaiting congregation that this very Israeli hero, Ariel Sharon, the "Lion of God," was the *one* person who must die before the Messiah would return. Within weeks, Sharon lay comatose in an Israeli hospital.

Some said the tragedy was a judgment from God.

9

ARIEL SHARON'S COMA—
A JUDGMENT FROM GOD?

Ariel Sharon's stroke in January 2006 came about because of his role in disengagement from Gaza.

—Eretz Yisrael Shelanu

After a convincing win in the 2003 elections, the Likud party saw a major split in 2005, when Likud leader Ariel Sharon left the party to form the new Kadima party. A mostly moderate coalition from the Likud party established Kadima on November 24, 2005, largely to support the policies of Ariel Sharon's unilateral disengagement plan. Predictably, when Ariel Sharon suffered his crippling stroke

and finally lost all consciousness, his detractors and various self-proclaimed sages quickly declared it was "God's judgment." Haaretz.
com, advertising itself as "the world's leading English-language
website for real-time news and analysis of Israel and the Middle
East," printed the following in an article titled "Israeli Campaign:
Ariel Sharon's Stroke Was 'Curse of Gaza Disengagement'":

> Former Prime Minister Ariel Sharon's stroke in January 2006
> came about because of his role in disengagement from Gaza,
> according to a campaign to be launched on December 31 by
> an extreme right-wing religious party, Eretz Yisrael Shelanu.
>
> The campaign, also sponsored by the organization
> Hamateh Lehatzalat Ha'am Hayehudi, is to be launched
> on the sixth anniversary of Sharon's stroke according to the
> Hebrew calendar. It will hang posters in synagogues and
> publish advertisements in the party's pamphlet, also called
> Eretz Yisrael Shelanu, using quotes by Shas spiritual leader
> Rabbi Ovadia Yosef about the causes of Sharon's condition.
>
> In so doing, the group says it seeks to warn the current
> government against evacuating settlements.
>
> One of Yosef's quotes about Sharon states: "How cruel
> is this evil man, for doing things like this . . . God will strike
> him so he will never rise again."
>
> Yosef also said: "And those who carry out his bidding—
> their time will come."
>
> Eretz Yisrael Shelanu's chairman, Rabbi Shalom Dov
> Wolpo, said: "The campaign is a warning to politicians and the
> prime minister not to be dragged into adventures like Sharon
> was. The price they will pay will be too heavy to bear."[1]

Jew and Christian alike proclaimed Sharon to be a traitor.
His turning over of Gaza to the Palestinians was considered a
violation of the biblical warning against *dividing the land* of Israel,
found in Joel 3:2, which states, "I will gather all the nations, and
bring them down to the valley of Jehoshaphat. Then I will enter

into judgment with them there on behalf of My people and My inheritance, Israel, whom they have scattered among the nations; and they have divided up My land" (NASB).

Many scholars believe this prophecy, written around 800 BC, is a pronouncement of God's retaliation against those who have taken the Jewish people from their land, or divided His land in the last days. This is the land God promised to Abraham, then Isaac, and then Jacob.

One blogger, expressing the sentiments of many others, stated the matter like this: "Former Israeli Prime Minister Ariel Sharon, born Ariel Scheinermann in Russia, went from Zionist to traitor, selling out Israel and destroying Jewish settlements (never forget Gush Katif) for lucrative foreign interests culminating in the treacherous creation of Kadima—a corrupt to the core political party."[2] Gush Katif was a bloc of seventeen Israeli settlements in the southern Gaza strip. It was specifically mentioned by Yitzhak Rabin, the Israeli prime minister who fell victim to an assassin in 1995, as being essential to Israel's security border. In August 2005, under the orders of Prime Minister Sharon, the 8,600 residents of Gush Katif were evicted from the area by the Israeli army, and their homes were demolished as part of Israel's plan to disengage Jewish residents from the Gaza Strip portion of the Palestinian territories. The displaced were moved to Israel.[3]

Another prognosticator, on a website dedicated to prophecy, speculated on the possibility of Sharon being under the judgment of God in this manner:

> Not only was this decision by Mr. Sharon against the will of his own people but was also against that of the God of Israel. Ariel Sharon gave away God's Covenant land that was given only to the children of Israel. Some people are of the opinion that the former prime minister may be paying the price for that very action of his.[4]

WND.com ran a stunning investigative report in July 2005, just six months before Sharon's stroke. In an article titled "Sharon Targeted with 'Death Curse,'" Aaron Klein, WND's senior staff reporter and Jerusalem bureau chief at the time, wrote:

Fringe activists held a midnight Kabbalistic ritual in an ancient cemetery calling for angels of death to kill Israeli Prime Minister Ariel Sharon and thwart his Gaza withdrawal plan, participants in the ceremony told WND.

The same individuals used the ritual against Prime Minister Yitzhak Rabin one month before his assassination in 1995.

The activists said they performed a "Pulsa Dinura"—a Kabbalistic ceremony in which God is asked to curse a sinner, usually an enemy of the Jewish people—and prayed for a death curse to be placed on Sharon.

They argued Sharon's Gaza evacuation will "destroy Israel and the Jewish people" and will cause Jewish deaths.

Rabbi Yosef Dayan, one of the leaders of the ceremony, told WND, "I said ten months ago that I am willing to do the Pulsa Dinura if rabbis are going to instruct me to do that. We decided now it is time. Sharon is endangering the entire Jewish population. He is giving land to the enemies who will use it to attack us. He has let them fire on us with bullets and rockets without retaliation because it serves his purposes. He is going to expel my mother-in-law from Gush Katif [Gaza's Jewish communities]."

The Pulsa Dinura was held late Thursday night in an ancient cemetery in the town of Rosh Pina. It was performed by a Kabbalist, who recited prayers that were repeated by twenty men, who, in line with Kabbalistic tradition, were all over the age of forty, bearded and first purified themselves in a ritual bath.

Describing the ceremony, participant Baruch Ben Yosef, an activist attorney, told WND, "It was done in a beautiful cemetery with a thick forest around it, under a full moon. We performed it near the graveside of Shlomo Ben Yosef [the first

Jew to be hanged by the British in Palestine after carrying out a revenge attack on an Arab bus.]

"The actual prayer of the Pulsa Dinura was read by the Kabbalist. There was a quorum of people that read back the prayer as he read it. And the hope we expressed is that the angels of Kaballah will remove Sharon from continuing to destroy the Jewish people and the land of Israel.

. . .

National Religious Party Chairman Zevulun Orlev said, "I vehemently condemn those who carried out the 'Pulsa Dinura' ceremony against Prime Minister Ariel Sharon. The 'Pulsa Dinura' prior to Rabin's assassination caused indescribable and irreversible damage to the religious public and the settlement enterprise, and repeating this act would hurt the legitimate struggle against the pullout."

"We have absolutely nothing to do with this craziness," said a leader of the Yesha settler's council. "It's a handful of nut cases who get a lot of publicity and then it serves to discredit us. Some even think they work for the government."[5]

Then just one month after the "Death Curse" had been performed, on the evening of August 15, 2005, Prime Minister Ariel Sharon addressed his stunned nation concerning the Gaza pullout. Following are the first several paragraphs and the final several paragraphs of his speech (translated from Hebrew):

Citizens of Israel,
The day has arrived. We are beginning the most difficult and painful step of all—evacuating our communities from the Gaza Strip and Northern Samaria.

This step is very difficult for me personally. It was with a heavy heart that the Government of Israel made the decision regarding Disengagement, and the Knesset did not lightly approve it.

It is no secret that I, like many others, believed and hoped that we could forever hold on to Netzarim and Kfar

Darom. However, the changing reality in this country, in this region, and in the world, required another reassessment and changing of positions.

Gaza cannot be held onto forever. Over one million Palestinians live there, and they double their numbers with every generation. They live in incredibly cramped refugee camps, in poverty and squalor, in hotbeds of ever-increasing hatred, with no hope whatsoever on the horizon.

It is out of strength and not weakness that we are taking this step. We tried to reach agreements with the Palestinians which would move the two peoples towards the path of peace. These were crushed against a wall of hatred and fanaticism.

The unilateral Disengagement Plan, which I announced approximately two years ago, is the Israeli answer to this reality. This Plan is good for Israel in any future scenario. We are reducing the day-to-day friction and its victims on both sides. The IDF will re-deploy on defensive lines behind the Security Fence. Those who continue to fight us will meet the full force of the IDF and the security forces.

Now the Palestinians bear the burden of proof. They must fight terror organizations, dismantle its infrastructure and show sincere intentions of peace in order to sit with us at the negotiating table.

. . .

Citizens of Israel,

The responsibility for the future of Israel rests on my shoulders. I initiated the Plan because I concluded that this action is vital for Israel. Believe me, the extent of pain that I feel at this act is equal only to the measure of resolved recognition that it was something that had to be done.

We are embarking on a new path which has many risks, but also a ray of hope for all of us.

With the help of God, may this path be one of unity and not division, of mutual respect, and not animosity between brothers, of unconditional love, and not baseless hatred.

I will do my utmost to ensure that it will be so.[6]

The Pulsa Denura curse was performed in July 2005. In August, the Gaza pullout by Israel was complete. Prime Minister Sharon addressed the nation of Israel, explaining that Gaza had been handed over to the Palestinians. Sharon was comatose by January of the next year. As of this writing, he remains in a permanent vegetative state.

SHARON'S LAST WORD OF INTERVIEW— ONE DAY BEFORE HIS STROKE

Just one day before his second stroke, Prime Minister Ariel Sharon gave what would be his last interview to the Japanese economic newspaper *Nikkei*. Sharon's words echoed the sentiments of many of Israel's citizens who desperately desired peace with its neighbors, while at the same time preserving Israel's sovereignty:

> If the Palestinians combat terror, I believe there is a chance to move forward in accordance with the Road Map initiative, which, with God's help, will bring peace.
>
> I am a Jew, and that is the most important thing for me. Therefore when it comes to security, Israel will not make any compromises; I don't see any situation where Israel will not be sitting on the Golan Heights.
>
> Our position is that Jerusalem is not negotiable. We are not going to negotiate on Jerusalem. Jerusalem will be forever a united and undivided capital of Israel.[7]

While some Israelis see Sharon as a traitor, and his enemies brand him a butcher and a terrorist, many others still see him as an indisputable and indispensable national hero. They believe his move to implement the Road Map was a prudent maneuver to bring lasting peace to Israel, and to them, he is still *Israel's savior*. In fact, to this day there are those in Israel who expect Sharon to rise from his bed and once again lead modern Israel.

The chances of this becoming a reality, however, appear slimmer with each passing day.

Unless, of course . . . something supernatural occurs.

10

BITTER IRONIES, STUNNING CONNECTIONS

In one of history's bitter ironies, Sharon was more respected by many of his Arab enemies than he was by some of his countrymen.
—*Australia/Israel and Jewish Affairs Council*

There is a certain quirk of fate in the juxtaposed names Ariel ("Lion of God") and Sharon ("pleasant and prosperous"). The irony has not gone without notice.

An article posted by the Australia/Israel and Jewish Affairs Council summed up the difficulty of defining Sharon's life as follows:

In one of history's bitter ironies, Sharon was more respected by many of his Arab enemies than he was by some of his countrymen. An Egyptian military intelligence assessment of Sharon in the lead up to the 1973 Yom Kippur War described him as: "Full bodied silvery hair, very calm, confident, enamored with the act of self-sacrifice, a talented officer, stubborn, dynamic, brave, in love with the Paratroopers and the Special Forces, a believer in the element of surprise, prone toward violence, loves to learn and to know."

Gilad Sharon comments on the above assessment of his father in his own biography of his father, Sharon: The Life of a Leader: "I would sign off on this description of my father, except for 'prone towards violence.' However, from the Egyptian perspective, they would see this as a trait of my father's. After all, one isn't victorious in battle by sending flowers."[1]

STUNNING CONNECTIONS

Once Kaduri's astounding prophecies of the coming Messiah were out, and once Ariel Sharon's life was connected to the prophecy, speculation abounded. The Internet was abuzz with theories, as well as name, event, and word associations. Bible researchers, endtime theorists, and even Jewish sages noted many interesting correlations. While it is not my purpose to validate any of the particular observations, I have catalogued a few for you to evaluate.

Some of the observations and correlations are astounding indeed. They may simply be matters of coincidence. There are those, however, who believe that too many striking coincidences may point to the actual *non-coincidental* nature of a thing. You can be the judge of that. I will point out several of the connected ironies here. But first, let us examine Sharon's name in light of certain biblical revelations.

Again, the name *Ariel* means "Lion of God." Of course, Christian students of the Bible will recognize the messianic connections to that name, as Jesus Christ is called the Lion of the tribe of Judah: "And one of the elders saith unto me, Weep not: behold, the Lion of the tribe of Judah, the Root of David, hath prevailed to open the book, and to loose the seven seals thereof" (Rev. 5:5). *Sharon*, the former prime minister's last name, again, means "pleasant and prosperous." These certainly would be messianic descriptions as well, and as a matter of fact, Bible commentators see the reference to the "rose of Sharon" in Song of Solomon 2:1 as a messianic intimation.

Further, one cannot help but notice the additional Messianic connection thrust upon him when he was nicknamed "the King of Israel." Along with this nickname eventually came the dastardly designation of "Butcher of Beirut." Sharon was given this last title of disrepute largely because of his reputation as a fierce and sometimes ruthless warrior. Yet, without condoning his several allegedly brutal actions as a warrior through the years, could not the same things be said of the exploits of the great and venerated King David?

As you may remember, King David was the most beloved *king of Israel*. He could play the harp and sing love songs to God, and at the same time, completely annihilate his enemies with his mighty military. David, King of Israel, was also, at times, ruthless and brutal. Do not forget: Israel had never fought a war without Ariel Sharon in the front lines or in command, or both. So in the eyes of many Israelis, Sharon was a modern-day King David—almost a messianic figure, because the Messiah Himself was prophesied to come through the line of King David. Additionally, it is prophesied that when Messiah comes, He will be seated upon the throne of David. Yes, many have seen hints of the Messiah in the name and character of Ariel Sharon. And for many, for Rabbi Kaduri to directly connect Sharon's life with the coming of the Messiah was not too far of a stretch for the imagination. Consider these comments from Tzaly Reshef, founder of the left-wing Israeli group Peace Now, as reported in a *New York Times* article written right after Sharon lapsed into a coma: "'I think it is a big tragedy that we lose him now,' Reshef said. The same 'power and personality,' he said, that caused Mr. Sharon to command the bloody invasion of Lebanon in 1982 'could maybe have made him the *savior of Israel* in the next four years.'"[2]

Another interesting and striking observation noted by some of the news followers of the Kaduri Messiah death message/Ariel Sharon connection is that in the Old Testament book of Isaiah, Jerusalem, the city of David, is called *Ariel*. This is the only place in Scripture where Jerusalem is given this name. Unbelievably, this passage makes mention of the Lord putting Ariel into a "deep sleep" and *shutting his eyes*. Not only that, but the passage also speaks of a book, or scroll, that is then sealed. When the message is delivered, says the passage, the receivers are *unable to read it*—their hearts are hardened. This scenario holds a striking parallel to what took place concerning Sharon's "deep sleep" and Rabbi Kaduri's sealed Messiah message, which was largely disregarded by the Jewish world.

> *Woe to Ariel, to Ariel,* the city where David dwelt! add ye year to year; let them kill sacrifices. *Yet I will distress Ariel, and there shall be heaviness and sorrow: and it shall be unto me as Ariel.* And I will camp against thee round about, and will lay siege against thee with a mount, and I will raise forts against thee. And thou shalt be brought down, and shalt speak out of the ground, and thy speech shall be low out of the dust, and thy voice shall be, as of one that hath a familiar spirit, out of the ground, and thy speech shall whisper out of the dust. Moreover the multitude of thy strangers shall be like small dust, and the multitude of the terrible ones shall be as chaff that passeth away: yea, it shall be at an instant suddenly. Thou shalt be visited of the LORD of hosts with thunder, and with earthquake, and great noise, with storm and tempest, and the

flame of devouring fire. And the multitude of all the nations that fight against Ariel, even all that fight against her and her munition, and that distress her, shall be as a dream of a night vision. It shall even be as when an hungry man dreameth, and, behold, he eateth; but he awaketh, and his soul is empty: or as when a thirsty man dreameth, and, behold, he drinketh; but he awaketh, and, behold, he is faint, and his soul hath appetite: so shall the multitude of all the nations be, that fight against mount Zion. Stay yourselves, and wonder; cry ye out, and cry: they are drunken, but not with wine; they stagger, but not with strong drink. *For the* LORD *hath poured out upon you the spirit of deep sleep, and hath closed your eyes: the prophets and your rulers, the seers hath he covered. And the vision of all is become unto you as the words of a book that is sealed,* which men deliver to one that is learned, saying, Read this, I pray thee: and he saith, I cannot; for it is sealed: And the book is delivered to him that is not learned, saying, Read this, I pray thee: and he saith, I am not learned. *Wherefore the Lord said, Forasmuch as this people draw near me with their mouth, and with their lips do honour me, but have removed their heart far from me, and their fear toward me is taught by the precept of men.* (Isa. 29:1–13; emphasis added)

Of course, the immediate and biblical/historical context of this passage is the Lord's pronouncement of the invasion of ancient Judea by Sennacherib, ruler of the Assyrian Empire, and then Jerusalem's sudden deliverance at the hand of God. The second part of the prophecy is God's reproof of the Jews for their infidelity and impiety. The Assyrian Empire covered much of what is now modern-day Iraq, Iran, Lebanon, Syria, Turkey, and Egypt—the very nations aligning themselves against Israel today.

Another obvious connection that many have noticed and frequently commented on is the aforementioned Yom Kippur relationship. You will remember that Ariel Sharon was, indeed, considered Israel's savior in that now-historic 1973 war. As a matter of fact, his involvement in that war was Sharon's final act of *saving Israel*. After the Yom Kippur war, Sharon entered the political arena. Others have pointed out that it was just over thirty-two years later, the approximate age of Jesus when he went to the cross (thirty-two to thirty-three, depending on when one sets His date of birth), when Rabbi Kaduri made his Yom Kippur prediction that the Messiah would come to Israel when Sharon was dead. As previously mentioned, just weeks later, Ariel Sharon was seemingly near death. In Sharon's Yom Kippur, he was Israel's "savior." But Kaduri's decree named Sharon's *demise* as the precursor to Israel receiving her long-awaited and *genuine* savior.

AN EXACT DATE?

Did Rabbi Kaduri set an exact date for the Messiah's arrival through the link with Ariel Sharon? Did he actually *nail down* a date, at all? This is where some say his prophecies become a bit muddled. Consider the following assertion by Rabbi Yosef Hayim Zakkai:

> It was on Chanukah, 5766 (2006), about a month before the passing of the elder Mekubal Rav Yitzhak Kaduri, we sat and learned the Holy Zohar as is our custom every evening. And then, I (Rabbi Yosef Hayim Zakkai, from the city Beitar Illit) understood that the rabbi (Kaduri) is interested that we speak about the Moshiach (Messiah).
>
> I got the courage and asked him, "Our rabbi! When will Moshiach come?" The Rav answered me, "I cannot reveal," and laughed a big laugh. I asked him again, "Our rabbi! When will Moshiach come?" The Rav answered in 2 words, "בשנת תשעב [in the year 5772]," and he repeated this twice.
>
> I was very shocked by his words, and immediately, when I left the Rav's home, I went up to the Kollel of Kabbalists in the Rav's Yeshiva, and told over what the Rav had said—they were all amazed.

About 2 weeks later, in the beginning of Tevet, 5766, the rabbi was admitted to Bikur Cholim Hospital in Yerushalayim. I would arrive daily to the hospital to learn with the Rav. And then, I asked him again, "Our rabbi! In what month and in what year will Moshiach come?" And the Rav answered me, "In the month of Av, 5772." And he repeated this twice. It is important to note that Rav Kaduri retained consciousness until 2 weeks before his passing. Rav Kaduri passed away on 29 Tevet, 5766.[3]

The Hebrew year 5772 ended on Elul 29 (September 16, 2012). The following day, Tishrei 1 (Rosh Hashanah) began the New Year 5773. Obviously, there was no messianic appearance in the year 2012. Of course, there are those who insist that Kaduri did not necessarily mean that Messiah would appear to the *world* on this date—only that he would come to Israel, preparing to ultimately reveal Himself when the time is right.

AFTER THE DEATH OF ARIEL SHARON . . .

Many who are following the case of Rabbi Kaduri's messianic predictions point out that, though Kaduri undoubtedly declared Sharon's death to be a very definitive marker for the arrival of Messiah, he did not say *when* or *how long* after Sharon's death Messiah would appear—only that it *would* be after. By inference, they assert, the only definitive thing is that Messiah will not appear *before* Sharon's death. As of this writing, Ariel Sharon is still in a coma—yet he has only recently exhibited signs of increased brain wave activity and the possibility of waking.[4]

Numerous followers of Kaduri's prophecies, especially as they relate to Ariel Sharon, have watched and waited with anxious anticipation.

Others, however, expect something even more sinister to occur.

11

ARIEL SHARON—
THE ANTICHRIST?

And I saw one of his heads as it were wounded to death; and his deadly
wound was healed: and all the world wondered after the beast.
—Revelation 13:3

There are some in Israel, and around the world, who
are hoping and praying for Sharon's full recovery and
return to power as prince and leader of Israel. While this
possibility certainly seems slim, the mere mentioning
of it has caused a furor of speculation that Sharon might be a
candidate for the fulfillment of the biblical Antichrist prophecy.
In fact, some have come to view Rabbi Kaduri's direct linkage

of Sharon's death with the revealing of the Messiah as a clear tie to an Antichrist scenario. A quick entry of *Sharon the Antichrist* in any Internet search engine reveals a multiplicity of sites passionately dedicated to this speculation. While there are several proffered Antichrist scenarios regarding Sharon, I have assembled a brief synopsis that I feel accurately represents the main points of the more prominent theories.

The idea seems to begin with the prophecy in Revelation 13, which Bible scholars interpret as a direct reference to the coming reign of the Antichrist. The Sharon-Antichrist theory merges this passage with other Scriptures, Kaduri's prophecy, and Sharon's current condition as of the printing of this book.

> And the beast which I saw was like unto a leopard, and his feet were as the feet of a bear, and his mouth as the mouth of a lion: and the dragon gave him his power, and his seat, and great authority. And I saw one of his heads as it were wounded to death; and his deadly wound was healed: and all the world wondered after the beast. And they worshipped the dragon which gave power unto the beast: and they worshipped the beast, saying, Who is like unto the beast? who is able to make war with him? (Rev. 13:2–4)

Usually, the point is made that according to this passage the Antichrist will have a mouth *like a lion*. Of course, Sharon's predominant nickname is the *Lion of God*. Further, some see the references to the leopard and the bear as indications of the Antichrist's ability and agility to make debilitating war against his enemies. Naturally, those who hold to this view see these characteristics as strikingly fulfilled in the life of Ariel Sharon.

Verse 3 is the part of the prophecy that draws the most striking parallel to Sharon's life. It speaks of an apparent wound, of some type, to the head. The wound would appear to be fatal—yet prove not to be so. Many see an allusion to some type of resurrection for the Antichrist. When Sharon suffered a stroke and lapsed into a coma, there were those who pointed to this *head wound* as a possible fulfillment. The theory goes on to assert that if Sharon does recover and then returns to power, of course the whole world would be amazed—thus fulfilling another very important element of this prophecy. Some have further speculated that, once recovered, Sharon could then claim to have communicated with the *Almighty* during his state of earthly unconsciousness—and even received special instructions or power from Him. This, they assert, could unite Christians and Jews and most likely would drive the Muslim world into the arms of the waiting Gog and Magog—Russia. Since Kaduri directly tied Ariel Sharon's death with the coming of the Messiah, they say, this points to Sharon's rise as the Antichrist of the Bible. They would then say that what Kaduri saw in his vision was not the coming of Messiah, but perhaps the coming of the Antichrist, mistaken by Kaduri to be the Messiah.

THE WORTHLESS SHEPHERD?

Another Sharon-Antichrist speculation that has gained much popularity during this saga comes from Zechariah's description of the *worthless shepherd*. Some Bible students, and even several scholarly Bible commentators, see this passage as a prophecy of the Antichrist. If that is so, it presents an interesting descriptive feature of the Antichrist.

> And the LORD said unto me, Take unto thee yet the instruments of a foolish shepherd. For, lo, I will raise up a shepherd in the land, which shall not visit those that be cut off, neither shall seek the young one, nor heal that that is broken, nor feed that that standeth still: but he shall eat the flesh of the fat, and tear their claws in pieces. Woe to the idol shepherd

that leaveth the flock! the sword shall be upon his arm, and upon his right eye: his arm shall be clean dried up, and his right eye shall be utterly darkened. (Zech. 11:15–17)

As you can see, the shepherd in these verses has a crippled arm and a useless right eye. Some have seen an allusion to Sharon's stroke and recovery, yet with obvious limitations.

Additionally, while many Bible scholars hold to the theory that the Antichrist will be a Gentile, Sharon/Antichrist theorists believe there is biblical evidence that he will be a Jew. As proof, they point to John 5:43: "I am come in my Father's name, and ye receive me not: if another shall come in his own name, him ye will receive."

However, Dr. David Reagan, a renowned and longtime Bible scholar, prophecy conference speaker, teacher, founder of Lamb & Lion Ministries (1980), and host of the weekly television program *Christ in Prophecy*, has refuted the possibility of an Antichrist of Jewish lineage, *especially* with regard to Jesus's statement in John. (Obviously, then, he does not hold to the view that Ariel Sharon is a potential Antichrist candidate.) Concerning the Antichrist, Dr. Reagan says,

> Scholars have been divided as to whether or not this person of Roman heritage will be a Gentile or a Jew. Many have pointed to John 5:43 to argue that the Antichrist will be a Jew.
>
> That verse quotes Jesus as saying, "I have come in My Father's name, and you do not receive Me; if another shall come in his own name, you will receive him." The argument drawn from this statement is that the Antichrist must be a Jew in order for the Jews to accept him as their Messiah.
>
> But other prophecies in the Bible make it clear that the Jews will never accept the Antichrist as their Messiah. In fact we are told point blank that when the Antichrist declares himself to be God at the mid-point of the Tribulation, the

Jews will be outraged and will reject him, causing him to turn on them in fury with the purpose of annihilating them (Rev. 12:13–17).

THE GENTILE ARGUMENT

So what did Jesus mean when He said, "If another shall come in his own name you will receive him?" Those who argue the Antichrist will be a Gentile respond by saying that the Antichrist will be accepted by the Jewish people as their political savior when he implements a treaty that will guarantee their security and enable them to rebuild their Temple (Dan. 9:27). But the Jews will never receive the Antichrist as their spiritual savior. Thus, when he declares himself to be God, they will reject him.

There is other scriptural evidence that the Antichrist will be a Gentile. For example, Revelation 13:1 pictures him as a beast arising "out of the sea." The sea is used in Scripture to symbolize the Gentile nations (Daniel 7:3 and Luke 21:25).

In contrast, the Antichrist's right-hand man and spiritual leader is pictured in Revelation 13:11 as rising up out of the land (or the earth, in some translations). This reference to the land is an indication that the False Prophet will be a Jew who will rise out of the Promised Land of Israel.[1]

While speculation abounds on the matter, it appears, at this point, it can *only* be that—*speculation*. I have merely attempted to provide a fair representation of the undeniably existent Sharon/Antichrist conjecture. There is also a plethora of scholarly material that refutes the connection entirely.

BETWEEN LIFE AND DEATH—NEITHER HERE NOR THERE

"Ariel Sharon: Still Alive, but Only Just": this was the headline of an ABC News article published in October 2008. Following are selected excerpts from that article:

The man whose inspired military leadership and controversial policies earned him the nickname "the Bulldozer" today lies silent and motionless in the Sheba Medical Center outside Tel Aviv.

"His predicament is like a Greek tragedy," said Dr. Raanan Gissen, his longtime spokesman and friend, in an interview with ABC News. "He is between life and death. He is neither here nor there."

. . .

"People don't like to think about it, it's just too painful," Gissen said. "He was a real leader. People were prepared to follow him. He made mistakes but he always got back up and carried on. People appreciated that."

. . .

"Sharon was a real leader. The real predicament of his absence is that he left no obvious heir. Right now it would be good to have someone of his stature to lead us, to guide us," he said.

. . .

Gissen clearly misses his old boss. He said Sharon was one of the last "founding fathers of Israel," part of the generation of soldiers and politicians who helped establish the Jewish state in the 1940s. Despite their decades-long relationship, Gissen has chosen not to visit Sharon's hospital room.

"I don't want to see him in this condition. It's very sad, it's tragic. I don't believe he himself would ever have wanted to end up like this."[2]

As of the writing of this book, Ariel Sharon is eighty-five. He is a farmer, a shepherd, a warrior, and a politician. He is known as the Butcher of Beirut, the Bulldozer, the King and Savior of Israel, the Lion of God, and thanks to Rabbi Yitzhak Kaduri's purported messianic vision, the precursor to the coming of the Messiah. Ariel Sharon has arisen over and over from an apparent defeat to a position of prominence and power.

Now, there are those who hope he will *rise again*.

12

THE SHARON/KADURI
ZIONISM CONNECTION

For Zion's sake will I not hold my peace, and for Jerusalem's sake I will
not rest, until the righteousness thereof go forth as brightness, and the
salvation thereof as a lamp that burneth.

—*Isaiah 62:1*

From what we have learned thus far, it appears *Zionism* is an integral part of our story—especially as it may relate to the connectivity of Prime Minister Ariel Sharon and Rabbi Yitzhak Kaduri. So it would be prudent at this point to examine the topic, at least briefly. We will do this historically, politically, and biblically.

Zionism as a movement is most often described as a type of

deeply passionate nationalist fervor predominantly among the Jews, but even among non-Jews, who support the existence of the nation of Israel in the Middle East, specifically within the territorial boundaries most often defined as the *Land of Israel*. The movement has its roots in both the political and the religious realms of Jewish life, and there are scores of formally organized groups around the world that are dedicated to the advancement of Zionism.

In a secular sense, Zionism's historical emergence is usually credited to the late nineteenth century, when it purportedly commenced as a nationalistic revival movement in Central and Eastern Europe. This is the movement of which Ariel Sharon's father was a part as a young man in Georgia. Many of the early movement's most prominent leaders associated the main goal of Zionism with re-creating the desired state of Israel within Palestine, at the time controlled by the Ottoman Empire.

There are a couple of other, less common ways the term *Zionism* is used. It is sometimes applied to a type of *cultural Zionism*, focused more on preserving the cultural aspects of ancient Jewish life, rather than on establishing a particular nation-state. Additionally, the term *Zionism* is used by Christians who distinctly ascribe to, and passionately support, the existence of Israel as a nation. This movement is most commonly known as *Christian Zionism.* There are several major Christian ministries devoted specifically to the cause of assisting Jews in returning to Israel. These ministries see the return of Israel as the partial fulfillment of endtime prophecy. But the common, foundational belief among all true and zealous Zionists is the claim to *Eretz Israel* (the Land of Israel) as the national homeland of the Jews.

Defenders of Zionism say it is predominantly a national liberation movement advocating the repatriation of a dispersed social group to a homeland from which they were brutally driven many centuries ago. Yet critics of Zionism say it is colonialist and/ or racist and predicated upon the violent and illegal occupation of certain territory.

There are some, even many Jews, who believe the basic tenets of political Zionism are evil and are not of God. They think that Israel should be reborn only by a specific, identifiable act of *HaShem*, not through the directives of the United Nations and the input of outside political forces. There are those within the Christian faith who believe similarly, claiming that the true Israel will come into existence only after the return of Jesus Christ—the Messiah. They assert that Jesus will then sit upon His earthly throne and will literally rule the earth from Jerusalem, Israel.

At one website, claiming to be an anti-Zionist Jewish site, the header reads, "Traditional Jews Are Not Zionists." The article goes on to say, "Although there are those who refuse to accept the teachings of our Rabbis and will continue to support the Zionist state, there are also many who are totally unaware of the history of Zionism and its contradiction to the beliefs of Torah-True Jews."[1]

A similar anti-Zionist site proclaims, as its foundational statement: "The State of Israel DOES NOT represent Jews or Judaism."[2] An article offered on this page bears the title "The State of Israel: The Most Dangerous Place for a Jew."[3]

Conversely, Christians United for Israel (CUFI) is the largest pro-Israel organization in the United States, with more than a million members. Posted on their home page, where they claim to conduct over forty pro-Israel events every month, is the following pledge:

> **We believe** that the Jewish people have a right to live in their ancient land of Israel, and that the modern State of Israel is the fulfillment of this historic right.

We maintain that there is no excuse for acts of terrorism against Israel and that Israel has the same right as every other nation to defend her citizens from such violent attacks.

We pledge to stand with our brothers and sisters in Israel and to speak out on their behalf whenever and wherever necessary until the attacks stop and they are finally living in peace and security with their neighbors.[4]

At the top of this page is their banner Scripture, Isaiah 62:1, which reads: "For Zion's sake will I not hold my peace, and for Jerusalem's sake I will not rest, until the righteousness thereof go forth as brightness, and the salvation thereof as a lamp that burneth." Interestingly, Isaiah 62 goes on to speak in distinctly messianic terms, speaking of Zion as a place where Jew and Gentile alike will see God's righteousness and will be called by a new name. Both of these statements allude to the ultimate reign of Messiah in Jerusalem.

And the Gentiles shall see thy righteousness, and all kings thy glory: and thou shalt be called by a new name, which the mouth of the Lord shall name. Thou shalt also be a crown of glory in the hand of the Lord, and a royal diadem in the hand of thy God. Thou shalt no more be termed Forsaken; neither shall thy land any more be termed Desolate: but thou shalt be called Hephzibah, and thy land Beulah: for the Lord delighteth in thee, and thy land shall be married. For as a young man marrieth a virgin, so shall thy sons marry thee: and as the bridegroom rejoiceth over the bride, so shall thy God rejoice over thee. (vv. 2–5)

Note that at Christ's coming, the land is to be called "Beulah." Beulah is a Hebrew word meaning "land of marriage"—yet another messianic symbol. This is the only place in the entire Bible where one finds the specific reference to a land called

Beulah—yet it has become the theme of one of the most beloved southern gospel songs of all time, "Beulah Land."[5]

Of course, in the New Testament, believers in Jesus Christ as Messiah are called the *bride*, and the messianic theme of bride and bridegroom abounds:

> Ye yourselves bear me witness, that I said, I am not the Christ, but that I am sent before him. He that hath the bride is the bridegroom: but the friend of the bridegroom, which standeth and heareth him, rejoiceth greatly because of the bridegroom's voice: this my joy therefore is fulfilled. (John 3:28–29)

The book of Revelation speaks of the wedding feast of the Lamb of God. One can certainly understand the connection, then, of the Christian message with that of Zionism.

> And a voice came out of the throne, saying, Praise our God, all ye his servants, and ye that fear him, both small and great. And I heard as it were the voice of a great multitude, and as the voice of many waters, and as the voice of mighty thunderings, saying, Alleluia: for the Lord God omnipotent reigneth. Let us be glad and rejoice, and give honour to him: for the marriage of the Lamb is come, and his wife hath made herself ready. And to her was granted that she should be arrayed in fine linen, clean and white: for the fine linen is the righteousness of saints. And he saith unto me, Write, Blessed are they which are called unto the marriage supper of the Lamb. And he saith unto me, These are the true sayings of God. (Rev. 19:5–9)

Some Christian Zionist groups believe that the current *ingathering* of Jews in Israel, from all over the world, is a biblical prerequisite for the Second Coming of Jesus Christ and a prophetic proof that we are now living in the last days. In many Christian circles, it is preached that true believers should actively support the Jewish return to the land of Israel, encouraging the returning Jews to become Christian, since salvation is available only to those who believe upon Jesus as Lord and Messiah. As evidence of this attestation, they cite New Testament passages such as these:

> Jesus saith unto him, I am the way, the truth, and the life: no man [Jew or Gentile] cometh unto the Father, but by me. (John 14:6)

> Neither is there salvation in any other: for there is none other name under heaven given among men [Jew or Gentile], whereby we must be saved. (Acts 4:12)

Accordingly, the Jewish ingathering, coupled with the conversion of Jews to Jesus as the Christ, is viewed as a means of fulfilling endtime biblical prophecy. Many Christian Zionists believe that the people of Israel who acknowledge Jesus as Messiah remain part of the chosen people of God, along with the ingrafted Gentile Christians. This, they claim, is in accordance with the teachings of the apostle Paul:

> And if some of the branches be broken off, and thou, being a wild olive tree, wert grafted in among them, and with them partakest of the root and fatness of the olive tree; boast not against the branches. But if thou boast, thou bearest not the root, but the root thee. Thou wilt say then, The branches were broken off, that I might be grafted in. Well; because of unbelief they were broken off, and thou standest by faith. Be not highminded, but fear: for if God spared not the natural branches, take heed lest he also spare not thee. Behold therefore the goodness and severity of God: on them which fell, severity; but toward thee, goodness, if thou continue in his goodness: otherwise thou also shalt be cut off. And they also, if they abide not still in unbelief, shall be grafted in: for God

is able to graft them in again. For if thou wert cut out of the olive tree which is wild by nature, and wert grafted contrary to nature into a good olive tree: how much more shall these, which be the natural branches, be grafted into their own olive tree? (Rom. 11:17–24)

ZIONISM IN THE OLD TESTAMENT

Numerous Bible scholars claim, "God Himself was the first Zionist, and if God is a Zionist, every believer should be a Zionist." They make this assertion because *Zion* is a distinctly biblical term, first appearing in 2 Samuel 5:7, which says, "Nevertheless David took the strong hold of Zion: the same is the city of David." The term's use in this book would put it at well over 2,500 years old.

The word *Zion* is from the Hebrew word *tsiyuwn*, meaning "marker," "guidepost," or "sign."[6] Its first appearance in the Bible ties the place to the Mountain of God, or what would eventually become known as the city of Jerusalem.

There are many passages of Scripture that refer to the unique and special place Zion holds in the hearts of the Lord and His people. One such example, which many believe gives biblical credence to the modern Zionist movement, is found in Psalms, a book that is more than three thousand years old:

> This shall be written for the generation to come: and the people which shall be created shall praise the LORD. For he hath looked down from the height of his sanctuary; from heaven did the LORD behold the earth; to hear the groaning of the prisoner; to loose those that are appointed to death; to declare the name of the LORD in Zion, and his praise in Jerusalem; when the people are gathered together, and the kingdoms, to serve the LORD. (Ps. 102: 18–22)

Note the reference to *when the people are gathered together.* The term *the people* (*Am* in Hebrew) most often refers specifically to the Israelites, the people of God. In that biblical vein of understanding, many see this passage as a prophetic utterance from the Lord Himself, declaring that His people will return to the land in the last days. Hence, Zionism is seen as a biblical dream and mandate from God—especially in light of the clear words of verses 18 and 22.

ZIONISM IN THE NEW TESTAMENT

The term *Zion* becomes *Sion* in older English translations of the New Testament, such as the King James Version. From Matthew to Revelation, the term is used exactly seven times, appearing first in Matthew: "Tell ye the daughter of Sion, Behold, thy King cometh unto thee, meek, and sitting upon an donkey, and a colt the foal of a donkey" (Matt. 21:5). (Here, *daughter of Sion* refers specifically to the people of Israel—the People of God.) The last occurrence in the New Testament is found in the book of Revelation: "And I looked, and, lo, a Lamb stood on the mount Sion, and with him an hundred forty and four thousand, having his Father's name written in their foreheads" (Rev. 14:1). There is even a messianic reference in the New Testament book of Romans that points back to the Old Testament as an attestation that the Messiah would come out of Israel and would be specifically presented in Jerusalem: "As it is written, Behold, I lay in Sion a stumblingstone and rock of offence: and whosoever believeth on him shall not be ashamed" (Rom. 9:33).

The reference in Romans 9 to the Old Testament is twofold:

> And he shall be for a sanctuary; but for a stone of stumbling and for a rock of offence to both the houses of Israel, for a gin and for a snare to the inhabitants of Jerusalem. (Isa. 8:14)

Therefore thus saith the Lord GOD, Behold, I lay in Zion for a foundation a stone, a tried stone, a precious corner stone, a sure foundation: he that believeth shall not make haste. (Isa. 28:16)

The apostle Peter also referred back to these Isaiah passages when he wrote of the Messiah coming from Israel—and specifically, from Jerusalem: "Wherefore also it is contained in the scripture, Behold, I lay in Sion a chief corner stone, elect, precious: and he that believeth on him shall not be confounded" (1 Pet. 2:6).

***

Zionism figures strongly into the United States' political scene and climate. There has never been a presidential race in my lifetime that did not include, at times, extensive discussion surrounding America's pledge of support for the nation of Israel. Even Sarah Palin, vice-presidential candidate in Senator John McCain's 2008 presidential campaign, donned a Star of David as she toured the Statue of Liberty in 2011. When asked why she, a Charismatic Christian, was wearing a distinctly Jewish symbol, Palin responded, "Today is the 44th anniversary of Jerusalem being reunited. We want to call attention to that."[7]

While I was writing this book, I attended the 2013 Conservative Political Action Conference (CPAC) in Maryland. Sarah Palin was one of the keynote speakers. I had a seat about fifty feet from the dais. Mrs. Palin wore a necklace, prominently displayed, boasting a large and shiny Star of David.

To this day, many Christians see the term *Zion* as a euphemism for the Church, as well as for heaven, the dwelling place of the Lord. Many hymns and songs of praise were written with this Zionist theme in mind. Perhaps the most famous of them all is titled "Marching to Zion":

Come, we that love the Lord,
And let our joys be known;
Join in a song with sweet accord,
Join in a song with sweet accord
And thus surround the throne,
And thus surround the throne.

Refrain

We're marching to Zion,
Beautiful, beautiful Zion;
We're marching upward to Zion,
The beautiful city of God.[8]

I am certain that, armed with the preceding scriptural, historical, and political/cultural knowledge, the reader can see why the Zionist movement is so strong today, among both Jew and Christian, and especially in the United States of America.

SHARON AND KADURI—UNITED BY ZIONISM?

Apparently, the rabbis of Israel have long been divided over the issue of Zionism and thus fall in distinctly separate camps. There are those who favor a strong nationalistic Israel and see its existence as the direct hand of God; and there are those who believe that Zionism should refer only to religious and cultural practices and that the Lord Himself will bring about the true Israel in His own way. As one might expect, the Christian world is also divided into similar factions.

As stated earlier, Ariel Sharon was an ardent nationalistic Zionist—in every sense of the word. From the training his parents imparted to him, he acquired his deep desire for Israel to be a strong and independent nation. It was Sharon's zealous Zionism that helped to earn his several nicknames—both the noble ones and the ignoble ones.

You will also remember from an earlier chapter that after Rabbi Yosef Chaim, Kaduri's childhood Kabbalah teacher, died, young Kaduri then migrated to the British Mandate of Palestine at the advice of the Jewish elders of Baghdad, who hoped he might *ebb the incursion of Zionism* in the post–World War I state. Apparently, somewhere along the way, Kaduri converted to the stronger Zionistic view of Israel and its modern political and geographical existence. This is evidenced in Kaduri's strong support of Ariel Sharon's government, and even Sharon's Israeli pullout from Gaza.

Observe, again, this quote from an earlier chapter: "If we give them a small thing and there will be peace with them, we can leave Gush Katif. We can trust Sharon, he is okay. It can cede territories in Gaza. I have no faith in the Arabs but we must have a little quiet."[9]

Furthermore, at Kaduri's death, Israeli president Moshe Katsav declared the old and revered rabbi to be a "distinguished" Zionist, and I have yet to find a reputable news source to repudiate such a claim. Said President Katsav: "Rabbi Kaduri was distinguished for his Zionism, his modesty, his way of life, and he gave an example to all of us to denounce materiality. He was an example of Jewish spirituality and morality that accompanied the Jewish people for generations."[10]

Some speculate that perhaps these strong nationalist and Zionist ties between Yitzhak Kaduri and Ariel Sharon help to keep the messianic fervor alive in Israel today—certainly for the nationalistic Jew . . .

But especially for the Christian Zionist.

13

WHO IS KADURI'S MESSIAH— *REALLY?*

And I answered, Who art thou, Lord? And he said unto me, I am Jesus of Nazareth, whom thou persecutest.

—Acts 22:8

I t would be wise at this point to take a more in-depth look at the *Jesus* whom Rabbi Kaduri supposedly revealed in his mysterious messianic death note. As already stated, the note sent shock waves through both the Jewish and Christian communities because the name of the revealed Messiah was supposedly *Yehoshua* or *Yeshua*, which, transliterated in English, is *Jesus*.

The Christian community, looking for the imminent return of *Jesus Christ*, was delighted beyond description to see the initial reporting on the note. To them, Rabbi Kaduri had clearly pegged *Jesus Christ* as the *true* Messiah. Of course, those of the Jewish faith quickly renounced that distinctly Christian claim. The religious Jews, and even some Christians, declared that the *Jesus* supposedly revealed by Kaduri's note could be *anyone*. They pointed out the various and difficult language variations involved in arriving at the name. Additionally, they reminded enthusiasts of the commonness of the Hebrew name that is often translated into English as *Jesus*. On these two points, the detractors are technically correct: *the Jesus*, or *Joshua*, of the note could be almost anyone in the Hebrew community—specifically because there was no other identifier included with the name. They claim that in saying the Messiah's name is simply *Yeshua* in Hebrew would have the same impact as if the note had said in English, "The Messiah's name is Joshua." With nothing else to specifically identify *which* Joshua to whom one is referring, the message would be enigmatic at best and utterly meaningless at worst.

So who was *Kaduri's Messiah?* The answer to this question is still hotly disputed and persistently debated. There are so many language considerations involved in the matter, and the detractors make a big deal out of the fact that the English name Jesus is an *invented name* and therefore not relevant to the mysterious message.

Let us now do a more in-depth study of the name found within Kaduri's note.

NO SMALL MATTER—A DEEPER WORD STUDY

Here is the crux of the problem: In all honesty, Kaduri did not say that Messiah's name was *Jesus of Nazareth* or *Jesus the Christ*, as represented in the New Testament. Actually, he did not even say the Messiah's name is *Jesus*. And to cynics of the note, this is no small matter. *Jesus* truly is an *invented* English word—specifically. On this point of technicality, the critics are also correct. What the note actually said, provided one holds that the key to understanding the note was to take the first *Hebrew* letter of each of the *Hebrew* words from the sentence—"He will lift the people and prove that his word and law are valid"—was that the name of Messiah is *Yehoshua*. That's it. The coded message simply said, "Yehoshua." There was no other identifier attached to the name. As previously stated, *Yehoshua* and *Yeshua* are, in effect, the same name, derived from the same Hebrew root of the word *salvation*. They actually translate directly to English as *Joshua*. However, the Hebrew name *Yeshua* was apparently a very common name from Old Testament times through the days of first-century Judea and the time of Jesus and His disciples. The name *Jesus*, as we use it, comes from the transliteration of *Yeshua* into Greek, and then from Greek into Latin, and then from Latin into English (more on this in a moment).

It is widely reported that archaeologists have unearthed the tombs of well over sixty Yeshuas from the period of time that dates to Jesus's ministry. The short name *Yeshua* (transliterated with a *J*) also appears dozens of times in the Old Testament and in reference to four separate characters—including a descendant of Aaron who helped distribute offerings of grain: "And next to him were Eden, and Miniamin, and *Jeshua* . . . in the cities of the priests, in their set office, to give to their brethren by courses, as well to the great as to the small . . ." (2 Chron. 31:15; emphasis added). Another person by that name accompanied former captives of Nebuchadnezzar back to Jerusalem: "Now these are the children of the province that went up out of the captivity, . . . which came with Zerubbabel: *Jeshua*, Nehemiah, Seraiah, Reelaiah, Mordecai, Bilshan, Mispar, Bigvai, Rehum, Baanah (Ezra 2:1–2; emphasis added).

The longer version of the name, Yehoshua, appears a little over two hundred times in the Old Testament and refers most notably to the legendary conqueror of Jericho and the guide of the children of Israel into the Promised Land—Joshua. This long version corresponds to *Strong's Hebrew Dictionary* reference number 3091 and is phonetically pronounced Ye–ho–shoo'–ah.

The Hebrew name Yehoshua is apparently quite common among Jews today. One of the most infamous people with that name is an American rabbi named Milton Yehoshua Balkany. Rabbi Balkany, of Brooklyn, New York, was dubbed the Brooklyn Bundler in November 2010, when he was found guilty of extortion, blackmail, wire fraud, and making false statements in a federal court in Manhattan.

It is also claimed that one of Rabbi Kaduri's closest spokesmen is named Yehoshua.[1] In light of this interesting revelation, some have joked that Kaduri actually informed us that his own spokesman was the *real* Messiah! But back to our brief language study.

Why is it, then, that we call the Hebrew warrior of the battle of Jericho *Joshua* and the Christian Messiah *Jesus?* It is because the New Testament was originally written in Greek, not Hebrew. The earliest written Greek version of the name Jesus is Romanized today as *Iesus* (pronounced Ee-ay-sooce). In the Latin of the early New Testament days, *Jesus* would have appeared as *Iesus*. This is why the Catholic version of the modern-day crucifix bears the inscription *INRI*. The initials stand for "Iesus Nazarenus Rex Iudaeorum," or "Jesus of Nazareth, King of the Jews." Also note the *I* used for the *J* in the Latin word for "Jews"—*Iudaeorum*.

On another interesting note, the English name *Jesus* is not used in the original 1611 King James Version of the Bible—not even once. Neither are the names Jehovah, Judah, Joseph, Joshua, Jerusalem, or John found in the original 1611 KJV. The word that is used in the *original* KJV is *Iesus*, the shortened Hebrew equivalent of the Hebrew name *Yehoshua.* The letter *J* did not come into use until much later. The peculiar sound of the *J* was, in fact, unfamiliar to Aramaic, Hebrew, Greek, and Latin. Not even the English language distinguished *J* from *I* until the mid-seventeenth century. That is why the *original* 1611 King James Bible refers to Jesus as *Iesus* and his father as *Ioseph,* the book of Joshua as *Ioshua* and the book of Judges as *Iudges.* Same goes for the books of Iob, Ieremiah, Ioel, Ionah, Iohn, and Iudeth.

Observe the first two verses of John 3 from an early English version for an example of this early English phenomenon. Note the other strange English word variations of the time:

> There was a man of the Pharisees, named Nicodemus, a ruler of Iewes: the same came to Iesus by night, and said vnto him, Rabbi, wee know that thou art a teacher come from God: for no man can doe these miracles that thou doest, except God be with him.[2]

The name *Yeshua* means "the Lord's Salvation," or "Salvation is from the Lord." Matthew 1:21 says, "And she shall bring forth a son, and thou shalt call his name JESUS [Yeshua]: for he *shall save his people from their sins*" (emphasis added). It is solely from this name, Yeshua, that the Greek word *Iesus* derives its meaning. Through multiple language translations and cultural changes in pronunciation, the tradition of calling the New Testament Messiah *Jesus* has firmly taken hold. However, today's English word *Jesus* is not to be found anywhere in the original languages in which the Bible was first written.

Here is another thought: What was Jesus's last name? His last name certainly was not *Christ.* The name *Christ* is a title—

it means "the Anointed." The *Anointed*, of course, carries with it the connotation of the *Messiah*.

> And Jacob begat Joseph the husband of Mary, of whom was born Jesus, who is called Christ [the Anointed]. (Matt. 1:16)

No, people from Jesus's day wishing to distinguish him from another Jesus (or Yeshua) would have called him *Yeshua Bar Yehosef* (Jesus son of Joseph) or *Yeshua Nasraya* (Jesus of Nazareth).

> Philip findeth Nathanael, and saith unto him, We have found him, of whom Moses in the law, and the prophets, did write, Jesus of Nazareth, the son of Joseph. (John 1:45)

> And they said, Is not this Jesus, the son of Joseph, whose father and mother we know? how is it then that he saith, I came down from heaven? (John 6:42)

> And when he was gone out into the porch, another maid saw him, and said unto them that were there, This fellow was also with Jesus of Nazareth. (Matt. 26:71)

> And I answered, Who art thou, Lord? And he said unto me, I am Jesus of Nazareth, whom thou persecutest. (Acts 22:8)

The New Testament–period Galileans distinguished themselves from others with the same first names by adding either "son of" and their fathers' names, or their birthplace. Jesus of the New Testament was called Christ, by those who knew who He was, to delineate Him specifically as the Messiah of God.

> And they said, Some say that thou art John the Baptist: some, Elias; and others, Jeremias, or one of the prophets. He saith unto them, But whom say ye that I am? And Simon Peter answered and said, Thou art the Christ, the Son of the living

God. And Jesus answered and said unto him, Blessed art thou, Simon Barjona: for flesh and blood hath not revealed it unto thee, but my Father which is in heaven. (Matt. 16:14–17)

Here is yet another interesting thought: What would Mary, Jesus's mother, have called Him? Now you know the answer, if you did not already know it before reading this chapter. Since she was Jewish and spoke Hebrew or Aramaic, she would have called Him *Yeshua*.

WHO WAS RABBI KADURI'S MESSIAH?

On the one hand, the only name Kaduri's note left was *Yehoshua*. That's it. There was no added "of Nazareth," or "of the New Testament," or "the Christ." Just *Yehoshua*, or *Joshua*, if the word were translated directly to English from Hebrew. His note merely left one of the most common of Hebrew names with no other hint as to whom this common name might be attached. As difficult as this may be for some to accept, it is the pure linguistic fact of the matter.

BUT WAIT . . .

It cannot be denied, however, that the name revealed by the supposed Kaduri note *did* leave strong pointers to *Jesus the Christ* of the New Testament. After all, Kaduri said he was leaving the name of the *real Messiah* for the entire world to see. There is only *one Jesus*, or *Yehoshua*, commonly held as the name for *Messiah* in the entire world. That name is *Jesus the Christ*—of the New Testament. Even the Muslim world acknowledges that name as distinctly belonging to Jesus of the New Testament Scriptures. If this were not so, there would be no controversy over the Kaduri note. And do not forget that the *initial* reaction of several of

Kaduri's followers and his son David, according to the *Israel Today* investigative report, was that the note held no credibility as being authentic. The outrage was over the fact it *obviously* pointed to the Christian understanding of the Messiah. This is what caused Kaduri's son and other Jewish leaders to begin calling the note a forgery or a fake. The fact that the controversy vehemently rages is prima facie evidence that many religious adherents—Jew, Christian, Muslim, and otherwise—saw what numerous people believe Kaduri *wanted* them to see in his messianic revelation: the name of Jesus Christ of Nazareth—*the Messiah.*

Accordingly—and predictably—the debate still rages.

14

PROPHETIC UTTERANCES OR A MESSIANIC MESS?

*The worldwide reaction to the news of Kaduri's note has been "crazy."
I have never received so many emails and calls from around the globe.[1]
—Aviel Schneider, author of the original Israel Today story*

ust how accurate have Rabbi Kaduri's Messiah prophecies
been thus far? How can we know whether or not to put
stock in his supposed visions and his subsequent predictions? Does the Bible have anything to say about how to
discern a true prophet from a false prophet? In examining the
Rabbi Kaduri story, it is important that we do the following study,
because it is upon this particular theologically profound point,

of prophets and prophecies, where the story currently hangs in the minds of many. Both Jew and Christian know that the Old Testament has some very specific instructions and even several dire warnings concerning the pronouncement of prophecies or heavenly visions supposedly to have come from the Lord. Even the strict Torah-only Karaite Jew knows the first five books of the Bible contain particularly strict instructions for interpreting prophecies and identifying true prophets. So, before we take a closer look at Rabbi Kaduri's specific messianic prophecies, let's first sample a few of the Old Testament instructions as we examine the following five highlighted Biblical truths:

1. A prophet of God can hear from the Lord in a dream or vision.

As unusual as it may sound to one who is not a student of the Bible, the Bible is clear on the matter. Many prophetic revelations of God have come through a supernatural vision or a dream. Apparently, the true prophet of God understands and knows when the Lord of Hosts has truly spoken to him: "And he said, Hear now my words: If there be a prophet among you, I the LORD will make myself known unto him in a vision, and will speak unto him in a dream." (Num. 12:6)

2. A prophet of God is responsible for turning people from wickedness.

While this may not always be the overall purpose of a prophecy, it certainly must be the overall purpose of the ministry and life of the true prophet.

> I have not sent these prophets, yet they ran: I have not spoken to them, yet they prophesied. But if they had stood in my counsel, and had caused my people to hear my words, then

they should have turned them from their evil way, and from the evil of their doings. (Jer. 23:21–22)

I have sent also unto you all my servants the prophets, rising up early and sending them, saying, Return ye now every man from his evil way, and amend your doings, and go not after other gods to serve them, and ye shall dwell in the land which I have given to you and to your fathers: but ye have not inclined your ear, nor hearkened unto me. (Jer. 35:15)

To the law and to the testimony: if they speak not according to this word, it is because there is no light in them. (Isa. 8:20)

I have seen also in the prophets of Jerusalem an horrible thing: they commit adultery, and walk in lies: they strengthen also the hands of evildoers, that none doth return from his wickedness: they are all of them unto me as Sodom, and the inhabitants thereof as Gomorrah. (Jer. 23:14)

3. There are tests to determine a prophet's genuineness, as well as dire warnings against false prophets.

The following four passages, according to most biblical experts, contain perhaps the most important tests in the entire Bible for examining the accuracy of a prophecy or a prophet. As such, people often refer to them when someone appears on the scene claiming to be a modern-day prophet. Bible scholars the world over have examined Rabbi Kaduri's prophecies in the strict light of the following declarations of the Lord (emphasis has been added):

But the prophet, which shall presume to speak a word in my name, which I have not commanded him to speak, or that shall speak in the name of other gods, even that prophet shall die. And if thou say in thine heart, How shall we know the word which the LORD hath not spoken? *When a prophet speaketh in the name of the Lord, if the thing follow not, nor come to pass, that is the thing which the Lord hath not spoken, but the prophet hath spoken it presumptuously*: thou shalt not be afraid of him. (Deut. 18:20–22)

For from the least of them even unto the greatest of them every one is given to covetousness; *and from the prophet even unto the priest every one dealeth falsely*. They have healed also the hurt of the daughter of my people slightly, saying, Peace, peace; when there is no peace. *Were they ashamed when they had committed abomination? nay, they were not at all ashamed,* neither could they blush: therefore they shall fall among them that fall: at the time that I visit them they shall be cast down, saith the LORD. (Jer. 6:13–15)

There is a conspiracy of her prophets in the midst thereof, like a roaring lion ravening the prey; they have devoured souls; they have taken the treasure and precious things; they have made her many widows in the midst thereof. *Her priests have violated my law, and have profaned mine holy things*: they have put no difference between the holy and profane, neither have they showed difference between the unclean and the clean, and have hid their eyes from my sabbaths, and I am profaned among them. *Her . . . prophets have daubed them with untempered mortar, seeing vanity, and divining lies unto them, saying, Thus saith the Lord GOD, when the LORD hath not spoken.* (Ezek. 22:25–28)

Then the LORD said unto me, The prophets prophesy lies in my name: I sent them not, neither have I commanded them, neither spake unto them: they prophesy unto you a false vision and divination, and a thing of nought, and the deceit of their heart. Therefore thus saith the Lord concerning the prophets that prophesy in my name, and I sent them not, yet they say, Sword and famine shall not be in this land; by sword and famine shall those prophets be consumed. And the people to whom they prophesy shall be cast out in the streets of Jerusalem because of the famine and the sword; and they shall have none to bury them, them, their wives, nor their sons, nor their daughters: for I will pour their wickedness upon them. (Jer. 14:14–16)

4. People tend to gravitate toward false prophets who tickle their ears.

Sadly, this is a fact of human nature. When solid scriptural truth is deemed too difficult for people to bear, they often begin to look for prophets who will tell them what they want to hear. This has been humankind's tendency since the most ancient of days. And frequently, in such cases, an abundance of these so-called prophets are ready to come forward.

> The prophets prophesy lies, the priests rule by their own authority, and my people love it this way. But what will you do in the end? (Jer. 5:31 NIV)

5. God can use a false prophecy to test His people!

This is surprising to many students of the Bible, but the Scripture is clear. God's Word is unambiguous regarding false prophets and their fictitious messages. Even so, prophecies abound and prophets abound. Yet, God declares that He is sovereign—in spite of the prophet who claims to have heard from God but has not. God may even perform a work through the mouth of a false prophet, or perhaps bring a *test* to His people through a false prophecy. The admonition is that God's people are to stay true to the contextually interpreted Word of the Lord. In this way, they are less prone to stray from the true Word or to be fooled by a false prophet.

If a prophet, or one who foretells by dreams, appears among you and announces to you a miraculous sign or wonder, and if the sign or wonder of which he has spoken takes place, and he says, "Let us follow other gods" (gods you have not known) "and let us worship them," you must not listen to the words of that prophet or dreamer. The LORD your God is testing you to find out whether you love him with all your heart and with all your soul. It is the Lord your God you must follow, and him you must revere. Keep his commands and obey him; serve him and hold fast to him. That prophet or dreamer must be put to death, because he preached rebellion against the Lord your God, who brought you out of Egypt and redeemed you from the land of slavery; he has tried to turn you from the way the Lord your God commanded you to follow. You must purge the evil from among you. (Deut. 13:1–5 NIV)

WHAT DOES THE NEW TESTAMENT SAY ABOUT THIS MATTER?

Now that we have this firm Old Testament understanding concerning prophets and prophecies, dreams, and visions, let us examine several key New Testament instructions concerning the same. This will be an especially important study for the Christian reader. Since so many people believe that Rabbi Kaduri may have been pointing to Jesus the Christ, or Jesus of Nazareth, of New Testament fame, as the *true Messiah*, let's have a quick look at what Jesus and some of the New Testament writers had to say about this very topic.

BEWARE: A FALSE PROPHET MAY DO WONDERFUL WORKS!

This is a startling truth that some people find hard to accept. Jesus declared that some people would come forth who would actually do *good things*. They will perform wonderful and miraculous feats.

And some of these people, and perhaps organizations, will declare that they are working in *the name of the Lord*—yet they do not really belong to the Lord. They are false prophets:

> Beware of false prophets, which come to you in sheep's clothing, but inwardly they are ravening wolves. Ye shall know them by their fruits. Do men gather grapes of thorns, or figs of thistles? Even so every good tree bringeth forth good fruit; but a corrupt tree bringeth forth evil fruit. A good tree cannot bring forth evil fruit, neither can a corrupt tree bring forth good fruit. Every tree that bringeth not forth good fruit is hewn down, and cast into the fire. Wherefore by their fruits ye shall know them. Not every one that saith unto me, Lord, Lord, shall enter into the kingdom of heaven; but he that doeth the will of my Father which is in heaven. Many will say to me in that day, Lord, Lord, have we not prophesied in thy name? and in thy name have cast out devils? and in thy name done many wonderful works? And then will I profess unto them, I never knew you: depart from me, ye that work iniquity [lawlessness]. (Matt. 7:15)

> And many false prophets shall rise, and shall deceive many. (Matt. 24:11)

> For there shall arise false Christs, and false prophets, and shall show great signs and wonders; insomuch that, if it were possible, they shall deceive the very elect. (Matt. 24:24)

As you can see, the Christian is warned very specifically of these so-called prophets, whose main desire will be to make money from their deceitful trade. The Christian is also warned that many will be deceived and will turn to the false prophets. The believer is admonished not to go running after them simply because they have amassed a great following. Consider these passages:

But there were false prophets also among the people, even as there shall be false teachers among you, who privily shall bring in damnable heresies, even denying the Lord that bought them, and bring upon themselves swift destruction. And many shall follow their pernicious ways; by reason of whom the way of truth shall be evil spoken of. And through covetousness shall they with feigned words make merchandise of you: whose judgment now of a long time lingereth not, and their damnation slumbereth not. (2 Pet. 2:1–3)

Preach the word; be instant in season, out of season; reprove, rebuke, exhort with all longsuffering and doctrine. For the time will come when they will not endure sound doctrine; but after their own lusts shall they heap to themselves teachers, having itching ears; and they shall turn away their ears from the truth, and shall be turned unto fables. (2 Tim. 4:2–4)

THE MESSIANIC PROPHECIES OF RABBI KADURI, IN REVIEW

Let us reexamine various prophetic components of some of Kaduri's most prominent Messiah statements. We will take a quick look at what Kaduri *said* would happen and compare it to what has *actually* happened.

He Will Wear the Star of David

In September 2001, Kaduri stated that in the garments of the coming Mashiach is hidden the Magen David, which supposedly will empower the Mashiach with the necessary leadership anointing. The anointing and power, Kaduri claimed, will be concealed until the proper time of revelation.

> . . . and the secret of his [Mashiach's] power is a Star of David hidden in his attire.[2]

The Star of David is known in Hebrew as the *Shield of David* or the *Magen David* (*Magen* is the Hebrew word for "shield"). An example of this Hebrew term is found in Psalm 3:3: "But thou, O LORD, art a shield for me; my glory, and the lifter up of mine head."

Rabbi Kaduri said the Messiah would receive his power by wearing a Star of David. *Could it be a kabbalistic amulet?* Notice that this Star of David will be *hidden* in the Messiah's garments. Here is another allusion to a distinctly kabbalistic element—that of hidden mysteries and hidden power. One can see why this particular prophecy would cause unease for the Christian but perhaps at the same time an added note of joy to the Jewish seeker of the Messiah. The Star of David is a generally recognized and cherished symbol of Jewish identity and Judaism.

The shape of the Star of David is that of a hexagram. Many have pointed out that the hexagram, when enclosed in a circle, is a universal symbol used in witchcraft and freemasonry. In witchcraft it is used to call forth the spirit world for earthly communication. Of course, Judaism denies any connection between the Magen David and the practice of witchcraft. The Jewish Encyclopedia references a twelfth-century document as the earliest Jewish literary source to make note of the symbol. The use of the star as an actual and official symbol of the Jewish community dates to the seventeenth century.[3]

He Is Already in Israel and Will Soon Bring Peace

> The Mashiach is already in Israel. Whatever people are sure will not happen, is liable to happen, and whatever we are certain will happen may disappoint us. But in the end, there will be peace throughout the world.[4]

If this Kaduri prophecy is true, then the Messiah has been in Israel since at least early 2005. The inference is that He is just waiting for the right time to be revealed. Until then there will be much confusion in the world—resulting ultimately in *world peace*.

This cryptic message appeals much more to the Jewish mind than to the Christian mind. The Christian would point to the New Testament Scriptures proclaiming that when the Messiah returns, the whole world will see Him at once. Based on this one Kaduri statement alone, many Christians have dismissed all of his Messiah prophecies, seeing a possible Antichrist connection, rather than a Messiah prophecy.

The following New Testament passage is the one most often cited in disputing a *gradual* or *secret* coming of the Messiah: "For there shall arise false Christs . . . Wherefore if they shall say unto you, Behold, he is in the desert; go not forth: behold, he is in the secret chambers; believe it not. For as the lightning cometh out of the east, and shineth even unto the west; so shall also the coming of the Son of man be." (Matt. 24:24–27)

He Is Already at Work

> Jews must come to the land of Israel to receive our righteous Mashiach (Messiah), who has begun his influence and will reveal himself in the future.[5]

Again, here is a clear declaration, uttered in October 2005, that the Messiah must already be *dwelling* in Israel—because He is already *influencing* people and events as He prepares to reveal Himself.

His Soul Is Attached . . .

With the help of God, the soul of the Mashiach has attached itself to a person in Israel.[6]

For many Bible students, this was an odd declaration indeed. Messiah's soul is, in this prophecy, *attached* to a *mere human being*. There appears to be nothing biblical about this prophecy at all—Old or New Testament. However, interestingly enough, there is a potential and distinctly Jewish *traditional* interpretation to this cryptic message. In actuality, a large number of Jews believe that there are *two Messiahs* to come to Israel. I will expand on this well-documented fact in a later chapter. But for the sake of the above-referenced prophetic utterance of Rabbi Kaduri, let me point out that some Jews believe Kaduri was revealing that the second and ultimate Messiah, known as *Messiah ben David*, was now making himself present in the first Messiah, *Messiah ben Joseph*, who is already present in Israel. Again, this is a foreign concept to most New Testament Christians—but a concept that would hold validity in the Jewish mind. Kaduri, of course, was speaking primarily to the Jews with his purported prophecies.

The Temple Must Be Rebuilt

This declaration I find fitting to issue for all of the Jews of the world to hear. It is incumbent upon them to return to the Land of Israel due to terrible natural disasters which threaten the world. In the future, the Holy One, Blessed be He, will bring about great disasters in the countries of the world to sweeten the judgments of the Land of Israel.

I am ordering the publication of this declaration as a warning, so that Jews in the countries of the world will be aware of the impending danger and will come to the Land of Israel for the building of the Temple and revelation of our righteous Mashiach (Messiah).[7]

This Kaduri pronouncement very clearly emphasized the nationalistic goal of Israel, as well as making the goal a part of the messianic prophecy process. Israel has long been engaged in a recruiting campaign to have as many Jews as possible return to the region and bolster the nation's strength. Some viewed this particular prophecy almost as a prophetic *threat*. The warning appeared to be that Jews who did not hurry back to Israel would suffer the wrath of God that was certain to be soon falling upon all the other nations of the world. Bible scholars, however, took note of Kaduri's call for the rebuilding of the Jewish Temple—a prominent desire among both Jews and Christians. The rebuilding of the Temple on the Temple Mount, in the very last days, is a major prophetic theme within certain Christian last-days scenarios.

He Will Come in the Year 2012

And then, I (Rabbi Yosef Hayim Zakkai, from the city Beitar Illit) understood that the rabbi (Kaduri) is interested that we speak about the Moshiach (Messiah).

I got the courage and asked him, "Our rabbi! When will Moshiach come?" The Rav answered me, "I cannot reveal," and laughed a big laugh. I asked him again, "Our rabbi! When will Moshiach come?" The Rav answered in 2 words, [in the year 5772]," and he repeated this twice. I was very shocked by his words, and immediately, when I left the Rav's home, I went up to the Kollel of Kabbalists in the Rav's Yeshiva, and told over what the Rav had said—they were all amazed.

About 2 weeks later, in the beginning of Tevet, 5766, the rabbi was admitted to Bikur Cholim Hospital in Yerushalayim. I would arrive daily to the hospital to learn with the Rav. And then, I asked him again, "Our rabbi! In what month and in what year will Moshiach come?" And the Rav answered me, "In the month of Av, 5772." And he repeated this twice.[8]

As previously noted, the Hebrew year 5772 ended on Elul 29 (September 16, 2012). The following day, Tishrei 1 (Rosh Hashanah), began the New Year 5773. To the disappointment of many followers of the old rabbi's prophecies, there was no messianic appearance in the year 2012.

He Will Save Us from Islam and Christianity

Kaduri was also quoted as saying the Messiah will "save Jerusalem from Islam and Christianity that wish to take Jerusalem from the Jewish Nation—but they will not succeed, and they will fight each other."[9] For the Christian, this statement is nonsensical. Christianity, of course, is linked *directly* to Jesus Christ. To be a Christian is to be a follower of Messiah—or Christ. How can the true Messiah be Jesus (Yehoshua) Christ, yet fight against *Christians*—those who follow Jesus Christ?

He Will Communicate to Us through *the Media*

> As leader, the Messiah will not hold any office, but will be among the people and use the media to communicate. His reign will be pure and without personal or political desire.[10]

Some have chuckled concerning Kaduri's claim that the Messiah would *use the media* as His method of communicating with the world. One could only hope not, considering the current and continually growing distrust of mainstream media sources the world over.

He Will Perform Magic and Have a Strong Self-Essence

One Hebrew-based blogspot, seemingly dedicated to promoting Kaduri's messianic visions, claims to have access to direct quotes from the rabbi. The next alleged Kaduri quote, derived from that blogspot, is a particularly interesting one (emphasis added):

Not everyone will believe the first stages of his revelation and his actions as the Mashiach. This is detailed in the many books, but his genuine test will not be in *his ability to perform magic*, but in his *self-essence* and in his actions. These actions will change him from the level of Chezkat Mashiach to the unquestionable Mashiach.[11]

The Hebrew word *Chezkat* means *candidate* or *presumed*. It would seem, then, from this quote and others like it, that Kaduri's Messiah is, at first, merely a candidate. Only later, through works of *magic* and a magnetic personality, will he finally be *proclaimed* the unquestionable Mashiach. Of course, the Christian Bible student immediately has visions of a strikingly undeniable New Testament *Antichrist* figure portrayed in this Kaduri description of the Messiah. Consider the following New Testament passages:

For there shall arise false Christs, . . . and shall shew great signs and wonders. (Matt. 24:24)

Then said Jesus . . . , Except ye see signs and wonders, ye will not believe. (John 4:48)

And he doeth great wonders, so that he maketh fire come down from heaven on the earth in the sight of men, and deceiveth them that dwell on the earth by the means of those miracles which he had power to do in the sight of the beast; saying to them that dwell on the earth, that they should make an image to the beast, which had the wound by a sword, and did live. And he had power to give life unto the image of the beast, that the image of the beast should both speak, and cause that as many as would not worship the image of the beast should be killed. (Rev. 13:13–15)

Let no man deceive you by any means: for that day shall not come, except there come a falling away first, and that man of sin be revealed, the son of perdition; who opposeth and exalteth himself above all that is called God, or that is worshipped; so that he as God sitteth in the temple of God, shewing himself that he is God. Remember ye not, that, when I was yet with you, I told you these things? And now ye know what withholdeth that he might be revealed in his time. For the mystery of iniquity doth already work: only he who now letteth will let, until he be taken out of the way. And then shall that Wicked be revealed, whom the Lord shall consume with the spirit of his mouth, and shall destroy with the brightness of his coming: Even him, whose coming is after the working of Satan with all power and signs and lying wonders, and with all deceivableness of unrighteousness in them that perish; because they received not the love of the truth, that they might be saved. And for this cause God shall send them strong delusion, that they should believe a lie. (2 Thess. 2:3–11)

Subsequently, it would appear, upon a closer examination, that Kaduri's Messiah prophecies leave the true *Messiah-return* hopeful, whether Jew or Christian, a bit wanting. However, the Jew would certainly find many more elements of his or her understanding of the Messiah in Kaduri's prophecy, whereas many Christians, once having truly studied the issue, would not be overly thrilled with the revelations. When the prophecies are parsed and examined in the light of where we are at this moment in history, to many people, there does not seem to be much meat on the bones of the old rabbi's prophetic declarations. Except . . . perhaps, one remaining prophecy—that of the return of the Messiah *in connection with* the death of Ariel Sharon. Because Mr. Sharon's life still hangs in the balance at this writing, the mystery still holds weight with many, the world over. And as has already been noted, even if Sharon has passed by the time you read this book, the question still remains: Just how long *after* Sharon's death was Messiah expected to return?

Now we must ask: Were Rabbi Kaduri's messianic pronouncements biblically prophetic utterances given to the world, through the Lord, by the mouth of a true prophet of God? Or, did his messages merely make a mess of the true biblical understanding, both Old and New Testaments, of the coming of Mashiach? As one might imagine, there are loyal and passionate pundits in each camp . . .

Which is why the next chapter is so crucial.

15

WHO IS LOOKING FOR A MESSIAH?

[My mission is to] pave the path for the glorious reappearance of Imam Mahdi, may Allah hasten his reappearance.[1]
— *Iranian president Mahmoud Ahmadinejad, in a speech in Tehran, November 16, 2005*

ust who is looking for a Messiah anyway? What religious groups are expecting the coming of, or the return of, a messianic figure? The answer to that question probably explains why Rabbi Kaduri's claim that he had a vision of the soon-coming Messiah resonated so vividly throughout the religious world. This will be a particularly important chapter to consider as we continue our journey of discovery. By the next chapter, you will notice another possible—and shocking—link between Kaduri's messianic prophecy and Ariel Sharon. I have a feeling a bright light will pop on when you see the potential connection. Prepare yourself.

THE WORLD OVER, PEOPLE ARE WAITING

Practically all the world's prominent faith systems are expecting a messianic figure—and what's more, they are expecting him to appear soon. Is it any wonder, then, that when Rabbi Kaduri claimed to have met the Messiah and to know His name, where He is, and what specific event has to happen before He appears, he had the ear of almost the whole world? Kaduri's message was especially intensified when it was revealed that it was *the death of Ariel Sharon* that must precede the Messiah's coming. This was a shocking revelation indeed. However, his pronouncement became even more electrifying when, just weeks after he made the declaration, Ariel Sharon lapsed into a deep and potentially deadly coma. And, to further intensify the matter, Sharon's vegetative state ensued a mere six months after the kabbalistic death curse of July 2005 was spoken upon him. As each of these surreal events unfolded, the world took note.

WHOM IS THE WORLD EXPECTING?

Buddhism, Hinduism, and Zoroastrianism each include doctrines that teach that the world is going through a *cosmic cycle* in which morals and religion have gradually decayed. Each of these faith systems is looking for a new earth age of enlightenment and peace, largely brought about through the appearance and subsequent teachings of a *Coming One*. The Hindus are expecting a new *Avatar*. The Buddhists are looking for the *Maitreya*, and those holding to Zoroastrianism are anticipating their *Saoshyant*. Three other major world religions, each claiming to be monotheistic, are Christianity, Islam, and Judaism. The Muslims are awaiting their *Mahdi*; the Jews are seeking the long-awaited Messiah of Israel, *Mashiach ben David*. The Christians are longing for the *return* of *Jesus Christ—Yeshua*.

The major and distinctly distinguishing feature of the Christian expectation of the Messiah is that it insists Jesus Christ, the true Messiah, has *already* come once—the first time as Savior. The next time He appears, it will be to gather His elect, pour out His wrath on the ungodly, and then finally, to rule and reign on the earth as righteous Judge and King. However—*and this is significant*—Christianity teaches that just before the return of Jesus the Christ—an *antichrist* figure will appear. This antichrist will claim to be the true Christ but will actually rule in the spirit and power of Satan. The purpose of the Antichrist will be to deceive the world into thinking that he is the genuine Christ of God: "Little children, it is the last time: and as ye have heard that antichrist shall come, even now are there many antichrists; whereby we know that it is the last time" (1 John 2:18).

Perhaps you can now understand more clearly why Rabbi Kaduri's cryptic prophecy of the messianic revelation both thrilled and alarmed the Christian world—almost at once. Many Christians were, of course, thrilled when it was initially unveiled that the ancient kabbalistic rabbi declared in his note that *Yehoshua*, or Jesus, was the name of the real Messiah. To countless Christians around the world, this revelation was reminiscent of the apostle Paul's Damascus Road conversion. Perhaps the old kabbalistic rabbi had been converted. Maybe he had met the resurrected Jesus, just as the Jewish rabbi Paul had done some two thousand years ago. On the other hand, once the questionable tidbits of Kaduri's messianic illuminations began to circulate within the Christian community, a sampling of which I outlined in the previous chapter, others began to see shades of the soon-coming *Antichrist.* Numerous Christians began to ask if it was possible that Kaduri, desperately longing for a messianic vision, had actually received a *demonic* vision. Could he then have uttered a false prophecy that, instead of the Messiah, will actually reveal the prophesied *antichrist?* Some Christians today are answering, "Yes, that is exactly what Kaduri envisioned." Other Christians, however, still insist that Kaduri's vision was of Yeshua—Jesus, the Christ of God.

THE ISLAMIC MESSIAH

Devout Muslims were more than a little concerned when Rabbi Kaduri's messianic pronouncement went public and resounded throughout the Internet world.

The Islamic world is looking for their messiah as well; they call him the Mahdi (MA-dee). In English, the Arabic word translates to "the Guided One." Depending on the particular sect of Islam,[2] it is taught that the Mahdi will rule the earth for a period from seven to nineteen years. After his reign is complete, he will bring final judgment and rid the world of evil. This "evil," of course, largely refers to Christianity and Judaism.

In the Shia (or Shiite) sect of Islam, the Mahdi is believed to be the *Twelfth Imam* (the twelfth ruling descendant from Muhammad), Muhammad al-Mahdi, whose return will mark the appearance of Mahdi. Islam teaches that the Mahdi was actually born hundreds of years ago but vanished, one day to return and establish justice on earth.

The Sunni sect of Islam teaches that the Mahdi—largely a political and conquering-king figure—is the successor of Muhammad. However, many Sunnis reject the idea of a *returning* Mahdi because, not only is the Mahdi not spoken of in the Quran, but the notion of his *return* does not conform to the strictest interpretations of the Hadith, the sayings of Muhammad. Therefore, belief in the return of the Mahdi is much more prevalent in Shiite Islam.

Interestingly, those Muslims who do anticipate a returning Mahdi expect Jesus (of New Testament fame) to return just ahead of him. So in effect, they, like Christians, are also awaiting the return of Jesus. Of course, Jesus is *not* the Christ, according to Islam, but only an exalted prophet who was first sent to the Jews to convince them that they needed to turn to Allah as the one true God. Therefore, Christians are quick to point out that the Islamic version of Jesus does not even closely resemble the New Testament identification of Jesus the Christ.

One particular subgroup within the Shia sect, known as the *Twelvers*, is particularly zealous in their convictions regarding the imminent return of the Mahdi, including the belief that the world must be *prepared* for the Mahdi's arrival. Much of this preparation involves the purposed elimination of the state of Israel and the forced submission of Christians and Jews the world over. Iranian president Mahmoud Ahmadinejad is probably one of the most famous Twelvers on the planet. In a January 2006 article, just days before Rabbi Kaduri's death and only a few weeks before Ariel Sharon's massive stroke, WND ran a story about the Iranian leader's self-proclaimed messianic mission. Following is an excerpt from that article:

> Iranian President Mahmoud Ahmadinejad's mystical preoccupation with the coming of a Shiite Islamic messiah figure—the Mahdi—is raising concerns that a nuclear-armed Islamic Republic could trigger the kind of global conflagration he envisions will set the stage for the end of the world.
>
> While Mahmoud Ahmadinejad has been making headlines lately by questioning whether the Holocaust actually

happened, by suggesting Israel should be moved to Europe and by demanding the Jewish state be wiped off the face of the earth, his apocalyptic religious zealotry has received less attention.

. . .

Shiite writings describe events surrounding the return of the Mahdi in apocalyptic terms. In one scenario, the forces of evil would come from Syria and Iraq and clash with forces of good from Iran. The battle would commence at Kufa—the Iraqi town near the holy city of Najaf.

Even more controversial is Ahmadinejad's repeated invocation of Imam Mahdi, known as "the Savior of Times." According to Shiite tradition, Imam Mahdi will appear on Judgment Day to herald a truly just government.

Missed by some observers in Ahmadinejad's speech at the U.N. was his call to the "mighty Lord" to hasten the emergence of "the promised one," the one who "will fill this world with justice and peace."

Who stands in the Mahdi's way?

A top priority of Ahmadinejad is "to challenge America, which is trying to impose itself as the final salvation of the human being, and insert its unjust state [in the region]," says Hamidreza Taraghi, head of the conservative Islamic Coalition Society.

Taraghi says the U.S. is "trying to place itself as the new Mahdi." This may mean no peace with Iran, he adds, "unless America changes its hegemonic . . . thinking, doesn't use nuclear weapons, [or] impose its will on other nations."[3]

Ibn Q. Al-Rassooli is Iraqi born (as was Rabbi Kaduri) and a native speaker of Arabic. He is the author of the book *Lifting the Veil: The True Faces of Muhammad and Islam.* I. Q. was raised as a Muslim. But when his parents sent him to London, England, as a young man, to complete his university studies, he renounced the Islamic faith. He has spent the last thirty years on a quest to *expose the Islamic danger sweeping the world.*

On several occasions, I have extensively interviewed I. Q. on my radio program. When asked to comment, for this book, on the concept of the Islamic Mahdi, I. Q. provided the following:

> The concept of al Mahdi (the Rightly Guided or Redeemer) was—as usual with Muhammad and his followers—plagiarized, plundered, pirated and/or perverted from the Christian Messiah by Shia Muslims (the followers of Ali, the cousin and son-in-law of Muhammad).
>
> Muhammad ibn al-Hasan (869 in Occultation since 874 AD), titled al-Mahdi, is believed by Twelver Shi'a Muslims to be the ultimate savior of humanity and the final Imam (Leader) of the Twelver Shia (similar to the twelve apostles of Jesus).
>
> *Occultation* (Arabic *al Ghaybah*, meaning "Hidden") in Shia refers to a belief that the messianic figure, or Mahdi, the infallible male descendant of the founder of Islam (Muhammad), was born but disappeared, and will one day return to fill the world with justice.
>
> Twelver Shi'a believe that al-Mahdi did not die but rather was hidden by Allah in 874 AD and will emerge in the future with Jesus Christ (terminating a worldwide Armageddon-like conflagration) in order to fulfill their mission of bringing peace and justice to the world.
>
> Muhammad ibn al-Hasan assumed the *Imamate* (leadership of Islam) at five years of age. Not all Shi'ite schools believe him to be the Mahdi, although the majority sect *Twelvers* do.
>
> Sunnis (who represent 85% of the followers of Muhammad) and other Shi'ites accept as true that the Mahdi has not yet been born, and therefore his exact identity is only known to Allah.
>
> Based on their belief, the Mullahs and Ayatollahs of Iran represent a present and clear danger to all of humanity if they are allowed to gain Weapons of Mass Destruction because they will try to bring about the arrival of their Mahdi as "predicted" through a Nuclear Holocaust.[4]

The Islamic expectation of the Messiah truly is an international one. Even the late Hugo Chávez, president of Venezuela—and a professed Catholic—made a public statement captured on video, in which he wished for the Mahdi to come soon. In March 2013, WND reported on the Chávez video:

> Chavez, in a meeting with Mahmoud Abbas, the president of the Palestinian National Authority, talked of his belief in the Coming of Mahdi, according to the video, and said, "The ultimate war of them all is the war in Gaza."
>
> In the video, which is not dated, but appears to have been captured during a signing of agreements at the Miraflores presidential palace in Caracas, Nov. 27, 2009, Chavez told his audience "Quds (Jerusalem) is a holy place for all of us Christians. I spoke with (Iranian President Mahmoud) Ahmadinejad about the day that Islam's Quran says both (Mahdi and Christ) will return. Jesus, holding hands with the 12th Imam, Mahdi. . . . Then peace will come upon the world. I tell Christ and Mahdi to come sooner, rush now, come sooner . . . because we witness the threats posed to the world, my God!"[5]

Jesus "holding hands" with the Mahdi? You may recall that Rabbi Kaduri's prophecy of the soon-appearing Messiah of Israel was accompanied by the announcement that Messiah would "save Jerusalem from Islam."[6]

Obviously, the Islamic world was less than thrilled with Kaduri's vision.

16

THE JEWISH MESSIAH:
ARE THERE TWO?

ome readers will be surprised to learn that, as mentioned in chapter 14, Israel is actually looking for two Messiahs: *Mashiach ben Joseph* and *Mashiach ben David*.[1] This fact may be extremely important in interpreting Rabbi Kaduri's messianic vision.

The Hebrew word *ben* means "son of." Accordingly, the two messianic figures would be, in English, Messiah the son of Joseph and Messiah the son of David. Jewish messianic tradition refers to the two redeemers as *Mashiach*, and both are important in ushering in the messianic age.

Messiah ben Joseph is said to be a hero of Israel who, after much suffering, eventually dies as a sacrifice of atonement and then ultimately rises from the dead. He is called the *suffering Messiah*.[2] Ancient Jews wrote about the Messiah ben Joseph coming into the world in light of a parallel understanding of the Joseph, son of Jacob, or Israel, in the book of Genesis. This Joseph of Genesis was the favorite son of Israel. He was one who foresaw the future, yet was hated by his Jewish brethren for his gift. His own brothers sold him into slavery, and thought him to be as good as dead. However, years later, Joseph was ultimately revealed to his brothers as the *second* most powerful person in the world, second only to Pharaoh. Though his brothers did not recognize him at first, Joseph would be the one who would save them. Accordingly, following this biblical parallel, the Jews believe that a militaristic *King of Israel* will arise along the lines of Joseph. He will be a *Lion of God*, so to speak, who will deliver his brothers from danger, even though they initially despise him. He will rise to be a prominent and successful political figure. Messiah ben Joseph, in other words, will arise from among the people of Israel in order to save them. Then, after he is finished with his work, Messiah ben David will appear.

THE LIGHT POPS ON

You probably see it now. Many others have seen it as well. This understanding could be one of the keys to discovering what Rabbi Kaduri meant when he said the ultimate Messiah (Messiah ben David) could not appear until after the death of Ariel Sharon. Could it be that Kaduri believed Sharon to be Messiah ben Joseph? Some speculate so. They claim this rendering of the prophecy makes sense. For if Sharon was Messiah ben Joseph (after the example of Joseph of Genesis), then Messiah ben David is soon to follow—perhaps after Messiah ben Joseph is gone—or dead.

Examples of this line of thinking can be found all over the Internet, in chat rooms and on blogs. Following is a blog post from a user claiming to be a Jew. Apparently, a Christian had been trying to convince him or her that Jesus Christ was the true Messiah. The user left the following response:

> You're misunderstanding the Jewish concept of the Messiah. You're also trying to make the scripture fit Jesus' biography but it doesn't.
> There's 2 Jewish Messiahs. The first messiah Messiah ben Joseph will be a warrior (which is why Ariel Sharon is a good candidate). [O]nly later will Messiah ben David come.[3]

Think of it. The Jewish mind, including this blogger's, could easily envision Sharon as Israel's Messiah ben Joseph. You will recall that Sharon was called the Lion of God, the King of Israel, and even the Savior of Israel. In the political realm, he was fearfully called the Bulldozer. Dignitaries, the press, and the man in the street bestowed these terms to him. And indeed, Sharon was a valiant warrior, a statesman, and a military hero. He is said to have literally saved Israel from certain destruction in the Yom Kippur War. Furthermore, Sharon was rejected by his "brothers." From his earliest days in the little socialist village where he was raised, he was tormented and bullied. But Sharon had a dream, or a vision, of a restored Israel—strong and mighty. The dream seemed impossible, yet it was fulfilled, and Sharon himself helped bring about its fulfillment. And though little Arik Sharon was despised as a boy, he went on to become the most powerful man in Israel—second only in power, in the minds of some, to the coming Messiah ben David. Furthermore, for seven long years at this writing, he has been *suffering*, in a coma—perhaps to *rise* again.

Again, this may be a key to unlocking some, at least, of the Jewish excitement over Rabbi Yitzhak Kaduri's Messiah prophecy. While certainly not all religious Jews hold the position that Sharon is the Messiah ben Joseph, some apparently do. Now the only thing for which Israel is waiting, according to this analysis, is Sharon's passing and the coming of Messiah ben David. The Jewish understanding of Messiah ben David is much closer to the understanding of the Christian Messiah—Jesus the Christ. Messiah ben David is said to be the ultimate and final King of the universe. Jews who are looking for Messiah ben David point to the prophecy of Daniel as an example of Messiah's authoritative reign:

> I beheld till the thrones were cast down, and the Ancient of days did sit, whose garment was white as snow, and the hair of his head like the pure wool: his throne was like the fiery flame, and his wheels as burning fire. A fiery stream issued and came forth from before him: thousand thousands ministered unto him, and ten thousand times ten thousand stood before him: the judgment was set, and the books were opened. I beheld then because of the voice of the great words which the horn spake: I beheld even till the beast was slain, and his body destroyed, and given to the burning flame. As concerning the rest of the beasts, they had their dominion taken away: yet their lives were prolonged for a season and time. I saw in the night visions, and, behold, one like the Son of man came with the clouds of heaven, and came to the Ancient of days, and they brought him near before him. And there was given him dominion, and glory, and a kingdom, that all people, nations, and languages, should serve him: his dominion is an everlasting dominion. (Dan. 7:9–14)

When Messiah ben David comes, according to Jewish teaching, he will avenge the death of Messiah ben Joseph, raise him from the dead, and usher in the messianic era of everlasting and universal peace. Of course, Israel will be restored as the *Nation of God*, and Jerusalem will be restored as the *City of God*—from where Messiah ben David will rule and reign in glory and power.

One Bible expositor succinctly explains the Jewish Messiah mindset in the following manner:

> When Jews typically think of "the" Messiah, however, they generally have in mind Mashiach ben David of the tribe of Judah who shall rule in the messianic age. Mashiach ben Yosef is said to be of the tribe of Ephraim (son of Joseph), and is also sometimes called Mashiach ben Ephraim.
>
> Mashiach ben Yosef will come first, before the advent of Mashiach ben David, to prepare the world for the coming of the kingdom of the Lord. He will fight God's wars (against "Edom," collectively understood as the enemies of Israel) in a time preceding the fulfillment of the Messianic Kingdom (this is sometimes referred to as Ikvot Mashiach, (the "footsteps of the Messiah").
>
> The Rabbis derive this understanding of Mashiach ben Yosef from their exegesis of Obadiah 1:18, "The house of Jacob shall be a fire, and the house of Joseph a flame, and the house of Esau stubble; they shall burn them and consume them, and there shall be no survivor for the house of Esau, for the Lord has spoken." Moreover, they understand the confrontation between the "house" of Joseph and the "house" of Esau to be prefigured in the birth of Joseph himself, where Rachel indicated that God would "add a son" who would be anointed for battle in the End of Days.
>
> However, Mashiach ben Yosef will be killed during the war against evil, as described in the prophecy of Zechariah, who says of this tragedy that "they shall mourn him as one mourns for an only child" (Zech. 12:10). His death would

be followed by a period of great calamities and tribulations for Israel, and shortly after this Mashiach ben David would appear to avenge his death and inaugurate the Messianic kingdom on earth.[4]

THE TWO JEWISH MESSIAHS—TOGETHER IN JESUS?

Of course, by now Christian students of the Scriptures have had yet another lightbulb pop on. It is apparent that the traditional Jewish teaching of the *two Messiahs* fits neatly with the singular understanding of Jesus Christ of Nazareth.

Jesus of the New Testament is revealed as having come and lived among men as a man—*the first time*. He came as Jesus, son of Joseph, his earthly father, and Mary, his mother, both from the tiny village of Nazareth. Jesus is presented as having been rejected by his own brothers and family. The writers of the Gospels (all of them Jewish) went to great lengths to point out this fact—drawing the parallel of Messiah ben Joseph:

> After these things Jesus walked in Galilee: for he would not walk in Jewry, because the Jews sought to kill him. Now the Jews' feast of tabernacles was at hand. His brethren therefore said unto him, Depart hence, and go into Judaea, that thy disciples also may see the works that thou doest. For there is no man that doeth any thing in secret, and he himself seeketh to be known openly. If thou do these things, shew thyself to the world. For neither did his brethren believe in him. (John 7:1–5)

> He was in the world, and the world was made by him, and the world knew him not. He came unto his own, and his own received him not. (John 1:10–11)

The New Testament account of Jesus goes on to describe Him as one of *great vision* for the future. He often spoke in a prophetic manner. In fact, Jesus's appearance as a man, His ability to draw large multitudes, His miraculous power, His continual rejection by His own brethren and family, His direct challenging of the religious/political elite of His day—may have served to convince His disciples that perhaps Jesus was the *Messiah ben Joseph* of Jewish tradition. The disciples, early on, anyway, hoped that Jesus would take His rightful throne, restore Israel's sovereignty, and deliver her from her enemies.

In Matthew, we discover that the mother of John and James came to Jesus, asking for a special place of authority in His new kingdom that was soon to come. The implication is that the mother and the boys thought Jesus would set up a political/theocratic kingdom. They wanted to have a guaranteed place of authority within it: "Then came to him the mother of Zebedee's children with her sons, worshipping him, and desiring a certain thing of him. And he said unto her, What wilt thou? She saith unto him, Grant that these my two sons may sit, the one on thy right hand, and the other on the left, in thy kingdom" (Matt. 20:20–21).

In fact, from the beginning of Jesus's life on earth, people mistakenly identified Him as the new "political" *King of the Jews*—implanting into the Jewish mind the image of *Messiah ben Joseph.* After all, this Jesus of Nazareth was commonly known among the people as the *son of Joseph.* Many people of power were concerned that He would indeed prove to be Israel's long-expected King of the Jews:

> Now when Jesus was born in Bethlehem of Judaea in the days of Herod the king, behold, there came wise men from the east to Jerusalem, saying, Where is he that is born King of the Jews? for we have seen his star in the east, and are come to worship him. When Herod the king had heard these things, he was troubled, and all Jerusalem with him. (Matt. 2:1–3)

And Jesus stood before the governor: and the governor asked him, saying, Art thou the King of the Jews? And Jesus said unto him, Thou sayest. (Matt. 27:11)

And when they had platted a crown of thorns, they put it upon his head, and a reed in his right hand: and they bowed the knee before him, and mocked him, saying, Hail, King of the Jews! (Matt. 27:29)

And there was one named Barabbas, which lay bound with them that had made insurrection with him, who had committed murder in the insurrection. And the multitude crying aloud began to desire him to do as he had ever done unto them. But Pilate answered them, saying, Will ye that I release unto you the King of the Jews? For he knew that the chief priests had delivered him for envy. (Mark 15:7–10)

And Pilate wrote a title, and put it on the cross. And the writing was, JESUS OF NAZARETH THE KING OF THE JEWS. This title then read many of the Jews: for the place where Jesus was crucified was nigh to the city: and it was written in Hebrew, and Greek, and Latin. Then said the chief priests of the Jews to Pilate, Write not, The King of the Jews; but that he said, I am King of the Jews. Pilate answered, What I have written I have written. (John 19:19–22)

There can be no doubt that many of the Jewish mind-set of two thousand years ago saw in Jesus a potential candidate for *Messiah ben Joseph*. As Jesus's ultimate and true mission became more apparent to His followers, He was seen as the possible *Messiah ben David* as well:

The book of the generation of Jesus Christ, the son of David, the son of Abraham. (Matt. 1:1)

And when Jesus departed thence, two blind men followed him, crying, and saying, Thou Son of David, have mercy on us. (Matt. 9:27)

Then was brought unto him one possessed with a devil, blind, and dumb: and he healed him, insomuch that the blind and dumb both spake and saw. And all the people were amazed, and said, Is not this the son of David? (Matt. 12:22–23)

And, behold, a woman of Canaan came out of the same coasts, and cried unto him, saying, Have mercy on me, O Lord, thou Son of David; my daughter is grievously vexed with a devil. (Matt. 15:22)

And the multitudes that went before, and that followed, cried, saying, Hosanna to the Son of David: Blessed is he that cometh in the name of the Lord; hosanna in the highest. (Matt. 21:9)

While the Pharisees were gathered together, Jesus asked them, saying, What think ye of Christ? whose son is he? They say unto him, The Son of David. (Matt. 22:41–42)

To further compound the New Testament emphasis upon Jesus as the *complete* Messiah—in one person—Matthew records Jesus's earthly father, Joseph, as also called the *son of David* . . . thus sealing the deal that in Jesus Christ, both Jewish messianic prophecies were fulfilled. Even though the messianic term *Son of David* is used in the New Testament to distinctly describe Jesus's messiahship, it can also be said Jesus was the *son of Joseph*:

But while he thought on these things, behold, the angel of the Lord appeared unto him in a dream, saying, Joseph, thou son of David, fear not to take unto thee Mary thy wife. (Matt. 1:20)

And they said, Is not this Jesus, the son of Joseph, whose
father and mother we know? how is it then that he saith,
I came down from heaven? (John 6:42)

And so, the message of the Christian's outreach to the religious Jew, the Jew who is fervently seeking the Jewish Messiah, is that the Messiah has already come—in Jesus of Nazareth. He is Jesus the Christ of God, Savior of Israel, and Savior of the world.

Christians point out that the New Testament was written entirely by Jews, most of them Jewish religious zealots. A Pharisee who was a highly respected Jewish rabbi, and one who had a Kaduri-type encounter with Jesus as Christ, wrote the vast majority of the New Testament documents. That rabbi's name was Saul—later to become known as Paul. Christians also insist to the Jew that in Jesus Christ, all the Old Testament Scriptures concerning the Christ are fulfilled—to the letter, and that in Jesus the true Messiah is wrapped up in *one*—Messiah ben Joseph, in his first coming, and Messiah ben David, in his second coming.

Of course, Orthodox Jews reject all of this argument. They maintain that Jesus of Nazareth was an imposter and a heretic and that Israel is still waiting for its Messiah. One prominent website dedicated to this theme is called *Jews for Judaism*. The headline reads, "The Jewish Messiah . . . And Why Jesus Does *Not* Qualify." The website goes into great detail, outlining step-by-step the Jewish reasoning as to why Jesus Christ cannot possibly be the Messiah. Here is an excerpt from that page:

Anyone can claim to be the Messiah or a group of people can claim that someone is the Messiah.

However, if that person fails to fulfill all the criteria found in the Jewish Bible, he cannot be the Messiah. According to the Christian scriptures, Jesus seems to have understood this. As he was being crucified by the Romans, he cried out "My God, my God, why have You forsaken me?" (Matthew 27:46)[5]

Amazingly enough, it is this very verse, Matthew 27:46, to which most Christians would point as *proof positive* that Jesus was, in fact, the Messiah of God. The verse in question presents Jesus on the cross, offering Himself as the sacrifice for the sin of mankind. There, on Golgotha, Jesus cried out the mournful words "Eli, Eli, lama sabachthani?" or "My God, my God, why hast thou forsaken me?"

The Christian would offer two striking rebuttals to the *Jews for Judaism* argument regarding this specific verse. First, the verse itself was written by a loyal and zealous Jew. Matthew's Gospel clearly presents Jesus as the Messiah of God who knew full well that He was the Messiah of God. Matthew's Jewish writing leaves no room for doubt on this matter. So, the question might be: *Why did Matthew include this accounting of Jesus's words on the cross?* The Christian would answer that it was because Matthew, being a devoted first-century Jew, knew the significance of Jesus's utterance just before He died. Jesus was referring the listeners, as a good rabbi would, to a particular psalm—by referring to the passage's *first line*. (Remember, the original Hebrew Scriptures did not have chapters and verses as they now appear in most modern Bibles.) Examples of this well-known practice, that of referring to an ancient Hebrew Scripture by a particular line, are found throughout the New Testament—during the time of Jesus. Following are several of the many examples:

> Now all this was done, that it might be fulfilled which was spoken of the Lord by the prophet, saying, Behold, a virgin shall be with child, and shall bring forth a son, and they shall call his name Emmanuel, which being interpreted is, God with us. (Matt. 1:22–23)

> For this is he that was spoken of by the prophet Esaias [(Isaiah)], saying, The voice of one crying in the wilderness,

Prepare ye the way of the Lord, make his paths straight. (Matt. 3:3)

That it might be fulfilled which was spoken by Esaias the prophet, saying, Himself took our infirmities, and bare our sicknesses. (Matt. 8:17)

As it is written in the prophets, Behold, I send my messenger before thy face, which shall prepare thy way before thee. (Mark 1:2)

And there was delivered unto him the book of the prophet Esaias. And when he had opened the book, he found the place where it was written, The Spirit of the Lord is upon me, because he hath anointed me to preach the gospel to the poor; he hath sent me to heal the brokenhearted, to preach deliverance to the captives, and recovering of sight to the blind, to set at liberty them that are bruised, to preach the acceptable year of the Lord. And he closed the book, and he gave it again to the minister, and sat down. And the eyes of all them that were in the synagogue were fastened on him. (Luke 4:17–20)

Accordingly, the Christian would argue, this is exactly what Jesus was doing when he cried out from the cross: the first line of Psalm 22 happens to begin with those heart-wrenching words: *My God, my God, why hast thou forsaken me?*

But what other words does Psalm 22 contain? Following is a sampling:

But I am a worm, and no man; a reproach of men, and despised of the people. All they that see me laugh me to scorn: they shoot out the lip, they shake the head, saying, He trusted on the LORD that he would deliver him: let him deliver him, seeing he delighted in him . . . They gaped upon me with their mouths, as a ravening and a roaring lion. I am poured out like water, and all my bones are out of joint: my heart is like wax; it is melted in the midst of my bowels. My strength is dried up like a potsherd; and my tongue cleaveth to my jaws; and thou hast brought me into the dust of death. For dogs have compassed me: the assembly of the wicked have inclosed me: they pierced my hands and my feet. I may tell all my bones: they look and stare upon me. They part my garments among them, and cast lots upon my vesture. (vv. 6–8, 13–18)

Stunningly, this passage reveals: the very words used by the religious elite to mock Jesus, His physical condition and extreme thirst while on the cross, the piercing of His hands and feet (*crucifixion* had not been invented at the time Psalms was written), and the gambling for His clothing that was literally taking place when He cried out. This passage was a direct prophecy of Jesus Christ, the Messiah who was to come, and was directly fulfilled in Him. Psalm 22 was written a thousand years before Jesus came—yet the passage strikingly refers to exceedingly specific events on the day of Jesus's execution. Jesus's reference to the 22nd Psalm on that fateful day was for one reason: to prove to those around Him, who were mostly Jews, that He was, indeed, the Christ who was to come.

So, the debate still rages. To many, Rabbi Kaduri's prophecy *still has life*.

And the world still waits . . . for its Messiah.

17

ZOHAR, THE CHRIST, AND THE ANTICHRIST

If this is not a demonic setup for the coming of the Antichrist, then I don't know what is.[1]
—*Stephen Yulish, former professor and Kabbalah instructor*

One of the greatest objections to Rabbi Kaduri's prophetic utterances, especially from the evangelical Christian world, is related to his practice of Kabbalah, a form of ancient Jewish mysticism. This mystical practice often involves what many would consider the application of magic, as well as deliberate attempts to contact the spirit world—both of which are specifically condemned in the

Bible. But further, the practice heavily relies upon extrabiblical texts—mystical, and some say mythical, literature—for the making of endtime prophecies. One such text is the Zohar, the foundational work in the literature of Kabbalah.[2]

Zohar is a Hebrew word meaning "Radiance" or "Splendor." The Zohar itself is actually a collection of books that includes commentaries on the mystical aspects of the Torah. The collection incorporates various esoteric scriptural interpretations as well as additional material dealing with mysticism, mythical cosmology, and mystical psychology. The Zohar contains numerous discourses on the true self and its relationship to the Light of God. Also included are sections dealing with the nature of God, the soul, and the relationship between man and universal energy. Additionally, the Zohar teaches its readers about astrology, reincarnation, and spirit guides.

The Zohar was believed to have first appeared on the scene of religious literature in the thirteenth century, in Spain. It was published by a Jewish writer who claimed the original work was actually completed by a rabbi named Shimon bar Yochai in the second century, the time of the Roman persecution of the Jews. According to Jewish legend, Rabbi Yochai hid in a cave for more than a dozen years and received spiritual revelations from the prophet Elijah. These revelations were then recorded as the work now known as the Zohar. Because of this purported history, Kabbalah is claimed to be the primary concealed part of the Oral Torah, or oral traditional teachings of Rabbinic Judaism.

The Zohar (vol. 1, p. 186) also contains teaching on the Nephilim (mentioned also in Genesis 6) and the giants of old, who, we are told, had physical relations with mortal women. The Nephilim bore children, whom they called Anakim (giants), while the Nephilim themselves were called "sons of God." The Zohar goes on to declare that up to this day the Nephilim still exist on earth and teach men the arts of magic.

More directly related to the interests of our account of Rabbi Kaduri, there are also teachings in the Zohar concerning the coming of Messiah. Kaduri's messianic predictions appear to have been heavily influenced by his knowledge of and reliance upon these teachings. A strikingly familiar, Kaduri-like messianic prophecy from the Zohar is as follows:

> In the *73rd year*, that is, seven years after the Messiah ben Joseph was revealed, *all the kings of the world shall assemble in the city of Rome.* And the Holy One, blessed be He, will shower *fire* and *hail* and *meteoric stones* upon them, until they are wiped out from the world. And only those kings who did not go to Rome will remain in the world. And they shall return and wage other wars. During this time, the *King Messiah will declare himself* throughout the whole world. And many nations will gather around him, together with many armies from all corners of the world. And all the children of Yisrael (Israel) will be gathered together from all their places.[3]

Rabbi Kaduri died in 2006, and Ariel Sharon went into his coma the same year. Some prophecy researchers have noted that if either Kaduri or Sharon were considered to be *Messiah ben Joseph*, then seven years later would be the year 2013. It so happens that in March 2013, a new pope (Pope Francis Bergoglio) was chosen after the resignation of Pope Benedict XVI, the first pope to resign from office in six hundred years. To further bolster the connection to the Zohar prediction and the pope, an amazing prediction was made in a best-selling book written by Chris D. Putnam and Thomas Horn, titled *Petrus Romanus: The Final Pope Is Here.* The book, quoting from the ancient prophecies of celebrated Catholic sage Saint Malachy, declared that the next to the last pope would resign in office, only to be followed by one who would be known as *Peter the Roman.* Following is a quote from the book's description as it appeared on *Amazon.com*:

> First published in 1595, the prophecies were attributed to
> St. Malachy by a Benedictine historian named Arnold de
> Wyon, who recorded them in his book, Lignum Vitæ. Tradi-
> tion holds that Malachy had been called to Rome by Pope
> Innocent II, and while there, he experienced the vision of the
> future popes, including the last one, which he wrote down
> in a series of cryptic phrases. According to the prophecy, the
> next pope (following Benedict XVI) is to be the final pon-
> tiff, Petrus Romanus or Peter the Roman. The idea by some
> Catholics that the next pope on St. Malachy's list heralds the
> beginning of "great apostasy" followed by "great tribulation"
> sets the stage for the imminent unfolding of apocalyptic
> events, something many non-Catholics would agree with.[4]

When Pope Bergoglio was selected, and took upon himself
the name *Pope Francis*, many thought perhaps the Malachy
prophecy held no weight. After all, they protested, the new pope
was born in Argentina and was not known as *Peter*.

However, it was quickly claimed and reported that Pope
Bergoglio's parents were both born in Italy, making Bergoglio
unquestionably of Italian or Roman descent. Furthermore, the
name the new pope took was borrowed from Saint Francis of
Assisi, who was baptized as *Francesco di Pietro di Bernardone*—his
middle name was *Peter*. Accordingly, many saw in Pope Francis
the qualifications for undeniably labeling him as the potential and
prophesied Peter the Roman. Prophetic speculation abounded
concerning the papal intrigue and the year 2013 as it may relate
to the rise of the biblical Antichrist.

As I mentioned before, numerous Bible and prophecy
scholars consider Rabbi Kaduri's messianic pronouncements
to be predictions of the antichrist figure of the Old and New
Testaments, rather than the true Christ of God. One amazing

testimony of that possible antichrist scenario comes from a man who represents himself as having been deeply involved in Kabbalah and Zohar teachings. He claims to have been a respected teacher in the movement, with a large following. Below is a selected section of his astounding insight:

> On Tuesday night, September 13, 2005, Rabbi Yitzchak Kaduri, a Rabbi steeped in Jewish Kabbalistic, mystical lore told his Yeshiva class (Jewish school) that Jews all over the world needed to return to Israel due to impending natural disasters, which threatened to strike the world. He had spoken of tsunamis . . . and other natural disasters. I asked myself how he could know what was going to happen? Probably because he used gematria (numerology) and other Kabbalistic divinations, witchcraft, and demonic practices that the Lord called detestable to Him in Deuteronomy 18:10–12. Satan knows that his time is short and he will give people just enough knowledge to condemn them to hell with him for eternity.
>
> . . .
>
> Back in 2005, Rabbi Kaduri said that the great Rabbi Schneerson (he also has since died) told him that Kaduri would live to see the coming of the Messiah. He said that the current government of Israel would be the last one of the old era. Sharon would be the last PM. The new leadership would be that of the Messianic era . . .
>
> Well, Schneerson was obviously incorrect and must therefore have been a false prophet. Rabbi Kaduri died in 2006 before the coming of the Messiah. Sharon was not the last Prime Minister of Israel. Before he died, however, Rabbi Kaduri told his followers that the spirit of Messiah had already attached itself to an Israeli and he also had been given the name of the coming Messiah but it was not to be revealed until one year after his death.
>
> The note when opened said that the coming Messiah will be called Yehoshua (Joshua) or the Aramaic, Yeshua (salvation). This name, Yeshua Hamashiach (literally Jesus the

Messiah or the Christ), is unbelievably what some of Rabbi Kaduri's followers called him.[5]

The returning Jesus (Yeshua Hamashiach) will not be an Israeli man but will come "in just the same way as you have watched Him go into heaven" (Acts 1:11). The Antichrist, however, will be a man. If this is not a false Messiah, a false Christ, a false Yeshua, then call me meshugeh (crazy).

If this is not a demonic setup for the coming of the Antichrist, then I don't know what is[.][6]

It cannot be denied that the Zohar plays a vastly influential role in the practice of Kabbalah. And given Rabbi Kaduri's involvement with the Kabbalah, again, you can understand how many from the more conservative branches of biblical scholarship would give very little credence to his prophecies, especially those concerning the coming of a Messiah. When one considers the kabbalistic and cryptic method by which the strange Messiah note was given, biblical credibility is called into question even more.

Now, let us turn our attention to one of the most hotly contested aspects of this entire matter . . . Jews coming to *Jesus Christ* as Savior and Messiah.

18

CHRISTIANS OUT OF JEWS?

One of the brightest flashpoints of contention concerning Rabbi Kaduri's purported messianic vision and his *Yehoshua* revelation is between Orthodox Judaism and Messianic Judaism. *Messianic Jews* is the term generally used to describe Jews who have proclaimed that Jesus of Nazareth, of New Testament record, is the only and true Messiah.

Messianic Judaism has its latest roots of origin in the 1960s and 1970s. However, many would argue that the entirety of the New Testament is a Messianic Jewish attestation emanating from the first century AD. It is a fact that every one of the New Testament writers was a hard-core Jewish believer who came to the realization that Jesus of Nazareth was, in fact, the long-awaited Messiah of Israel. The book of Acts goes to great lengths to demonstrate how the conversion of the apostle Paul, a Jewish rabbi and Pharisee, was used by God to turn the Jewish world upside down concerning the proclamation that Jesus (Yehoshua or Yeshua) was indeed the Christ.

Modern Messianic Judaism often blends the evangelical Christian understanding of the Scriptures with the customs, practices, feasts, and traditions of the more traditional Judaism. Most modern Messianic Jews, however, hold to the unwavering proposition that Jesus Christ is the true Messiah and that there is no entrance into heaven apart from full faith and trust in Jesus as Savior and Lord.

The traditions of Judaism, the Messianic Jew would claim, are mainly cultural considerations and have no bearing upon one's ultimate salvation. Accordingly, most mainstream evangelical Christian groups accept Messianic Judaism as a legitimate form of biblical Christianity. Many adherents of Messianic Judaism are Jewish by ethnicity. Numerous Messianic Jews claim that their religious group is also a legitimate sect of Judaism. Various Jewish organizations, and the Supreme Court of Israel in cases related to the Law of Return,[1] have rejected this claim, and instead consider Messianic Judaism to be merely a form of Christianity.[2] Here are their main arguments:

- Jesus did not fulfill the messianic prophecies.

- Jesus did not embody the personal qualifications of the Messiah.

- Biblical verses "referring" to Jesus are mistranslations.

- Jewish belief is based on national revelation.[3]

The Messianic Jewish movement is no small sect. It boasts a large membership and its ranks are growing every day. While there are apparently no exact figures, it has been estimated that in the United States alone, there are at least 175,000 Jewish believers in the Messiah Yeshua. Rabbinic Judaism estimates that more than a million Jewish people around the world believe that Yeshua is the Messiah. Messianic congregations are found in numerous countries the world over.[4]

There is a rather large push from the evangelical Christian community to evangelize Jews to this end. The missionary effort is seen by countless Christians to be a part of the fulfillment of biblical endtime prophecy. The prophetic understanding involves the idea that in the last days, a remnant of Jews will see the light and accept Jesus Christ as Messiah and Lord.

The New Testament is rife with declarations of the *remnant of Israel* coming to Jesus as Christ:

> Esaias [Isaiah] also crieth concerning Israel, Though the number of the children of Israel be as the sand of the sea, a remnant shall be saved: For he will finish the work, and cut it short in righteousness: because a short work will the Lord make upon the earth. And as Esaias said before, Except the Lord of Sabaoth had left us a seed, we had been as Sodoma, and been made like unto Gomorrha. What shall we say then? That the Gentiles, which followed not after righteous-

ness, have attained to righteousness, even the righteousness which is of faith. But Israel, which followed after the law of righteousness, hath not attained to the law of righteousness. Wherefore? Because they sought it not by faith, but as it were by the works of the law. For they stumbled at that stumblingstone; as it is written, Behold, I lay in Sion a stumblingstone and rock of offence: and whosoever believeth on him shall not be ashamed. (Rom. 9:27–33)

Here, Paul, a Jewish rabbi, used the Old Testament prophecy of Isaiah to prove that Jesus was the predicted stumbling stone. However, Paul proclaimed, there will be a remnant from among the Jews who will come to Jesus as Messiah.

Even the apocalyptic book of Revelation clearly portrays the idea of Jews coming to Jesus as Christ—especially in the very last of the last days. Notice how the apostle John, a devout Jew and the author of Revelation, identified the true Christian as one who *keeps the commandments and has faith in Jesus.*

Here is the patience of the saints: here are they that keep the commandments of God, and the faith of Jesus. (Rev. 14:12)

And the dragon was wroth with the woman, and went to make war with the remnant of her seed, which keep the commandments of God, and have the testimony of Jesus Christ. (Rev. 12:17)

The dragon of which John wrote is Satan. The woman, in the context of the passage, is Israel—or the Jews. The seed of the woman is the Jews who are living in the last days, and those who *keep the commandments of God and have the testimony of Jesus Christ* are the last days Christians, with an apparent special emphasis upon Jews who hold that Jesus Christ is Messiah. Certainly we can observe how the modern Christian community understands the importance of evangelizing the Jewish world as a fulfillment of certain Old and New Testament prophetic declarations.

As a result of the massive evangelism push from evangelical Christianity and the Messianic Jewish community, the number of Messianic Jews has dramatically increased. From 2003 to 2007, the movement grew from 150 Messianic houses of worship in the United States to as many as 438, with more than 100 in Israel and even more worldwide; individual congregations are often affiliated with larger Messianic organizations or alliances.[5]

Additionally, there are numerous Jews who are not ready to make the step of claiming Jesus as Messiah—yet hold a fairly high regard for the understanding of the Jesus of the New Testament.

CNN did an in-depth story on the massively controversial but worldwide movement of Jews looking deeper into the *Jesus phenomenon*. The title of the piece was "Jews Reclaim Jesus as One of Their Own." Following is an excerpt from that fascinating and lengthy news report:

> The relationship between Jews and Jesus has traditionally been a complicated one, to say the least.
>
> As his followers' message swept the ancient world, Jews who did not accept Jesus as the Messiah found themselves in the uncomfortable, and sometimes dangerous, position of being blamed for his death.
>
> Mainstream Christian theology's position held that Judaism had been supplanted, the Jewish covenant with the divine no longer valid, because of the incarnation of God as Jesus and his sacrifice on the cross.
>
> Jews, for their part, tended largely to ignore Jesus.
>
> That's changing now . . .
>
> And overwhelmingly, they are coming up with positive answers, urging their fellow Jews to learn about Jesus, understand him and claim him as one of their own.
>
> "Jesus is a Jew. He spent his life talking to other Jews," said Amy-Jill Levine, co-editor of the recently released *"Jewish*

Annotated New Testament."

"In reading the New Testament, I am often inspired, I am intrigued. I actually find myself becoming a better Jew because I become better informed about my own history," she said. . .

And Benyamin Cohen, an Orthodox Jew who spent a recent year going to church, admitted that he's jealous that Christians have Jesus.

"He's a tangible icon that everybody can latch on to. Judaism doesn't have a superhero like that," said Cohen, the author of the 2009 book *My Jesus Year.*

"I'm not advocating for Moses dolls," he said, but he argued that "it's hard to believe in a God you can't see. I'm jealous of Christians in that regard, that they have this physical manifestation of the divine that they can pray to.

"There could be more devout Jews than me who don't need that, but to a young Jew living in the 21st century, I wish we had something more tangible," he said.

The flurry of recent Jewish books on Jesus—including this month's publication of *The Jewish Gospels: The Story of the Jewish Christ* by Daniel Boyarin—is part of a trend of Jews taking pride in Jesus, interfaith expert Edward Kessler said.

"In the 1970s and 1980s, Christian New Testament scholars rediscovered the Jewish Jesus. They reminded all New Testament students that Jesus was Jewish," said Kessler, the director of the Woolf Institute in Cambridge, England, which focuses on relations between Jews, Christians and Muslims.

A generation later, that scholarship has percolated into Jewish thought, he said, welcoming the trend: "It's not a threat to Jews and it's not a threat to Christians."[6]

Rabbi Jonathan Cahn is a modern-day, and enormously popular, Messianic Jewish rabbi. He leads the Jerusalem Center/Beth Israel in Wayne, New Jersey. His worship center, he asserts, consists of Jews and Gentiles. In January 2012, Rabbi Cahn authored the

New York Times number one best-selling book: *The Harbinger: The Ancient Mystery That Holds the Secret of America's Future.*[7]

Rabbi Cahn was asked to provide his insight concerning the Messianic Jewish movement, as well as Rabbi Kaduri's prophecy and the naming of Yehoshua as the real Messiah. Following is Rabbi Cahn's response:

> For two thousand years it has been taught that the Jewish people cannot believe in Jesus/Yeshua and still remain Jewish. He has been the great dividing point and stumbling block of Jewish history. His name has been banned.
>
> Any serious consideration of the claim that he could be the Messiah has become taboo. It remains a striking irony that the one largely rejected by the people of his distinct heritage has become the central figure of human history.
>
> No less ironic that a world largely hostile to Jewish existence should so revere a Jewish rabbi. The issue is also prophetic.
>
> For the Nazarene said that his second coming would rest upon the turning of the Jewish people back to Him. It is therefore significant that we are now witnessing an unprecedented revival among the Jewish people, a turning to Jesus of historic proportions.
>
> The story of Rabbi Yitzhak Kaduri is thus a fascinating addition to this endtime phenomenon. To have a highly revered Orthodox Jewish rabbi declare that he has met the Messiah and knows his name, and then to reveal that name, and then to have that revelation point to Yehoshua or Yeshua—Jesus—is stunning—so much so that the revelation has been fought over ever since.[8]

HAS RABBI KADURI'S REVELATION BROUGHT JEWS TO JESUS?

The question is one of great importance. It is also one of enormous contention. Rabbi Kaduri's message, that Yehoshua was the name of the true Messiah, sparked the imaginations and the questions of many Jews who were longing for an authoritative declaration of the Messiah's identity. For some, Kaduri's revelation was all it took.

So has his revelation brought Jews to Jesus? The answer appears to be *yes*. Reportedly, a number of Jewish people claiming to be disciples of Kaduri have come to faith in Jesus Christ as Messiah as a result of his prophetic revelation. This, of course, is a matter of great celebration for the Christian and the Messianic Jewish world. But it is a matter of deep consternation for the Orthodox Jewish realm—but more on that later.

Tim LaHaye is a renowned American evangelical Christian minister, author, and speaker. He is best known for the enormously popular Left Behind series of apocalyptic fiction, which he coauthored with Jerry B. Jenkins. He has written more than fifty books, of both the fiction and nonfiction genres. *Time* magazine named Tim LaHaye one of the twenty-five most influential evangelicals in America.

I asked Mr. LaHaye what his views were on the possible influence of the Kaduri prophecy among the Jewish world. He responded:

> I do know that something significant is going on spiritually within the Jewish community. While there are many divisions among them, there seems to be a growing yearning for the coming of their Messiah. Due to their centuries of persecution and suffering, they of course longed for the Messiah that would deliver them from their captors, like the cruel Romans of the first century. This blinded them to many of their own prophecies that pointed out that before their Messiah came to rule he must first come to die for their sins as the Lamb of God to give them eternal life. This is clearly seen in the Prophecy of Isaiah 53, given almost 800 years before Jesus Christ was born miraculously of a Virgin, thus escaping the

sinful Adamic nature. Accordingly, Jesus alone was qualified to be the "Lamb of God" that takes away the otherwise sin of mankind, if they will accept Him by faith.

The remarkable revelation on April 30, 2007, published by *Israel Today*, of the note opened one year after his death, the highly respected Rabbi Kaduri indicated he believed "Yeshua (Jesus) is the Messiah." This revelation confirmed what I have come to believe for a long time . . . that many Jews, in Israel and throughout the world secretly believe, and hopefully have received Jesus as Savior and Lord.

There are of course many "Messianic Jews" or Christian Jews who proudly name the name of Christ openly as their Savior and Lord. When I was young, I seldom met a Jewish convert. In the last few years, I have met many and talked to those whose ministry is primarily to Jews and they tell of remarkable conversions to Christ.

One of the prophecy preachers I have worked with in the past, himself half-Jewish, who has cultivated a good relationship with several Rabbis in Israel, told of a Rabbi he had spent a lot of time with privately talking about what I call the claims of Christ as Messiah. My friend asked the Rabbi what he would do if "when Messiah comes, you discover he is Jesus Christ?" The Rabbi was silent a long time; then with tears in his eyes he replied, "I'm so glad it is you!"

For the Jews accept many prophecies of the over 109 of the Messiah that Jesus fulfilled in His first coming. In fact, I have made a careful list of them and find that no other man has fulfilled more than eight or ten such qualifications, from being born in Bethlehem against unbelievable odds, to the many in Isaiah 53 and to even being crucified between two thieves and being buried in a rich man's tomb. Yet Jesus fulfilled all 109 prophecies, several made seven and eight hundred years before His birth! That alone makes Him unique in the entire world and the only possible candidate for the Messiah. He is literally one out of the 13 billion or more people who have ever lived.

Jesus Himself gave over 140 prophecies, over half of which He fulfilled while still on the earth. The other half is End Time prophecies that are soon to be fulfilled. His most important prophecy is that He would be killed, buried, and in three days rise again. He did exactly that, which is celebrated every Resurrection Sunday by upwards of two billion people worldwide. The best proof of the resurrection is the foundation of the Christian faith—without which there would be no Christianity. Even today the resurrected Christ is still transforming the lives of those who put their trust in Him by inviting Him into their heart to forgive their sins and save their soul.

In this day when Jews and others read and study the Bible (including the New Testament), it is not hard for them to learn to love a man who healed all the sick he encountered, restored sight to blind eyes, healed ten lepers at once and according to those who were there, even raised the dead. Jesus, when understood who He really was in history and who He is today, is easy to love and serve. I should know; I have served Him joyfully for my entire life.[9]

A STUNNING REVELATION

As an example of the Jewish conversion phenomenon, an amazing YouTube video features a Messianic Jew interviewing a professing Jewish disciple of Kaduri in Tel Aviv, Israel. The interviewer is identified as Evangelist Zev Porat, of Messiah of Israel Ministries, who also is obviously fluent in Hebrew. The man being interviewed is dressed in traditional Hebrew religious garb and apparently does not speak English. Mr. Porat translates the entire conversation into English from Hebrew and back to English.

The Jewish Kaduri disciple gives his testimony of coming to faith in Jesus as the Christ and Messiah of God. He claims his journey to Jesus, as Messiah, was a result of Rabbi Kaduri's vision and teaching. In a striking revelation, Kaduri's disciple claims, in the video, that Kaduri actually taught in his yeshiva that *Yehoshua* was the Messiah. If this amazing attestation is valid, it is a stunning revelation indeed. Following is a paraphrased, translated version of what Kaduri's disciple claims:

> I studied in the Yeshiva of Rabbi Kaduri, who also believed in Yeshua. But Kaduri was afraid to say out in public what he believed concerning the Messiah.
>
> I was one of Kaduri's students, so I used to go around and tell everybody that Yeshua was the Messiah. I had a lot of debates with people who claimed that Yeshua was not the Messiah. But, I continued to declare that He was anyway.
>
> Yeshua was crucified and His blood is the redemption for the sin of mankind. No one else's blood will suffice—only Yeshua. And because Yeshua shed His blood for us, He is the Messiah, and He will save us. Yeshua is the way of salvation! Hallelujah!
>
> Rabbi Kaduri taught us in yeshiva that Yeshua is the Messiah. He did not, however, present the full picture. It was under Kaduri's teaching that the Holy Spirit gave me the full revelation of Yeshua as Messiah.
>
> My prayer is that everyone will believe that Yeshua is the Messiah, because He is the only one that was crucified for our sins. Please pray for the salvation of Israel.[10]

According to the Kaduri disciple, Isaiah 7:14 was the verse that opened his eyes to the full revelation of Messiah. The rabbi's Jewish disciple said, "This was a difficult process for me. But the revelation came to me." He then read aloud the verse in Hebrew, for the video presentation. The verse reads, "Therefore the Lord himself shall give you a sign; Behold, a virgin shall conceive, and bear a son, and shall call his name Immanuel."

Amazingly, the New Testament, written entirely by Jews,

opens with this identical prophecy as *the reason* that a Jew can believe that Jesus of Nazareth is the long-awaited Messiah of Israel:

> But while he [Joseph] thought on these things, behold, the angel of the LORD appeared unto him in a dream, saying, Joseph, thou son of David, fear not to take unto thee Mary thy wife: for that which is conceived in her is of the Holy Ghost. And she shall bring forth a son, and thou shalt call his name JESUS: for he shall save his people from their sins. Now all this was done, that it might be fulfilled which was spoken of the Lord by the prophet, saying, Behold, a virgin shall be with child, and shall bring forth a son, and they shall call his name Emmanuel, which being interpreted is, God with us. (Matt. 1:20–23)

"MESSIANIC 'JEWS' AND THEIR RABBI KADURI LIE"

As mentioned earlier, the Orthodox Jewish response to testimonies such as the one we just examined has been emotional, to say the least. "Messianic 'Jews' and Their Rabbi Kaduri Lie" is the title of an article posted on one such Jewish site.

The article, posted in December 2012, passionately proclaims:

> That missionaries have no limits to how low they'll stoop is nothing new to Yad L'Achim,[11] which has been battling them for decades. But their latest, despicable ploy is stunning in its audacity, deceit and sacrilege.
>
> The newest campaign features Yakov Damkani, a missionary and leader of the "Messianic Jewry" movement in Israel, who describes Harav Yitzchak Kadouri, zt"l, the elder of the mekubalim, as "one of the most prominent rabbis in the country's history." Damkani then goes on to say that a year after the Rav's death, in 2006, "a note was found which he left for his followers. In the note he wrote that the name of the mashiach is J."

In his farcical pitch, Damkani presents a forged note from Rav Kadouri with this "revelation" and adds that the Rav had met the mashiach in the final year of his life and was exhorting people to follow in the ways of J.

As expected, the spontaneous response among G-d-fearing Jews, especially those who had any connection with the Rav, was to dismiss the claim as utter nonsense. However, the missionaries aren't aiming their poisonous arrows at the Jews who know better; their target is ignorant Jews who give credence to the claim that "one of the most prominent rabbis in the country" was instructing them to join the "Messianic Jews."[12]

One can certainly feel the passion and anger displayed in the article concerning this highly controversial issue. The matter had its beginnings in the revelation of the Rabbi Yitzhak Kaduri Messiah note. Now, according to this same article, there may be potential legal proceedings taken against Messianic Jews who are actively evangelizing Jews in Israel:

To protect these potential victims, Yad L'Achim this week launched a counter campaign, discrediting the missionaries' ridiculous claims. The film presents each and every claim made by Damkani and refutes it with powerful testimony from Rav Kadouri's son and close disciples. Anyone who sees this film can have no doubt that the original is a lie from start to finish.

Featured in the Yad L'Achim film is the son of the elder of the mekubalim, Harav David Kadouri, rabbis who were close to him, his senior aides, and attorney Yoram Sheftel.

Meanwhile, Yad L'Achim's legal department is examining criminal aspects of the case, including the possibility of filing a libel suit in response to the false claims based on forged documents.

In a statement released this week, Yad L'Achim said: "We are familiar with the lies of the missionaries and their agents. At the same time we will not stand by idly and allow them to mislead innocent Jews. We will continue to use every legitimate means to block them and foil their spiritually destructive campaigns."[13]

Rabbi Kaduri's death note continues to shake the foundations of Judaism around the world, especially in Israel—the very place where Kaduri was the most adored. The battle, to many Christians and students of the New Testament, is eerily reminiscent of the days of Jesus, the disciples, and the apostle Paul. For today in Israel, over the issue of *Jesus as Messiah*, Jew is against Jew, threats of legal proceedings rage, and emotional pleas on both sides of the aisle ensue. Synagogues are debating the issue, Jews are coming to Jesus as Christ, and brothers are fighting brothers—just as Jesus predicted:

> Think not that I am come to send peace on earth: I came not to send peace, but a sword. For I am come to set a man at variance against his father, and the daughter against her mother, and the daughter in law against her mother in law. And a man's foes shall be they of his own household. He that loveth father or mother more than me is not worthy of me: and he that loveth son or daughter more than me is not worthy of me. And he that taketh not his cross, and followeth after me, is not worthy of me. He that findeth his life shall lose it: and he that loseth his life for my sake shall find it. (Matt. 10:34–39)

***

This chapter would not be complete without mentioning the ministry of Moishe Rosen, a controversial Jewish figure who converted to Christianity. He was the founder of the world-famous organization Jews for Jesus. His life, ministry, and the controversy surrounding his ministry serve to illustrate the great and divisive tension demonstrated between the Jews over the person of Jesus. This clash has continued, often in a heated rage, since Jesus first presented Himself as Messiah to the Jewish people, almost two thousand years ago.

Moishe Rosen was raised an Orthodox Jew. It is reported that, as a young man, he renounced his Jewish faith. When his wife, Ceil, also a Jew, became a Christian, Rosen promptly and enthusiastically followed, at age twenty-one. His family immediately disowned him.

Within four years, Rosen was ordained in the Baptist church. He then went to work for the American Board of Missions to the Jews. But in time, his eccentricity caused him to part ways with the board.

In 1973, he founded his own group, Jews for Jesus, which has been responsible for leading countless Jews to Christ. Reverend Rosen passed away on May 19, 2010.[14]

An article on the *Encyclopedia Britannica* blog serves as a perfect illustration of the two-thousand-year-old messianic battle in the world of Judaism. The battle fire was stoked to a roaring flame with Rabbi Kaduri's vision and his messianic proclamation. Here's an excerpt from that article:

> In a vitriolic editorial for The Jewish Journal, Rabbi Bentzion Kravitz outlines the arguments most Jews have with Jews for Jesus and its founder. In addition to accusing Rosen of needlessly aggresive [*sic*] methods, Kravitz also believes he and his organization have been deceptive in two major ways. First, "His most deceptive tactic promoted the notion that a Jew can be Jewish and Christian at the same time," while also condemning Judaism in many instances. Second, he accuses Rosen of instructing missionaries to ignore basic theological tenets of Christianity (such as the Trinity and the divinity of Christ), when reaching out to Jews, so as to make proselytism easier. He concludes: "Rosen's legacy will be that his deceptive

tactics have become the accepted protocol in the Evangelical Christian movement. It is now second nature for church members to tell their Jewish friends, and Christian students to tell their peers, that they can be Jewish and Christian at the same time."[15]

And that is the messianic message that is still so controversial among the Jews today: *that one can be Jewish and Christian at the same time.* That argument becomes quite ironic, the modern Christian would say, when one considers that all of the very first Christians were both Jew and Christian at the same time. The word *Christian* simply means *follower of Jesus as the Christ.* All of the original disciples were Jews. The first three thousand Christian converts were Jews. They were converted hearing a message preached by a Jew . . . *Peter*:

> And there were dwelling at Jerusalem *Jews*, devout men, out of every nation under heaven . . . Then Peter said unto them, Repent, and be baptized every one of you in the name of Jesus Christ for the remission of sins, and ye shall receive the gift of the Holy Ghost. For the promise is unto you [Jews], and to your children, and to all that are afar off, even as many as the Lord our God shall call. And with many other words did he testify and exhort, saying, Save yourselves from this untoward generation. Then they that gladly received his word were baptized: and the same day there were added unto them about three thousand souls. [All of them Jews] (Acts 2:5, 38–41; emphasis added)

Fourteen years later, the early church was still primarily Jewish. It would not be until the preaching of the apostle Paul, a Jew and Pharisee rabbi, that many from outside the Jewish faith were brought into the church. Even then, Paul's first place of preaching, whenever he entered a new town was the synagogue—for it was there that he could best reach his rabbinical Jewish brothers. Paul was a "Jew for Jesus." He was a *Messianic Jew*—both a *Christian and a Jew.*

But his rabbinical Jewish brethren also labeled him a *heretic.* He was often imprisoned, beaten, and mocked. He was continually slandered and falsely accused. Several times he was either run out of town or forced to escape in the night just before great harm threatened to befall him. On other occasions, Paul was dragged before tribunals and made to stand against criminal charges simply because he was a follower of Jesus as Messiah.

Never doubt—the battle Paul faced two thousand years ago still rages today. And Rabbi Kaduri's note has further ensured the stoking of the matter.

I wish to conclude this chapter by revisiting the CNN report previously mentioned. The report contains a startling nugget of revelation pertinent to this issue. Benyamin Cohen, the Orthodox Jew who spent a recent year going to a Christian church, is quoted as saying:

> I was shocked when I went to church and heard them give sermons about the Old Testament . . . I had no idea Christians read the Old Testament.
>
> One week, I went to church and the pastor gave exactly the same sermon my rabbi did the night before about Moses and the burning bush, and the pastor did it much better . . .
>
> "People ask me all the time if I believe in Jesus. Do I believe he exists? Sure. Do I believe he's your God? Sure, I have no problem with that," he said he tells Christians who ask.
>
> I understand Christians' love for Jesus and I respect that . . . If anything, I learned a lot from them and did become a more engaged Jew, a better Jew, and I appreciate my Judaism more because I hung out with Jesus.[16]

It seems apparent to many following this story that, just like Benyamin Cohen, the highly venerated Jewish kabbalistic Rabbi Yitzhak Kaduri *hung out with Jesus*. After all, they would claim, Kaduri clearly and publicly declared that he had *seen* the Messiah—and his decoded cryptic note plainly proclaims what has simultaneously thrilled and enraged millions . . .

Messiah's name is *Yehoshua*—Jesus.

19

THE ENDTIMES?

I think this is irresponsible preaching and very dangerous, and especially when it is slanted toward children, I think it's totally irresponsible, because I see nothing biblical that points up to our being in the last days, and I just think it's an outrageous thing to do, and a lot of people are making a living—they've been making a living for 2,000 years—preaching that we're in the last days.[1]

—*Charles M. Schulz*

WAS RABBI KADURI REALLY ONTO SOMETHING?

A prominent feature of Rabbi Yitzhak Kaduri's messianic prophecies included his dire warnings that we are currently living in the biblically prophesied *endtimes*. Rabbi Kaduri, as referenced previously, spoke of coming world tribulations, major calamities, the urgent need for Jews to return to Israel, messianic signs and wonders, and even the beginning of the famed last days Gog and

Magog war of the Bible. These apocalyptic prophecies, coupled with Rabbi Kaduri's promise that when Ariel Sharon dies, the Messiah will come, have Bible prophecy watchers of every ilk on guard. All manner of prophetic speculation has ensued. Following is an example of one such vein of speculation relating specifically to the Kaduri/Sharon prophecy connection:

> However, there may also be another reason why he [Sharon] survives multiple strokes and is still alive even today against all odds. Some reasoned that it might have to do with the symbolic meaning his name conveys.
>
> God planned to bring the flood of Noah after all the men who walked in the ways of the Lord had been removed. Methuselah lived during the construction of Noah's ark but died right before the flood, as God had promised him that he would not be killed with the unrighteous. The name Methuselah translates, "When he is dead it shall be sent"; meaning "the deluge" of judgment would come after his death. Therefore, Methuselah's death marked the end of mankind's grace period and the coming of the Great Flood.
>
> Since there is nothing new under the sun and history just repeats itself, sustaining the life of the man may once again serve God's purposes.
>
> Perhaps it will be that after the announcement of the death of Ariel Sharon whose name means "Lion of God" or "Jerusalem" or "Fertile Land," the fall of Jerusalem will follow, and at the same time, those who are alive and living for the Lord will not die but be raptured and be removed; just as Methuselah died before the flood so that he would not be "killed with the unrighteous" in the coming "flood of judgment." Just as Methuselah's death indicated the coming literal flood of judgment so might Ariel Sharon's death signify the coming flood of judgment upon an unrepentant world; or the redemption of the righteous in Christ![2]

As demonstrated in a previous chapter, Rabbi Kaduri's prophecies regarding specific endtime events appear to be nebulous at best and flatly incorrect at worst. Numerous Bible prophecy experts agree with this assessment. However, Kaduri's Messiah prophecies have specifically piqued the interest of those who are looking for the soon coming (or the second coming) of the Messiah. Furthermore, Kaduri's linking of the Messiah's return to the death of Ariel Sharon has, without doubt, taken the prophetic interest to a whole new level of intrigue.

NEVER A SHORTAGE OF PROPHETS OR PROPHECIES

There has never been a shortage of prophets who are willing to proclaim, "The end is near!" or "The Messiah is right around the corner!" Neither has there been a lack of folks more than eager to line up squarely behind a particular prophet and his prophecies. It is evident to many that endtime prophecy speculation is an exceptionally popular and even a worldwide spectator sport. There appears to be something about the human race that taps into the innate sense that things will not always continue as they are. There will be *an end*, and perhaps a new *beginning*—of biblical proportions.

And so, like the biblical flood recorded in the book of Genesis, prophetic speculations sweep the earth. However, in view of Rabbi Kaduri's endtime prophecies, the larger question is, *does the Bible really have anything to say, in a direct manner, concerning end-of-times prophecy and the specific era in which we live?* Many believe so. Rabbi Kaduri's dramatic, apocalyptic, and messianic prophetic proclamations certainly sparked off a firestorm of conjecture and fervent discussion. Judaism, Islam, and Christianity, the world's three largest monotheistic religions,[3] are each looking toward a coming Messiah, and each warns of endtime apocalyptic events—perhaps coming soon.

Charles M. Schulz was an American cartoonist best known for his comic strip *Peanuts*. He believed, as shown in this chapter's opening quote, that there is nothing at all, in the Bible or elsewhere, that indicates we are living in the endtimes. To teach otherwise, said Schulz, is "totally irresponsible."[4]

I am not aware of Mr. Schulz's credentials in biblical study, and particularly as his biblical knowledge may have related to matters of eschatology; however, I am aware that numerous people the world over share his stated view. Amazingly, the sentiment expressed by Mr. Schulz was long ago prophesied in the very Bible he insists does *not* point to our being in the last days! Apparently, even in New Testament times there were those who scoffed at the idea of a soon-coming apocalypse. Furthermore, Peter prophesied that, especially in the very last days, the mocking would intensify:

> Knowing this first, that there shall come in the last days scoffers, walking after their own lusts, and saying, Where is the promise of his coming? for since the fathers fell asleep, all things continue as they were from the beginning of the creation. For this they willingly are ignorant of, that by the word of God the heavens were of old, and the earth standing out of the water and in the water: whereby the world that then was, being overflowed with water, perished: but the heavens and the earth, which are now, by the same word are kept in store, reserved unto fire against the Day of Judgment and perdition of ungodly men. (2 Peter 3:3–7)

The chapter continues by explaining *why* for the last two thousand years, as Mr. Schulz opined, people have been preaching that we are in the last days:

> But, beloved, be not ignorant of this one thing, that one day is with the Lord as a thousand years, and a thousand years

as one day. The Lord is not slack concerning his promise, as some men count slackness; but is longsuffering to us-ward, not willing that any should perish, but that all should come to repentance. But the day of the Lord will come as a thief in the night; in the which the heavens shall pass away with a great noise, and the elements shall melt with fervent heat, the earth also and the works that are therein shall be burned up. (vv. 8–10)

INSIGHT FROM MODERN CHRISTIAN PROPHECY TEACHERS

To better appreciate why there was such a marked reaction among Christians to Kaduri's Messiah predictions, it is important to understand the typical Christian understanding of endtime prophecy. I asked Dr. David Reagan, a nationally prominent and highly acclaimed prophecy expert introduced in chapter 11, to briefly comment about Bible prophecy from the evangelical Christian perspective. Specifically, I asked him, "Are we really living in the last days? And if so, how can we be certain? Are there definitive biblical signs that might point us to this conclusion?"[5]

While I understand that there are several predominant views among evangelical Christians concerning eschatological time lines, I believe Dr. Reagan presents a fair assessment of the norm of evangelical Christian belief. Dr. Reagan told me:

I believe we are living in the season of the return of Jesus Christ, because the Bible—both the Old and New Testaments—gives us many signs to watch for which will signal His return. When I first started studying these signs, I found it difficult to get a handle on them. What I finally did was to group them by the following topics:

1) the signs of nature
2) the signs of society

3) spiritual signs
4) the signs of world politics
5) the signs of technology
6) the signs of Israel

I then asked Dr. Reagan to give a brief explanation of his insight concerning each of these six signs of the return of the Messiah. He responded:

With regard to the *signs of nature*, the Bible says that natural calamities will be like "birth pangs" in the endtimes. In other words, all forms of natural disasters, like earthquakes, tsunamis, and hurricanes, will increase in frequency and intensity. We are witnessing that today.

The *signs of society* refer to the fact that the Bible prophesies that the world will go full circle in the sense that society will become as evil as it was in the days of Noah. Those days were characterized by immorality and violence. That's exactly what we are witnessing today on the evening news.

The *spiritual signs* are the most numerous. On the negative side, the Bible says there will be an increase in occultic and demonic activity. And it warns over and over that there will be an explosion of heresy and apostasy within the Church. It also prophesies a great increase in the persecution of believers. On the positive side, the Bible says that the Gospel will be preached to the whole world, something that is now being accomplished through modern technology.

As a former professor of international law and politics, I am particularly interested in *the signs of world politics*. The Bible prophesies that in the endtimes, a particular pattern of international politics will emerge. It says the old Roman Empire will come back to life, something we are witnessing today in the establishment and growth of the European Union. The Bible further states that Israel will be reestablished and will become the focus of world politics, menaced from the north by Russia and constantly under attack by its Arab neighbors.

The *signs of technology* are particularly interesting because we are told in the Old Testament book of Daniel that many of the endtime prophecies will not be understood until the endtimes arrive. When I speak of such signs, what I have in mind are endtime prophecies that could never be understood apart from modern technological developments like satellite television. One that comes to mind is the prophecy in the book of Revelation that two great witnesses of God will be killed by the Antichrist in the middle of the Tribulation, and the entire world will be able to look upon their bodies. No one could understand that prophecy before the deployment of television satellites in the 1960s.

I was particularly interested in Dr. Reagan's reference to the nation of Israel, and modern-day events surrounding the relatively new nation, as a sign of biblical prophecy. Since Rabbi Kaduri also drew parallels to events in Israel with cataclysmic predictions and prophecies of a coming Messiah, I asked Dr. Reagan to expound upon his belief that Israel might be at the forefront of forecasting the return of the Messiah, Jesus Christ.

The most important signs—more important than all the rest put together—are those that relate to the *sign of the nation of Israel*. That's because Israel is used in the Bible as a prophetic time clock. By that I mean that the focus of endtime Bible prophecy is the nation of Israel.

There are many prophecies regarding Israel in the endtimes, several of which were fulfilled in the twentieth century, like the prophecies that the Hebrew language would be revived from the dead in the endtimes.

However, the four most important *signs of Israel* are these: (1) the regathering of the Jewish people from the four corners of the earth; (2) the reestablishment of the State of Israel; (3) the reoccupation of Jerusalem; and (4) the focusing of world politics on Israel and the control of Jerusalem.

I commented to Dr. Reagan that I thought it was most interesting that he believed Israel's existence in the land today was such an integral part of endtime prophecy. I asked him to expand on his previously mentioned four points concerning Israel. He replied:

> The regathering of the Jewish people began in the 1890s and has continued to this day. In 1900, there were only forty thousand Jews in the land of Palestine, as it was called then. By the end of World War II, the number had increased to eight hundred thousand. Today there are six million who have returned from all over the world. This regathering led to the fulfillment of the second prophecy, the reestablishment of the State of Israel on May 14, 1948. And the prophecy concerning the reoccupation of Jerusalem became a reality during the Six-Day War on June 7, 1967.
>
> Today, the last prophecy is being fulfilled before our very eyes as the world demands that Israel surrender all or part of Jerusalem. The United Nations desires to internationalize it. The Vatican would love to have control of it. The European Union, together with the United Nations and the United States, is demanding that the Jews surrender at least half of it. These demands are going to lead to the war described in Psalm 83, a war that Israel will win decisively, according to other prophecies in the Hebrew Scriptures. I believe the message of these signs is that we are living on borrowed time. Jesus is about to break from the heavens.

I am certain you can understand, even though Dr. Reagan has not endorsed Rabbi Kaduri's specific prophetic stances, how the elderly rabbi's utterances would have gained the focused interest of the evangelical Christian community—as well as the Jewish world. In Kaduri's predictions, there were also mentions of world strife, impending disasters, an Israel-centric geopolitical focus—and the promise of a soon-coming Messiah. Furthermore, when Kaduri's death note reportedly revealed that the name of the real and soon-to-come Messiah was *Yehoshua* or *Yeshua*, the Christian world was abuzz—at least initially.

For further elucidation on this matter, I solicited the prophetic insights of Joel Richardson, *New York Times* best-selling author of *Islamic Antichrist: The Shocking Truth about the Real Nature of the Beast*, and internationally recognized speaker and expert on Bible prophecy and the Middle East.[6] My first question was, "What do you say to those who claim, like Mr. Schulz, that prophecy teaching of impending endtime events is mere 'fear mongering'?"

He answered:

> When one surveys the range of opinions within the Church today concerning the return of Jesus, it is easy to identify extremes on both sides of the spectrum, neither of which is aligned with the orientation or perspective of the early Christian believers. We are all familiar with the type of Christian who declares in a rather fearful and frenzied manner that the end of the world is near, all hope is gone. These kinds of Christians are easy and frequent targets for those who most often take the extreme opposite position, those who mock the notion that the return of Jesus could, in fact, be drawing near.
>
> But while the fearmongers are most often highlighted for criticism, I would suggest that it is the latter group that not only dominates the Church today, but also . . . is in the greatest measure of error. While Jesus, the apostles, and the early church preached and practiced a gospel that was thoroughly apocalyptic in its orientation, very few ministers or lay people today proclaim the actual hope of the early church.

"Did not the early New Testament believers think that the endtimes were upon them as well?" I asked. "They lived two thousand years ago—yet the end did not occur within their lifetimes. Should this belief, this urgency, still be an important feature of the modern church and its message?"

Richardson responded:

Yes, early believers, in accordance with the message, emphasis, yearning, and hope of all the Hebrew prophets before them, were looking for the physical establishment of the kingdom of God here on the earth.

They were eagerly awaiting the time when the Messiah would rule and reign over the nations from Jerusalem. Their hope was firmly fixed upon the return of Jesus, the physical, bodily resurrection of the dead, the judgment and destruction of the wicked, and the subsequent restructuring of the whole natural order. But beyond simply looking for these things, the early believers clung to this hope with an urgency that is almost never seen among Christians today.

Yet it was this hope, this confidence in the fact that even in death, they would be bodily raised immortal to rule and reign with Jesus on the earth, that empowered this small movement to "turn the world upside down" in just a few short generations.

And it is precisely the lack of urgency and emphasis on the coming of Jesus that is at the root of why the Church today is largely so impotent. Any Gospel that does not proclaim a very real and very radical restructuring of this present order has nothing of any real substance to offer the world.

I then asked Mr. Richardson, "If the apostle Paul were with us today, what would be the focus of his message, his preaching?"

If the apostle Paul were alive today, I am confident that he would look to those who are fearfully focused on the imminent destruction of all things, and he would steer them toward a more hopeful orientation. He would redirect them toward the kingdom to come and the accompanying joys and glories to follow. I am sure he would encourage them to give themselves to the proclamation of the coming kingdom not only with their words, but also by demonstrating the nature of the age to come with their whole lives.

He would encourage facing the distress to come with courage, with action, and with an excited hope—not a frenzied fear. But to those who openly mock the notion that we are living in the last days, I am confident that Paul would reserve his harshest rebukes. For in denying the possibility that Christ could be coming soon, these so-called believers neuter the "gospel of the kingdom" of its very substance, its entire emphasis, its power and its relevance to all of us.

In conclusion, I asked Mr. Richardson, "In light of your answer to my previous question, what is the central focus of *your* prophetic message to the world in which we live?"

"For the past six thousand years," he said, "all of creation, all of the prophets, all of the apostles, and even Jesus Himself have all been pointing to the Day of the Lord. Being a Christian is to imitate Christ, and like Jesus, I will continue to proclaim to believers and unbelievers alike, 'Repent, for the kingdom of heaven is at hand!'"

Along a similar vein of questioning, I asked Dr. David Reagan why he believes the message of Christianity is so unique and, especially, why it is distinctly different from the Orthodox Jewish faith. Following is his response.

> The main feature that distinguishes Christianity from all the other world religions is that it teaches salvation is by grace through faith in Jesus Christ. The New Testament specifically states that no one can be saved by good works.
>
> All the other religions of the world, and particularly Judaism, teach that a person must earn his salvation through good works. But the Bible says that good works are like "filthy rags" with regard to the forgiveness of one's sins. That doesn't mean that good works are irrelevant. The Bible says we are saved to do good works that will bring honor and glory to God. But those works do not save us.
>
> Rather, we are saved by the work that Jesus Christ did

on the cross, when He, as a perfect man, died for the sins of mankind. He took our sins upon Himself, and those who put their faith in Him as their Lord and Savior receive the forgiveness of their sins. Salvation is a free gift of God, given by His grace to those who put their faith in His Son.

And there is no other way to be reconciled to God. Jesus, who was God in the flesh, said in John 14:6, "I am the way, and the truth, and the life; no one comes to the Father, but through Me." In other words, there is not a multiplicity of roads to God. Jesus Christ is the only way.

And there we have it. Now we can at least understand the root of the absolute furor that ensued in both the Jewish and Christian worlds of faith when Rabbi Kaduri's cryptic death note was decoded. Now we understand why many, even within the evangelical Christian world, believed that Kaduri might have been *onto something*. With all of his other predictions concerning the end of days and his warnings of certain and soon-coming judgments, he also included a specific prediction of the coming of the Messiah. And of all things, this aging Jewish rabbi proclaimed in writing, for the entire world to read, that the Messiah's name was *Jesus*.

The religious world, especially those dedicated to last days prophecy, let out a collective gasp . . . in amazement.

20

THE STORY ENDS,
THE STORY BEGINS

ome people suppose that Rabbi Yitzhak Kaduri simply wanted to ensure that his memory and legacy lived on for a long time, and *that's* why he wrote the Messiah death note. If that is so, he certainly accomplished his purpose. Others argue that the note only served to tarnish his legacy—deeply. But still others wonder, *Why would such a legendary rabbi want to tarnish the name and legacy he worked so hard to establish? It just doesn't make sense—unless the old rabbi really* did *have a messianic vision, and he really* did *believe that the true Messiah of Israel was one called Yehoshua.*

Supporters of Rabbi Kaduri's vision as a true sign from *HaShem* claim that time will vindicate the old rabbi. After all, they say, Messiah *will* come—and then we all will know.

A number of Jews insist that the old rabbi simply had lost his mind. His body had became feeble in his old age, and so had his reasoning ability, they would assert. After all, he was well over a hundred. How could anyone that old possess their sharpest mental agility?

Of course, the problem with that argument is that the

evidence seems to plainly indicate that Kaduri was as sharp as a tack, to the last, even within the final weeks of his life. In fact, it is widely reported that even in his old age Kaduri was renowned for his photographic memory and his celebrated memorization of massive amounts of kabbalistic and Torah teaching. Kaduri would frequently, it is claimed, astonish his students by reciting a truth from an instruction book, then reaching up on his shelf, pulling down that very book, turning to the correct page, and almost instantly placing his crooked and arthritic finger on the passage he had just recited. His eyes would gleam with delight, and a childlike grin would appear on his face as he gazed at his astounded onlookers. Not only did he know the passage, but he also clearly demonstrated that he knew the book, its place on the shelf, the page of the reference, and the line he had memorized.[1]

A Kaduri biographer, writing for the Sephardic Legacy Series at sephardiclegacy.com, wrote of the rabbi's mental agility in this way:

> Most of his life Rav Yitzhak was known only as *Yitzhak Korech* (Yitzhak the bookbinder)—a humble title that suggested nothing of his stature. When someone would bring him a *sefer* [religious book] to bind, he would ask permission to learn the contents of the sefer while binding its exterior. When he returned the *sefer* to the owner, often after a month or so, he would apologize for the delay, explaining that he had just finished learning it. He committed many of these *sefarim* to memory, including some ancient handwritten manuscripts.[2]

No, Rabbi Kaduri could not merely be passed off as a dawdling old man whose mind was wasting away.

In the same biography, the writer related a brief anecdotal story of the elderly Kaduri's desire to ensure his entrance into heaven:

Rav Yaakob Hillel *shlita*, presently the Rosh HaYeshivah of Yeshivat Hebrat Ahabat Shalom, once recalled a conversation that he had with Rav Yitzhak.

"Five years ago," he said, "Rav Kaduri gave me an envelope filled with shekels and dollars. The shekels were for Rav Yitzhak's yeshivah. The dollars he called '*tzedah laderech*—food for the journey ahead.'

"'When I go up to *Shamayim* [Heaven], I want some merit to accompany me,' Rav Kaduri had explained. He wanted the money to be distributed to *tzedakah* [charity] after he would leave this world, so that the extra *mitzvoth* [keeping of the Jewish law] would be a *zechut* [reward] for him.

"*He* needs extra! Imagine—such a great *talmid hacham* [wise student of the Word of God], and he is concerned that he does not yet have enough *zechut* to accompany him to Heaven!"

By the time Rav Yitzhak passed away, Rav Hillel had accumulated about fifty such envelopes from the *hacham*, containing cash totaling some one hundred thousand American dollars! Each envelope had a handwritten note inside stating, "This money is from Rabbi Yitzhak Kaduri, to be distributed as *tzedah laderech* [food for the journey ahead]."[3]

***

Who *was* Rabbi Kaduri? More importantly, who was his *Messiah*? And did Kaduri *see* the Messiah—or did he see the Antichrist? Did he have a vision at all? Or, did he simply feel the overwhelming need to self-fulfill the supposed prophecy made over him as a boy, and then again, in 1990, as an old man who still had not seen a vision of the Messiah?

Considering Kaduri's insistence that *Yehoshua* was Messiah, some speculate that he had come to the same realization of one of his ancient Jewish ancestors, the apostle Paul, who wrote: "But

God forbid that I should glory, save in the cross of our Lord Jesus Christ, by whom the world is crucified unto me, and I unto the world" (Gal. 6:14). In this life, we may never know. Kaduri's mysterious Messiah message is still an enigma, much like the man who wrote the message. Why would such an adored icon do such a thing if he were not convinced the vision was real?

It is incumbent upon every student of the Holy Scriptures, Old and New Testaments—Jew, Christian, and Messianic Jew alike—to search this matter deeply.

In a previous chapter, I referred to a passage from the Old Testament book of Jeremiah. It warned its readers of the need to discern false prophecies. The warning ended with a call to *personal responsibility*. This query is the most important feature of the passage. The warning still stands today: "The prophets prophesy lies, the priests rule by their own authority, and my people love it this way. But *what will you do in the end?*" (Jer. 5:31, emphasis added).

What will *you* do in the end? That is the eternal question.

ELDERLY RABBIS WITH VISIONS

An elderly Orthodox Jewish rabbi having a vision of Yeshua as Messiah and Lord is certainly not novel. Apart from the obvious New Testament example of the apostle Paul, I will present one more as I prepare to close this chapter. His name was Rabbi Daniel Zion, and his amazing story is reported in Dr. David Reagan's *Lamplighter* magazine.[4]

Briefly, Rabbi Zion was the chief rabbi of Sofia, Bulgaria, when the nation was taken over by the Nazis in 1941. Immediately after the Nazis took over, they began pressuring the Bulgarian government to start passing anti-Semitic laws, resulting in ever-increasing persecution of the Bulgarian Jews. Eventually, Rabbi Zion himself was arrested and confined to a concentration camp.

When World War II ended, miraculously Rabbi Zion had survived. He resumed his duties as chief rabbi of Sofia.

By now, however, the communists had replaced the Nazis in Bulgaria, and Jewish persecution resumed.

In 1949, one year after the nation of Israel was established, Rabbi Zion decided to emigrate to the Jewish homeland. He settled in Tel Aviv, where he was immediately accepted as the rabbi of the Bulgarian Jews.

But here's the catch: Rabbi Zion was a devout believer in Yeshua as the Messiah.

According to him, one morning when he was still in Sofia, he had a "road to Damascus experience." While he was praying, a man suddenly appeared before him—then left. This happened three times.

The third time, Rabbi Zion asked the man to identify himself. The man answered that he was Yeshua. This revelation compelled Rabbi Zion to examine the New Testament documents in detail. From his examination, he came to believe that Yeshua was the Messiah.

His belief that Yeshua—Jesus—was the Messiah became well-known within his congregation and even among other Jewish leaders. Even so, his position was so honored and his services so highly esteemed that none of the Jewish functionaries in Sofia would dare to openly criticize him.

In 1954, the new chief rabbi of Israel invited Rabbi Zion to become a judge in the Rabbinical Court in Jerusalem. But when rumors began to fly that Rabbi Zion believed in Yeshua, he was tried before that very court. Evidence of his faith in Yeshua was presented through statements he had made in four books he had written about the Messiah. Rabbi Zion told the court:

Yeshua conquered me, and with the New Man He honored me. He delivered me from my poverty-stricken self. With His great love, He cherished me.

Every day the canny devil aspires to grab my faith. I hold on to my faith and chase the devil away. I stand here alone in my faith, with the whole world against me. I give up all my earthly honor for the sake of the Messiah, my mate.

Rabbi Zion was stripped of his rabbinical title, but the Bulgarian Jews continued to honor him as their rabbi. One of his followers gave him a building in downtown Tel Aviv, and this became the synagogue where he taught until his death in 1979, at age ninety-six. He had written many songs about Yeshua being his Savior and friend.

Messianic Rabbi Joseph Shulam, in summarizing Rabbi Zion's life, said, "He lived a 100% Jewish lifestyle, and was a 100% follower of the Messiah Yeshua."

STILL WAITING FOR THE MESSIAH

And so we end this book where we began, asking the question, could Yehoshua—Jesus Christ—appear to a Jewish rabbi—even one involved in Kabbalah, *even* one who continued in his legalistic Judaism—and present Himself as the *one and true Messiah*?

The answer is yes . . . but *did* He? Did God hand-pick the insanely popular Kaduri—knowing he would ultimately have the most influence on the Jewish people—to be the one who would reveal the name and person of the real Messiah?

For many, this conundrum is difficult to resolve. The mystery has Jew and Christian alike scratching their heads in wonderment. And yet, Jew, Christian, and everyone in between—indeed, practically the whole world—is looking for a Messiah.

Hear what Orthodox Judaism has to say about the *Messianic Hope of Israel*:

The world is in desperate need of Messianic redemption. To the extent that we are aware of the problems of society, is the extent we will yearn for redemption. As the Talmud says, one of the first questions asked of a Jew on Judgment Day is: "Did you yearn for the arrival of the Messiah?"

How can we hasten the coming of the Messiah? The best way is to love all humanity generously, to keep the mitzvot [commandments] of the Torah (as best we can), and to encourage others to do so as well.

Despite the gloom, the world does seem headed toward redemption. One apparent sign is that the Jewish people have returned to the Land of Israel and made it bloom again. Additionally, a major movement is afoot of young Jews returning to Torah tradition.

The Messiah can come any day, and it all depends on our actions. God is ready when we are. For as King David says: "Redemption will come today if you hearken to His voice."[5]

Sadly, the religious Jew is looking to works, *the keeping of the Law*, in the hope that in so doing, the Messiah may soon come. Yet, the Christian would assert that all our works "and all our righteousnesses are as filthy rags" (Isa. 64:6)—and besides, the Messiah has *already* come, the Christian claims, in the person of Jesus Christ. The first time He came, He fulfilled the prophecies of *Messiah ben Joseph*. The second time He comes will be in fulfillment of the prophecies of *Messiah ben David*. He died on the cross, paid for our sins, rose from the grave, and provided the way—the *only* way—of salvation for mankind.

The Christian message, the New Testament Gospel message, is not that Messiah Yeshua is *coming*—but that He is *coming again*. And this time, He is not coming as Savior, but as the Righteous Judge, the Ruling King of kings and Lord of lords.

Rabbi Kaduri's note, for all the other mysteries surrounding his life, undeniably points to *Yeshua*——that is *Jesus*——

as Messiah. Was Rabbi Yitzhak Kaduri correct in his predictions of the *Coming One?* One thing is certain, according to both the Old and New Testament Scriptures: one day, and perhaps very soon, the true Messiah *will come.* But for now, the world waits—and wonders.

And so, our story ends. Or, perhaps . . . it has just begun.

But what will you do in the end? —*Jeremiah 5:31*

UNRAVELING THE MYSTERY

We have examined this story from practically all possible angles with the best information that currently exists. The question remains: Did Rabbi Kaduri have a vision of the *real* Messiah? Let us explore this question from a purely logical standpoint.

- Did Rabbi Kaduri claim he met the Messiah? *Yes.*

- Did Rabbi Kaduri claim he knew the real Messiah's name? *Yes.*

- Did Rabbi Kaduri leave this name in a note? *This attestation is disputed, but the very best documented evidence says yes.*

- According to the note, What was the Messiah's name? *Yehoshua. (English: Jesus)*

- What is the only faith system in the world (out of several hundred faith systems) that claims Yehoshua (Jesus) as the name for the Messiah? *Christianity.*

- In what documentation is Yehoshua (Jesus) most clearly revealed as the Messiah who fulfills all the Old Testament prophecies of the Coming One? *The New Testament.*

- Did at least some of Kaduri's students believe he was teaching, before he died, that the *Jesus* of New Testament fame was the true Messiah? *Yes. One such testimony is recorded in this book.*

- Could Rabbi Kaduri have simply made up the account of his vision? *Yes, but why? Again, this would be like Billy Graham or the pope leaving a deathbed note stating that the Islamic Mahdi was the real Messiah.*

- Why would Kaduri have left such a note if it would only serve to discredit him with the entire Orthodox Jewish world? *The only logical explanation is that Rabbi Kaduri had an experience similar to that of the apostle Paul, another Jewish rabbi. Kaduri had an encounter with the Messiah . . . Jesus.*

The debate concerning this sensational story will undoubtedly continue. However, the above facts cannot be denied. Certainly, other points of argument could be added as well. But of one thing there is no doubt: If the note was real, then Rabbi Kaduri proclaimed the real Messiah to be Jesus, or Yehoshua. And as a result of this Jewish rabbi's tremendous influence, which lives on to this day, Jews around the world are coming to Jesus Christ as Messiah, Lord, and Savior.

And this is no surprise. After all, the Christian faith was delivered first to the Jews, through the *Hebrew* nation of Israel, *Jewish* disciples, *Jewish* Scriptures, *Jewish* prophecies—and by a God who put on *Jewish* flesh in order to dwell among us—in the person of Jesus (Yehoshua) Christ.

NOTES

EPIGRAPH PAGE

1. Lawrence Joffe, "Obituary: Rabbi Yitzhak Kaduri," *Guardian* (UK), January 30, 2006, http://www.guardian.co.uk/news/2006/jan/31/guardianobituaries.israel.

INTRODUCTION

1. Many believe the monumental political and geographical restoration of the nation of Israel to be the fulfillment of a twenty-five-hundred-year-old end-time prophecy.

2. From the website of *Israel Today*: "*Israel Today* is a Jerusalem-based news agency providing a biblical and objective perspective on local news. Founded in 1978, when it began publishing a monthly German news magazine, the English language edition of *Israel Today* was launched in January 1999 in order to meet a growing demand for news from Israel to the English-speaking market. The Japanese edition was launched in 2004, and a Dutch edition is currently in the works, as well. *Israel Today* maintains a diverse staff of local journalists who live in the Land and therefore report from firsthand experience, offering a mix of information, interviews, inspiration and daily life in Israel." (http://www .israeltoday.co.il/More/AboutUs.aspx).

3. "Rabbi Reveals Name of the Messiah," *Israel Today*, http://www.israeltoday.co.il /default.aspx?tabid=128&view=item&idx=1347. No longer accessible. (Note: Though the original web address was not accessible at the time of the writing of this book, *Israel Today* has since restored the article to the following new web address: http://www.israeltoday.co.il/NewsItem/tabid/178/nid/23877/Default

.aspx?hp=readmore. (Accessed May 30, 2013. Screen captures of the page and word-for-word copies of the original article still appear in abundance on the Internet.)

4. Ryan Jones, e-mail message to author, in response to a requested quote for this book (April 2013).

5. Ryan Jones, e-mail message to author (May 29–30, 2013). The original article has been restored to: http://www.israeltoday.co.il/NewsItem/tabid/178/nid/23877/Default.aspx?hp=readmore.

1: THE YOUNG RABBI AND HIS VISION

1. Kaduri's authentic date of birth is still disputed, so his age at the time of death is unknown. According to *Wikipedia*, estimates range from 106 to 118 years old (http://en.wikipedia.org/wiki/Yitzhak_Kaduri). Several sources, though, put his age at death at 108. See, for example, http://rabbikaduri.blogspot.com/; http://www.yeshuahamashiach.org/Kaduri_names_Messiah.htm; and http://www.biblesearchers.com/hebrews/jewish/messiah5.shtml.

2. HaShem is a name for God that is literally translated "The Name." It is used by some Jews in place of Adonai ("Lord," "Master") in nonritual contexts. Wikipedia, s.v. "Names of God in Judaism," http://en.wikipedia.org/wiki/HaShem#HaShem.

3. According to the Bible and other historical sources, Saul, later named Paul, was trained in the elite rabbinical schools and traditions. Since he certainly was a "Pharisee of Pharisees" by his own description and wrote much of the New Testament, that he was considered a rabbi (a teacher of the Law) among the Jews cannot be disputed by serious scholars. (Jesus was often called *Rabbi* by those under His teaching.)

2: THE OLD RABBI AND HIS VISIONS

1. Baruch Gordon, "Leading Kabbalist Urges Jews to Israel—More Disasters Coming," *Arutz Sheva* (Channel 7), October 19, 2005, http://www.israelnationalnews.com/News/News.aspx/91417#.UYgOWqKsiSo.

2. The *kittel* is a simple white robe, also used as a shroud. The revered article is worn by the bridegroom in many Jewish weddings. The *tallit* is a prayer shawl with *tzitzis*, specially knotted ritual fringes, tied through each of the four corners.

3. The preceding narrative, as I have written it, is in part fiction, and certain elements are solely products of the author's imagination. However, the *fact* of the Yom Kippur synagogue revelation is heavily documented. The fictional narrative simply reflects these facts in a creative fashion. In October 2005, *Israel National News* published an online article, named in the previous note, in which the story is told as fact. Here is an excerpt from that extensive article:

During the afternoon Mincha prayer on Yom Kippur, the kabbalist scholar surprised his students and fellow worshippers with secrets relating to the coming of the Mashiach. During the service, Rabbi Kaduri lowered his head and entered a deep mystical concentration, which lasted uninterrupted for some 45 minutes. The Rabbi covered his eyes as though reciting the Sh'ma prayer and only his lips were seen moving.

Students who thought the elderly Rabbi was suffering an attack of sort tried to communicate with him, but he did not break his intense concentration for a moment, even to nod.

Only after some 45 minutes, the Rabbi raised his head and looked around the room at the students and worshippers who were gathered at his Nachalat Yitzhak Yeshiva, in the Bucharim neighborhood of Jerusalem. With a broad smile on his face, familiar to his students when he had a revelation, he declared, "With the help of G-d, the soul of the Mashiach has attached itself to a person in Israel."

4. A member of a Hasidic community founded in Russia in the late eighteenth century that stresses the importance of religious study.

5. Baruch Gordon, "Kabbalist Urges Jews to Israel Ahead of Upcoming Disasters," *Arutz Sheva*, September 21, 2005, http://www.israelnationalnews.com/News /News.aspx/89850#.UYj976KsiSp.

6. "Disaster, Redemption and the Tsunami," *Arutz Sheva*, December, 2004, http:// www.israelnationalnews.com/News/News.aspx/74451#.UYj_taKsiSo.

7. *Wikipedia*, s.v. "Yitzhak Kaduri," http://en.wikipedia.org/wiki/Yitzhak_Kaduri.

8. "Messiah Mystery Follows Death of Mystical Rabbi: Revered Israeli apocalyptic kabbalah leader shocks Jews, Christians with name 'Yeshua,'" WND, May 18, 2007, http://www.wnd.com/2007/05/41669/.

9. Megan Gannon, "Vegetative Ariel Sharon Shows 'Significant' Brain Activity," January 29, 2013, http://news.yahoo.com/vegetative-ariel-sharon-shows -significant-brain-activity-225039580.html.

10. Associated Press, "Scientists Say Comatose Former Israeli Leader Ariel Sharon Shows 'Robust' Brain Activity," Fox News, January 28, 2013, http://www.foxnews .com/world/2013/01/28/scientists-say-comatose-former-israeli-leader-ariel-sharon -shows-robust-brain/.

11. *Israel Today*, "Rabbi Reveals Name of the Messiah." (See intro., note 3.) This text can also be seen in David Mock's May 2007 article, "Secret Note from Torah Giant in Israel Gives Name of the Jewish Messiah—'Yehoshua'" at BibleSearchers .com: http://www.biblesearchers.com/hebrews/jewish/messiah5.shtml.

12. Gordon, "Leading Kabbalist Urges Jews to Israel."

13. Ibid.

14. Ibid.

15. "Obama wins 2009 Nobel Peace Prize," *BBC News Online*, October 9, 2009, http://news.bbc.co.uk/2/hi/8298580.stm.

16. Steven Erlanger and Sheryl Gay Stolberg, "Surprise Nobel for Obama Stirs Praise and Doubt," *New York Times*, October 9, 2009, http://www.nytimes .com/2009/10/10/world/10nobel.html?_r=0.

17.   "Farrakhan on Obama: 'The Messiah Is Absolutely Speaking," WND, October 9, 2008, http://www.wnd.com/2008/10/77539/; italics in the Farrakhan quotes are added for emphasis.
18.   Jerome R. Corsi, "Is Obama the Messiah? Websites Capture Wave of Transcendent Fervor," WND, February 23, 2008, http://www.wnd.com/2008/02/57090/.
19.   A striking example of this assertion is found at http://obamamessiah.blogspot .com, a site that appears to have catalogued the various messianic attributions and statements made by notable personalities regarding Barack Obama. Writing about this very website, WND senior staff reporter Jerome Corsi said, "The creator of a satirical blog that asks whether Barack Obama is the 'messiah' says he has a serious purpose, hoping the mainstream media will 'work through its childish infatuation' with the front-runner for the Democratic presidential nomination." Jerome R. Corsi, "'Obama Messiah' Creator: How Far Will 'Cult' Go?" WND, March 27, 2008, http://www.wnd.com/2008/03/60093/.
20.   Jeannine Hunter, "At Soul Train Awards, Foxx about Obama: 'Our Lord and Savior,'" *Washington Post*, November 26, 2012, http://www.washingtonpost .com/blogs/under-god/post/at-soul-train-awards-foxx-about-obama-our-lord-and -savior/2012/11/26/3e7d466a-37f5-11e2-b01f-5f55b193f58f_blog.html.
21.   Jesse Lee Peterson, "How Obama Replaced Christ Among Blacks," WND, December 11, 2012, http://www.wnd.com/2012/12/how-obama-replaced-christ -among-blacks/.
22.   Gordon, "Leading Kabbalist Urges Jews to Israel."

3: THE LAST OF A LOST GENERATION

1.   Ilan Marciano, "Rabbi Kaduri Laid to Rest," *ynet/Real Truth* magazine, January 29, 2006, http://www.ynetnews.com/articles/1,7340,L-3207585,00.html.
2.   The narrative that follows with regards to the young student Josiah and the myste-rious old man is fictional, a product of the author's imagination. However, the names of the various dignitaries and many of the details of the day are real. The eulogies in this narrative are quoted or adapted from Matthew Wagner, "Kaduri Funeral Draws Over 200,000," *Jerusalem Post*, January 28, 2006, http://www.jpost.com/Israel /Article.aspx?id=11488; and Ezra HaLevi, "Rabbi Yitzchak Kaduri Passes Away in Jerusalem at 108, *Free Republic*, January 28, 2006, http://www.freerepublic.com /focus/f-news/1567155/posts. Descriptions of the scene came from photographs of the actual event.
3.   Several sources report that Kaduri's was one of the most-attended funerals in the history of modern Israel. See, for example, http://www.raptureintheairnow.com /rita-main-discussion-forum/student-of-rabbi-kaduri-saved-messiah-revealed and http://ffoz.org/blogs/2008/01/yartzeit_of_yitzchak_kaduri.html.
4.   *Wikipedia*, s.v. "Yitzhak Kaduri," http://en.wikipedia.org/wiki/Yitzhak_Kaduri.
5.   Most of the content of this section is adapted from Matthew Wagner, "Judaism: The Magic of the Late Rabbi Yitzhak Kaduri," *Jerusalem Post*, February 2, 2006, http:// www.jpost.com/Features/Judaism-The-magic-of-the-late-Rabbi-Yitzhak-Kaduri.

NOTES

6. Roi Tov, "Promoting Armageddon: Rabbi Kaduri's Note," http://www.roitov.com /articles/kaduri.htm. See also http://www.clas.ufl.edu/users/murray/courses/Anth .of.Judaism/News.articles/Kabbalist.Kadouri.dies.htm.
7. For more than what is discussed here regarding Kabbalah, see "What Is Kabbalah?" at http://www.kabalatalisman.com/kabbalah/.
8. "Chuck Missler Goes 'Extraterrestrial' in Sermon," WND, March 9, 2013, http:// www.wnd.com/2013/03/chuck-missler-goes-extraterrestrial-in-sermon/.
9. See "Christian Kabbalah" at http://www.forgivenet.com/kabala.asp.
10. Gutman Lochs, "Imbued with Holiness," *Kabbalah Online*, www.kabbalaonline .org.
11. Andrew Guy Jr., "Madonna Claims the Hebrew Name 'Esther,'" *Houston Chronicle*, June 17, 2004, http://www.chron.com/entertainment/article/Madonna-claims -the-Hebrew-name-Esther-1516214.php.
12. Joseph Berger, "A Jewish Madonna? Is That a Mystery?" *New York Times*, June 18, 2004, http://www.nytimes.com/2004/06/18/movies/a-jewish-madonna-is -that-a-mystery.html?pagewanted=all&src=pm.
13. Wagner, "Judaism: The Magic of the Late Rabbi Yitzhak Kaduri."

4: KADURI'S JOURNEY: OUT OF BAGHDAD

1. Joffe, "Obituary: Rabbi Yitzhak Kaduri."
2. The preceding narrative is entirely fiction. It is a product of the author's imagination. However, the *fact* of the encounter is reportedly accurate. According to many historical sources, it was Rabbi Chaim who pronounced the blessing and prophecy upon young Kaduri that he would have a vision of the Messiah in his old age. The bulk of the remainder of this chapter was compiled from information found in several sources, but predominantly from Wikipedia's article on Kaduri (http://en.wikipedia.org/wiki/Yitzhak_Kaduri), and an article titled "Who Is Sephardic Orthodox Rebbe Yitzhak Kaduri," accessed from a link at http:// rabbikaduri.blogspot.com/.
3. Z"L is an abbreviation of the Hebrew words *Zichrono Livracha* used to indicate that the person has died. The abbreviation means *Of Blessed Memory.* It is very common to see Rabbi Kaduri's name in print with this designation following his name.
4. Gordon, "Leading Kabbalist Urges Jews to Israel."
5. Michael Tzadok Elkohen, "Hilulah HaRav Kaduri 5771," *An Aspiring Mekubal* (blog), January 4, 2011, http://mekubal.wordpress.com/2011/01/04/hilulah-harav -kaduri-5771/.
6. See "The Spheres" at http://www.forgivenet.com/kabala.asp.
7. *Wikipedia*, s.v. "Yitzhak Kaduri."
8. Ibid.
9. Joffe, "Obituary: Rabbi Yitzhak Kaduri."

10. "Kabbalist Kadouri Dies," *Jerusalem Post*, January 28, 2006, posted on the Notes to Students page, at http://www.clas.ufl.edu/users/murray/courses/Anth .of.Judaism/News.articles/Kabbalist.Kadouri.dies.htm.
11. Gordon, "Kabbalist Urges Jews to Israel Ahead of Upcoming Disasters."
12. "Kabbalist Kadouri Dies."
13. Joffe, "Obituary: Rabbi Yitzhak Kaduri."
14. "Kabbalist Kadouri Dies."
15. Sefi Rachlevsky, "Netanyahu and the Laws of Killing 'Goyim,'" *Haaretz*, April 23, 2013, http://www.haaretz.com/opinion/netanyahu-and-the-goyim .premium-1.517024; Joffe, "Obituary: Rabbi Yitzhak Kaduri."
16. Joffe, "Obituary: Rabbi Yitzhak Kaduri."
17. Ibid.
18. Ibid.
19. Ibid.
20. Who Is Sephardic Orthodox Rebbe Yitzhak Kaduri," accessed from a link at http://rabbikaduri.blogspot.com/.
21. Marciano, "Rabbi Kaduri Laid to Rest."

5: WORLD PEACE OR WORLD DISASTERS?

1. "Messiah Mystery Follows Death of Mystical Rabbi."
2. Interestingly, during his lifetime some of his followers had considered Schneerson to be the Jewish Messiah, but Rabbi Schneerson discouraged such talk. "Rabbi Schneerson Led a Small Hasidic Sect to World Prominence," June 13, 1994, *New York Times,* http://www.nytimes.com/1994/06/13/nyregion/rabbi-schneerson-led -a-small-hasidic-sect-to-world-prominence.html?pagewanted=all&src=pm.
3. Toby Janicki, "Yartzeit of Rabbi Yitzhak Kaduri," Firstfruits of Zion, *FFOZ Blogs*, January 22, 2009, http://ffoz.org/blogs/2009/01/yartzeit_of_rabbi_yitzchak_kad .html.
4. Gordon, "Kabbalist Urges Jews to Israel Ahead of Upcoming Disasters."
5. The Vilna Gaon was a venerated eighteenth-century kabbalist. Rabbi Kaduri was heavily influenced by his writings and teachings and often quoted from his material.
6. Gordon, "Kabbalist Urges Jews to Israel Ahead of Upcoming Disasters."
7. Ibid.
8. Ibid. See section titled "Postscript to This Article."
9. Gordon, "Kabbalist Urges Jews to Israel Ahead of Upcoming Disasters."
10. Who Is Sephardic Orthodox Rebbe Yitzhak Kaduri," accessed from a link at http://rabbikaduri.blogspot.com/.
11. This would be his second wife. Rabbi Kaduri's first wife, Rabbanit Sara, died in 1989. He remarried in 1993 to Rabbanit Dorit, a *baalat teshuva* who was just over half his age. The term *baal teshuva*, from the Talmud, literally means "master of repentance." The term is used to refer to a worldwide phenomenon among the Jewish people in which they are embracing Orthodox Judaism. The Baal

Teshuva movement is the return of secular Jews to religious Judaism (*Wikipedia*, http://en.wikipedia.org/wiki/Baal_teshuva; http://en.wikipedia.org/wiki/Baal _teshuva_movement). According to author Lisa Aiken, "Since the baal teshuva movement began in the 1960s, tens of thousands of Jews have become observant. The movement's effects were [greatly] noticeable by the 1980s." Lisa Aiken and Diane Ladderman, *The Baal Teshuva Survival Guide* (n.p.: Rossi Publications, 2009), 1.

12. Marciano, "Rabbi Kaduri Laid to Rest."
13. Ibid.

6: THE MYSTIFYING DEATH MESSAGE, *UNSEALED*

1. Quoted on the website of Shofar Be Tzion Ministries, http://www.shofarbetzion .com/01/RabbiYitzchakKaduri.html.
2. The preceding narrative is entirely fiction. It is a product of the author's imagination. However, according to many historical sources, the effect of Rabbi Kaduri's death message was profound and did produce such protestations as are reflected in the author's fictional account. See, for example, "Rabbi Kaduri Reveals Name of the Messiah," at the website of Yeshua Ha'Mashiach Ministries, April 30, 2007, http://www.yeshuahamashiach.org/Kaduri_names_Messiah.htm.
3. The bulk of the information and quotes in this chapter were derived from the *Israel Today* article posted on April 30, 2007. See intro., n. 3.
4. Tal Ilan, *Lexicon of Jewish Names in Late Antiquity Part I: Palestine 330 BCE–200 CE* (*Texte und Studien zum Antiken Judentum 91*) (Tübingen, Germany: J. C. B. Mohr, 2002), 129; David Stern, *Jewish New Testament Commentary* (Clarksville, MD: Jewish New Testament Publications, 1992), 4–5.

7: ISLAM, JESUS, MAHDI, AND THE ANTICHRIST

1. "Messiah Mystery Follows Death of Mystical Rabbi."
2. Ibid.
3. "Rabbi Reveals Name of the Messiah." See intro., n. 3. This quote can also be seen on the *Free Republic* website, at http://www.freerepublic.com/focus /f-news/1898697/posts.
4. "Messiah Mystery Follows Death of Mystical Rabbi."
5. Ahadith quotes sourced from Christopher Logan, "Islam 101: What Islam Really Says about Jesus and His Return," *Logan's Warnings* website, May 1, 2011, http:// loganswarning.com/2011/05/01/what-islam-really-says-about-jesus-and-his -return/.
6. "Jesus, Mahdi Both Coming, Says Iran's Ahmadinejad," WND, December 19, 2006, http://www.wnd.com/2006/12/39356/.
7. Posted by user NOTSOSUBTLE in response to the article titled "Rabbi Yitzhak Kaduri's AMAZING End Times PROPHECY of Ariel Sharon!" on the Bible Prophecy and Survival! Website, November 12, 2012, http://markofthetimes .com/rabbi-yitzhak-kaduris-amazing-end-times-prophecy-of-ariel-sharon/.

8. Joel Richardson, in an interview with the author in April 2013. Richardson is the *New York Times* best-selling author of *The Islamic Antichrist: The Shocking Truth about the Real Nature of the Beast* and *The Mideast Beast: The Scriptural Case for an Islamic Antichrist*; coauthor of *God's War on Terror: Islam, Prophecy and the Bible*, and coeditor of *Why We Left Islam: Former Muslims Speak Out*. Joel is also an internationally recognized speaker and expert on Bible prophecy and the Middle East. He is a regular columnist at WND, a human rights activist, and is deeply committed to the pro-life and adoption movements. His website is www .joels-trumpet.com.

8: THE LION OF GOD, THE KING OF ISRAEL, AND THE BUTCHER OF BEIRUT

1. Ariel Sharon, with David Chanoff, *Warrior: The Autobiography of Ariel Sharon* (New York: Simon & Schuster, 2001), 543.
2. The preceding narrative was written in fictional fashion, yet it encompasses the facts presented in the web book *Ariel Sharon Life Story: A Biography*, in the chapter titled "1928–1947 Childhood and Youth of Ariel Sharon," http://www .ariel-sharon-life-story.com/01-Ariel-Sharon-Biography-1928-1947-Childhood -and-Youth.shtml.
3. Ilan Marciano, "Rabbi Kaduri in Serious Condition," *ynetnews*, January 16, 2006, http://www.ynetnews.com/articles/0,7340,L-3200573,00.html.
4. *Encyclopaedia Britannica*, s.v. "Ariel Sharon," http://www.britannica.com /EBchecked/topic/538892/Ariel-Sharon.
5. Paul Monk, "The Biblio File: 'Arik: King of Israel,'" AIJAC, July 30, 2102, http:// www.aijac.org.au/news/article/the-biblio-file-arik-king-of-israel.
6. Answers Corporation, "What Is the Hebrew Word for Lion?" http://wiki.answers .com/Q/What_is_the_Hebrew_word_for_lion.
7. Michael Kramer, "Israel's Man of War," *New York* magazine, August 9, 1982, 19–24.
8. Ibid.
9. *Wikipedia*, s.v. "Ariel Sharon," https://en.wikipedia.org/wiki/Ariel_Sharon.
10. "Sharon Victory: An Arab Nightmare," BBC News, February 6, 2001.
11. Ze'ev Schiff and Ehud Ya'ari, *Israel's Lebanon War* (New York: Simon & Schuster, 1984), 283–84.

12. "Report of the Commission of Inquiry into the events at the refugee camps in Beirut—8 February 1983," Israel Ministry of Foreign Affairs, February 8, 1983. Retrieved April 2013, http://www.mfa.gov.il/mfa/foreignpolicy/mfadocuments /yearbook6/pages/104%20report%20of%20the%20commission%20of%20 inquiry%20into%20the%20e.aspx.
13. *Wikipedia*, s.v. "Ariel Sharon."
14. Uri Dan, *Ariel Sharon: An Intimate Portrait* (New York: Palgrave Macmillan, 2007), 59, 61.

9: ARIEL SHARON'S COMA—A JUDGMENT FROM GOD?

1. Ophir Bar-Zohar, "Israeli Campaign: Ariel Sharon's Stroke Was 'curse of Gaza disengagement,'" Haaretz, December 22, 2011, http://www.haaretz.com/print -edition/news/israeli-campaign-ariel-sharon-s-stroke-was-curse-of-gaza -disengagement-1.402829.
2. "Ariel Sharon," http://sharon-ariel.blogspot.com/2008/06/tribe-of-dan-shows-way .html.
3. *Wikipedia*, s.v. "Gush Katif," http://en.wikipedia.org/wiki/Gush_Katif.
4. "Ariel Sharon Mistakenly Declared Dead," *Look Up!*, November 7, 2011, http:// lookup.upway.com/?p=1769.
5. Aaron Klein, "Sharon Targeted with Death Curse," WND, July 26, 2005, http:// www.wnd.com/2005/07/31479/.
6. "Prime Minister Sharon Addresses the Nation" (transcript), Israel Ministry of Foreign Affairs, August 15, 2005, http://www.mfa.gov.il/MFA/Government/Spe eches+by+Israeli+leaders/2005/PM+Sharon+addresses+the+nation+15-Aug-2005 .htm.
7. Ronen Bodoni, "Sharon's Last Interview," *ynetnews*, January 6, 2006, http://www .ynetnews.com/articles/0,7340,L-3196291,00.html.

10: BITTER IRONIES, STUNNING CONNECTIONS

1. Paul Monk, "The Biblio File: 'Arik: King of Israel,'" AIJAC, July 30, 2102, http:// www.aijac.org.au/news/article/the-biblio-file-arik-king-of-israel.
2. James Bennet, "History Interrupted," *New York Times*, January 8, 2006, http:// www.nytimes.com/2006/01/08/weekinreview/08bennet.html?pagewanted =all&_r=0. Emphasis added.
3. From the publication *Or Elyon*, Gilyon no. 23, Cheshvan 5772, http://www .chabadtalk.com/forum/showthread.php3?t=12658. No longer accessible. A version of the same quote can be seen at *Yeranen Yaakov* (blog), http://yeranenyaakov .blogspot.com/2011/11/rav-kaduri-ztvkl-told-his-havruta-when.html.
4. Ashley Fantz and Jethro Mullen, "'Significant Brain Activity' in Comatose Ariel Sharon," CNN, January 28, 2013, http://www.cnn.com/2013/01/28/world /meast/israel-sharon-brain-activity/index.html.

11: ARIEL SHARON—THE ANTICHRIST?

1. David R. Reagan, "The Antichrist: Will He Be a Muslim?" Lamb & Lion Ministries, http://lamblion.com/articles/articles_islam4.php. Used by permission . Permission transmitted from Dr. Reagan in email dated 5-28-2013.
2. Simon McGregor-Wood, "Ariel Sharon: Still Alive—but Only Just," ABC News, October 27, 2008, http://abcnews.go.com/International /story?id=6118826&page=1.

12: THE SHARON/KADURI ZIONISM CONNECTION

1. "Jews against Zionism—Rightly Dividing the Word," rightlydividingtheword .com/articles/jewszionism.html. No longer accessible.
2. True Torah Jews against Zionism, http://www.truetorahjews.org/zionism.
3. You can read this article at http://www.truetorahjews.org/danger.
4. Christians United for Israel, http://www.cufi.org/site/PageServer.
5. "Beulah Land," words by Edgar Page Stites, music by John R. Sweney. This well-known gospel hymn, written in the 1800s, was based on Isaiah 62:4.
6. Strong's Hebrew dictionary #6725. As displayed in the computer Bible study program PC Study Bible, copyright 1993–1998, Biblesoft – Version 2.11, February 1998.
7. Roseanne Colletti, "Sarah Palin Dons Star of David Necklace for NYC Visit," MSNBC, June 2, 2011, http://www.nbcnewyork.com/news/local/SARAH -PALINS-STAR-122981193.html.
8. Words: Isaac Watts, Hymns and Spiritual Songs, 1707; refrain by Robert Lowry . Music: Robert Lowry, 1867.
9. Marciano, "Rabbi Kaduri in Serious Condition."
10. Marciano, "Rabbi Kaduri Laid to Rest."

13: WHO IS KADURI'S MESSIAH—*REALLY*?

1. "Handwriting Analysis of Rav Kaduri's Note," *Parshablog*, February 7, 2007, http://parsha.blogspot.com/2007/02/handwriting-analysis-of-rav-kaduris.html.
2. W. E. Henley, ed., *The English Bible*, the Tudor translations, vol. 6 (David Nutt), 144.

14: PROPHETIC UTTERANCES OR A MESSIANIC MESS?

1. "Messiah Mystery Follows Death of Mystical Rabbi."
2. Gordon, "Kabbalist Urges Jews to Israel Ahead of Upcoming Disasters."
3. Jewish Encyclopedia, s.v. "Magen Dawid," http://www.jewishencyclopedia.com /articles/10257-magen-dawid.
4. Gordon, "Leading Kabbalist Urges Jews to Israel."
5. Ibid.
6. Ibid.
7. Gordon, "Kabbalist Urges Jews to Israel Ahead of Upcoming Disasters."
8. From the publication *Ohr Elyon*, Gilyon no. 23, Cheshvan 5772, http://www .chabadtalk.com/forum/showthread.php3?t=12658, accessed May 6, 2013.
9. "Messiah Mystery Follows Death of Mystical Rabbi."
10. Ibid.
11. "Redemption from Rav Kaduri, z'sl," *Dreaming of Moshiach* (blog), September 3, 2007, http://dreamingofmoshiach.blogspot.com/2007/09/redemption-from-rav -kaduri-zsl.html.

15: WHO IS LOOKING FOR A MESSIAH?

1. "Iran Leader's Messianic End-Times Mission: Ahmadinejad Raises Concerns with Mystical Visions," WND, January 6, 2006, http://www.wnd.com/2006/01/34221/.
2. There are two predominant denominations within the Islamic faith: *Shia* Islam and *Sunni* Islam. There are several notable differences between their doctrinal stances, the largest probably being their respective views of Islamic leadership. The Shiites believe that only a direct, blood descendant of Muhammad should rule. Sunnis believe only a descendant of the original Caliphate (governing council—hand-picked by Muhammad) should rule. Thus, there has been a major power struggle within Islam for many hundreds of years.
3. "Iran Leader's Messianic End-Times Mission."
4. I. Q. Al-Rassooli, e-mail message to author with permission to reprint, March 9, 2013. I. Q.'s website is http://www.alrassooli.com.
5. Reza Kahlili, "Chavez: Mahdi Come Sooner!" WND, March 9, 2013, http://www.wnd.com/2013/03/chavez-mahdi-come-sooner-rush-now-come-sooner/#PXAb7KKL6PHQdm1A.99.
6. "Messiah Mystery Follows Death of Mystical Rabbi."

16: THE JEWISH MESSIAH: ARE THERE TWO?

1. *Wikipedia*, s.v. "Messiah ben Joseph," http://en.wikipedia.org/wiki/Messiah_ben_Joseph#cite_ref-schochet_moshiah_ben_yossef_2-0.
2. D. C. Mitchell, "Messiah ben Joseph: A Sacrifice of Atonement for Israel," *Review of Rabbinic Judaism* 10 (2007).
3. Posted by user Anglojew, on the thread "Ask a Jewish Zionist Freemason Anything," on the European Cultural Community The Apricity, at http://www.theapricity.com/forum/showthread.php?64734-Ask-a-Jewish-Zionist-Freemason-anything/page6.
4. John J. Parsons, "Mashiach ben Joseph: Joseph as a Type of the Messiah," Hebrew 4 Christians, http://www.hebrew4christians.com/Articles/Mashiach_ben_Yosef mashiach_ben_yosef.html. (Parsons writes the Hebrew Lesson column for the Zola Levitt Ministries newsletter.)
5. Jews for Judaism, http://www.jewsforjudaism.ca/resources-info/the-jewish-messiah.

17: ZOHAR, THE CHRIST, AND THE ANTICHRIST

1. Stephen Yulish (former professor at the University of Arizona), "Is Kabbalistic Rabbi Kaduri's Yeshua (Jesus) Really An Antichrist?" Dubroom, http://dubroom.org/articles/342.htm, p. 3 (342c).

2.   The information in this section is taken from *Wikipedia*, s.v. "Zohar," http://
      en.wikipedia.org/wiki/Zohar; Sol Scharfstein, *Jewish History and You II* (Jersey
      City, NJ: KTAV, 2004), 24; and http://en.wikipedia.org/wiki/Oral_Torah;
      Howard Schwartz, *Tree of Souls: The Mythology of Judaism* (Oxford University
      Press, 2004), iv.
3.   Quoted from the article "Two Jewish Mashiachs (Messiahs)," in paragraph 480
      under the heading "Zohar Volume 3 Vaera 34 'Signs Heralding Mashiach'" at the
      website of Discovering Islam, http://www.discoveringislam.org/jewish_messiahs
      .htm.
4.   *Petrus Romanus: The Final Pope Is Here*, "Book Description," Amazon, http://
      www.amazon.com/Petrus-Romanus-Final-Pope-Here/dp/0984825614.
5.   The following web address was referenced in the original article as the site on
      which Kaduri's followers supposedly called his Messiah *Jesus the Christ*: http://
      rabbiyeshuaswisdom.wordpress.com/2007/02/12/the-rebbes-name-is-the
      -revealed-name-of-mashiach. The site has since been deleted by the authors.
6.   Stephen Yulish, "Kabbalah, Satan and Me," Hearken the Watchmen, October 17,
      2011, http://www.hearkenthewatchmen.com/article.asp?id=635.

18: CHRISTIANS OUT OF JEWS?

1.   The Law of Return is Israeli legislation, passed on July 5, 1950, that gives Jews
      the right of return and settlement in Israel and the right to gain full citizenship.
2.   *Wikipedia*, s.v. "Messianic Judaism," http://en.wikipedia.org/wiki/Messianic
      _Judaism.
3.   Shraga Simmons, "Why Jews Don't Believe in Jesus," Aish.com, http://www.aish
      .com/jw/s/48892792.html.
4.   http://www.bethadonai.com/FAQ_number_jewish_believers.html.
5.   Evangelical Movement On The Rise, http://www.jewsforjudaism.org/index
      .php?option=com_content&view=article&id=268:evangelical-movement-on-the
      -rise&catid=110.
6.   Richard Allen Greene, "Jews Reclaim Jesus as One of Their Own," *CNN Belief
      Blog*, April 5, 2012, http://religion.blogs.cnn.com/2012/04/05/jews-reclaim-jesus
      -as-one-of-their-own/.
7.   *The Harbinger* (Lake Mary, FL: Frontline/Charisma House Book Group, 2012)
      stayed on the *New York Times* best-seller list longer than any other title. Cahn is
      also the inspiration for *The Isaiah 9:10 Judgment*, the number 1 faith movie of
      2012, produced by WND Films.
8.   Jonathan Cahn, e-mail message to author, March 8, 2013.
9.   Tim LaHaye, e-mail message to author, March 22, 2013. Used with permission.
10.   "Rabbi Kaduri Student Saved. www.messiahofisraelministries.org" (video), Youtube,
      http://www.youtube.com/watch?feature=player_embedded&v=zIldXZcs8pg#!.
      Note: As an added measure of caution and integrity, I downloaded this video and
      have archived it in my digital files in case it ever disappears from YouTube, or if I
      am ever called into question concerning my reporting of the video in this book.

11. Yad L'Achim was established in 1950 to help new immigrants adjust to the newly born country of Israel and to help them find a suitable religious framework. It is a nonprofit organization claiming no political affiliation.

12. Miriam Woelke, "Messianic 'Jews' and Their RABBI KADURI Lie," *Shearim* (blog), December 18, 2012, http://meashearim.wordpress.com/2012/12/18/messianic-jews-and-their-rabbi-kaduri-lie/.

13. Ibid.

14. William Pike, "Moishe ("Jews for Jesus") Rosen: A Messianic Jew Meets His Maker," *Encyclopedia Britannica Blog*, May 31, 2010, http://www.britannica.com/blogs/2010/05/moishe-rosen-a-messianic-jew-meets-his-maker/.

15. Ibid.

16. Greene, "Jews Reclaim Jesus as One of Their Own."

19: THE ENDTIMES?

1. Charles M. Schulz, *Conversations (Conversations with Comic Artists)* (Jackson: University Press of Mississippi, 2000), 114–15.

2. "Ariel Sharon Mistakenly Declared Dead."

3. Some Bible teachers claim that Islam is not a truly monotheistic faith system because in its earliest roots the religion featured a belief in a multiplicity of "gods."

4. Schulz, *Conversations*, 114.

5. All quotes from Dr. Reagan in this chapter were provided in email format in April 2013. Dr. David Reagan is the founder and president of Lamb & Lion Ministries in Dallas, Texas; host of the weekly television show *Christ in Prophecy*; and editor and publisher of *Lamplighter* magazine. Dr. Reagan is a nationally recognized and highly sought-after preacher and teacher on matters of biblical prophecy. Dr. Reagan's website is www.lamblion.com.

6. All quotes from Joel Richardson in this chapter were provided in email format in April 2013. Joel Richardson is the *New York Times* best-selling author of *Islamic Antichrist: The Shocking Truth about the Real Nature of the Beast*, and an internationally recognized speaker and expert on Bible prophecy and the Middle East.

20: THE STORY ENDS, THE STORY BEGINS

1. "Who Is Sephardic Orthodox Rebbe Yitzhak Kaduri," accessed from a link at http://rabbikaduri.blogspot.com/.

2. *Rav Yitzhak Kaduri*, sample chapter, http://www.sephardiclegacy.com/wp-content/uploads/2012/08/Sample-Chapter-R-Yitzhak-Kaduri.pdf, p. 276 from original.

3. Ibid., 281–82 of original.

4. The entire story of Rabbi Zion in this chapter is adapted from "Rabbi Daniel Zion," *Lamplighter* magazine, November–December 2010, 12–13, http://www.lamblion.com/xfiles/publications/magazines/Lamplighter_NovDec10_VirginBirth.pdf.

5. Simmons, "Why Jews Don't Believe in Jesus."

GLOSSARY

Adonai (Hebrew)—Adonai is the verbal parallel to Yahweh. Adonai is plural. The singular form of the word is *adon*. When referring to God the plural Adonai is employed. When the singular adon is used, it almost always refers to a human lord or master.

Ahadith (Arabic)—Plural of Hadith.

Am (Hebrew)—"The people."

Amulet—Usually necklaces, with writings of blessing or charms inscribed upon them, believed by many to bring healing and success.

Beulah (Hebrew)—"Land of marriage" or "married woman." Found once in the Old Testament. Isaiah 62:4.

Chezkat (Hebrew)—"Candidate or presumed." As in the Hebrew concept of the Chezkat Mashiach.

Christians United for Israel (CUFI)—The largest pro-Israel organization in the United States.

Dybbuk (Jewish Mysticism)—Said to be a lost soul that has strayed into the body of an unfortunate living person in order to torment that person.

Eretz Israel (Hebrew)—"The Land of Israel."

Hadith—The Islamic authoritative teachings or the sayings of Muhammad.

Haredi—The most theologically conservative streams of Orthodox Judaism. Haredim (plural) view themselves as the most religiously authentic group of Jews.

Hashem—(Hebrew)—The word many pious Jews use instead of the YAHWEH name, in casual conversations, which literally means The Name.

Hasidic Judaism or Hasidism—A branch of Orthodox Judaism that promotes spirituality through the popularization and internalization of Jewish mysticism as the fundamental aspect of the faith.

Hoshana Rabba—The seventh day of the Jewish holiday of Sukkoth (Feast of Booths or Feast of Tabernacles), 21st day of Tishrei, is known as Hoshana Rabbah. This day is marked by a special synagogue service.

Imam—The Imam for Sunni Muslims is the one who leads Islamic formal prayers. In the Shi'a sect, Imams have a meaning more central to belief, referring to leaders of the community.

Kabbalah—Kabbalah is a set of esoteric and mystical teachings meant to explain the deeper meanings of the Hebrew Scriptures.

Kadima party—A centrist and liberal political party in Israel. It was established on November 24, 2005, by moderates from the Likud party.

Karaite Judaism—A form of Judaism that does not acknowledge the oral law as a divine authority nor the Rabbinic procedures that are commonly employed to interpret Jewish scripture. Karaite Jews hold only to the Torah (the first five books of the Old Testament) as being the Word from God.

Kittel—A white robe worn over the clothing during a Yom Kippur service. Because it is similar to the burial shroud, it serves to remind the wearer of man's mortality and the need for *teshuvah* (repentance). The kittel must not be decorated with gold—this is because gold recalls the sin of the golden calf of idolatry formed in the Wilderness Journey.

Kohen Gadol (Hebrew)—"High priest."

Law of Return—Israeli legislation, passed on July 5, 1950, gave Jews the right of return and the right to live in Israel and to gain citizenship.

Likud party—A predominantly right-wing Israeli political party founded by Menachem Begin. Sometimes this party was in alliance with the Shas Party.

Lubavitch—The name "Lubavitch" is taken from the name of the Russian village Lyubavichi where the Lubavitch movement's leaders lived for over one hundred years. The name "Lyubavichi" means "Town of Love."

Lubavitch movement—A large missionary Hasidic movement known for their emphasis on religious study seeking wisdom and knowledge.

Magen David—Magen is the Hebrew word for "shield." Magen David is the emblem of the Shield or Star of David.

Mahdi—The Rightly Guided or Redeemer. The title of the Muslim "messiah."

Maitreya—The title of the enlightened one for whom the Buddhists are looking.

Mashiach (Hebrew)—"Messiah."

Messiah ben David and Messiah ben Joseph—Jewish tradition speaks of two separate redeemers, both called Mashiach. The two are involved in ushering in the Messianic age. They are called Mashiach ben David and Mashiach ben Joseph. Messiah ben Joseph will act as a precursor to Messiah ben David (the ultimate exalted Messiah) and will prepare the world for the coming of the final redeemer and savior of Israel.

Messianic Judaism —The term generally used to describe Jews who have proclaimed that Jesus of Nazareth, of New Testament record, is the only and true Messiah.

Mincha—The afternoon prayer service in Judaism. The name "Mincha" is derived from the meal offering that accompanied each sacrifice.

Mitzvoth (Hebrew)—"Keeping of the Jewish law."

Mizrahi Haredi—Mizrahi are Jews descended from the Jewish communities of the Babylonian era in the Middle East. The Haredi sect of Judaism is the most conservative form of Orthodox Judaism, often referred to, by those outside the Hebrew faith, as ultra-Orthodox.

Occultation (Arabic concept)—"Hidden." In the Shi'a sect of Islam the word refers to a belief that the messianic figure, or Mahdi, the infallible male descendant of the founder of Islam (Muhammad), was born but disappeared, and will one day return to fill the world with justice.

Orthodox Judaism—Also known as Torah Judaism, is the approach to a deeply devout Judaism, which adheres to the interpretation and application of the laws and ethics of the Torah as legislated by the Sanhedrin in the Talmudic texts.

Pharisees – The Pharisees were at various times a political party, a social movement, and a religious school of thought among Jews during the Second Temple period. They were known as the "party of the synagogue."

Pulsa Dinura [also Pulsa Denura] (Aramaic) —"Lashings of fire." A kabbalistic curse calling for the torment and ultimate death of the pronounced victim.

Rabbi (Hebrew)—"Teacher" or "master."

Rabbinical Judaism—Grew out of Pharisaic Judaism of New Testament fame. Rabbinic Judaism became the predominant Hebraic religious thought between the 2nd and 6th centuries. The oral law and the Talmud became the authoritative interpretation of Jewish scripture. Rabbinic Judaism encouraged the practice of Judaism in the absence of Temple sacrifice and other practices, which were no longer possible. Rabbinic Judaism is based on the teaching that at Mount Sinai, Moses directly received from God the Torah (The Law—the first five books of the Old Testament) as well as additional oral explanation of the revelation he received. Rabbinic Judaism contrasts with Karaite Judaism, which does not acknowledge the oral law as a divine authority nor the rabbinic procedures that are commonly employed to interpret Jewish scripture.

Rebbe (Yiddish)—"Master, teacher, or mentor." Derived from the Hebrew word Rabbi.

The Sadducees (Hebrew)— A sect of Jews that were active in Judea during the Second Temple period. They were identified mainly with the upper social and economic classes of Judean society. The Sadducees fulfilled various political, social, and religious roles, including maintaining the Temple. (See Sanhedrin Council)

Sanhedrin Council—An assembly of twenty to twenty-three men appointed in every city in the biblical Land of Israel. This court dealt only with religious matters. The Sanhedrin was governed by the Kohen Gadol or the High Priest. It was also made up of a vice chief justice and sixty-nine general members. The Sanhedrin is mentioned in the Gospels in relation to the trial of Jesus and several times in the Acts of the Apostles, including chapter 5 where Gamaliel appeared, and in the stoning death of Stephen the deacon in chapter 7. The Sanhedrin Council was made up of both Sadducees and Pharisees.

Saoshyant—The name of the Zoroastrianism "expected one."

Sefarim—Sefer in Hebrew means any kind of "book." The plural of the word is sefarim. It is derived from the same Hebrew root-word as sofer (scribe), sifriyah (library), and safrut (literature). Among Orthodox Jews it is used for books of the Tanakh, the oral law, or any work of Rabbinic literature.

Sephardi rabbis—Refers to the rabbis who are descendants of Jewish settlers, originally from the Near East, who lived in the Iberian Peninsula until the Spanish Inquisition. The term may also apply to those who use a Sephardic (Spanish) style of liturgy, or would otherwise define themselves in terms of Jewish customs and traditions originating from the Iberian Peninsula.

Shalom (Hebrew)—"Peace."

Shamayim (Hebrew)—"Heaven."

Shas Party—The ultra-orthodox religious political party in Israel. Sometimes this party was in alliance with the Likud Party.

Shas Council of Torah Sages—The Shas party was formed under the leadership of former Israeli Chief Sephardi Rabbi Ovadia Yosef. Rabbi Yosef then established a four-member (which included himself) Council of Torah Sages. Yosef remains the party's spiritual leader today.

Shi'a and Sunni Islam—The two major denominations of Islam. Approximately 80 percent of the world's Muslims are Sunni—the remaining 10 to 20 percent are Shi'a. Shi'a comprises the majority populations of Iran and Iraq. Pakistan is the largest Shi'a majority country in the world. The largest Sunni populations are in Southeast Asia, China, Africa, and the Arab World. Most Shi'as belong to the Twelvers tradition of Islam.

Star of David—Known in Hebrew as the Shield of David or the Magen David (Magen is the Hebrew word for "shield").

Sukkoth—Also called Feast of Tabernacles or Feast of Booths. Sukkoth begins on the 15th day of Tishri (in September or October), five days after Yom Kippur, the Day of Atonement. It is one of the three Pilgrim Festivals of the Hebrew Bible; the other two being the festivals of Passover and Pentecost.

Synagogue—Transliterated from the Greek. The word means "assembly." The common word for the Jewish gathering place for worship and scripture teaching.

Tallit—A Jewish prayer shawl. The tallit is worn over the outer clothes during the morning prayers and worn during all prayers on Yom Kippur.

Talmid hacham (Hebrew)—"Wise student of the Word of God."

Talmud—The central text of rabbinic Judaism. It is comprised of two important components, the *Mishnah* (the first written collection of Jewish oral law) and the *Gemara* (a massive elucidation upon the *Mishnah*, delving into all manner of Jewish life and practice.) The Talmud is often traditionally referred to as the *Shas*.

Torah—The first five books of the Old Testament. Also known as The Law or The Pentateuch.

Twelvers—The sect of Shiite Islam that believes the 12th Imam is the true and final ruler of Islam. They identify the 12th Imam as the Mahdi.

Twelfth Imam—In the Shi'a sect of Islam, the Mahdi is believed to be the 12th Imam (the twelfth ruling descendant from Muhammad) and the coming Islamic world ruler. Many Christians see a picture of the Biblical antichrist in the person of the Islamic Mahdi.

Tzaddikim (Hebrew)—A title given to personalities considered righteous in Jewish tradition.

Tzedah laderech (Hebrew)—"Food for the journey ahead."

Tzedakah (Hebrew)—"Charity."

Vilna Gaon—A Talmudist, kabbalist, and the foremost leader of non-Hasidic Jewry of the past several centuries. He is commonly referred to in Hebrew as ha-Gaon ha-Chasid mi-Vilna, "the saintly genius from Vilnius." He was often quoted by Rabbi Kaduri in Kaduri's endtime prophecies.

Yad L'Achim (Hebrew)—"Hand for brothers." A Jewish organization established in 1950 with the goal "to help new immigrants to the newly born country, and to help them find a suitable religious framework." It is primarily an antimissionary group devoted to preventing Christian evangelization in Israel and almost permanently in a heated dispute with the Israeli Messianic Jewish community.

Yarmulke—A skullcap worn principally by Orthodox and Conservative Jewish males in the synagogue and the home. The word is pronounced *yamaka*.

Yehoshua, or Yeshua (Hebrew)—Transliterated in English to— Jesus. The Hebrew words actually translate directly to English as Joshua. In the Romanized Greek of the early New Testament days, the term appeared as Iesus.

Yeshiva—An educational institution that focuses on the study of traditional religious texts, primarily the Talmud.

Yom Kippur (Day of Atonement)—Known as the highest of the holy feasts and holy days of Israel.

Z"l—An abbreviation for Hebrew zichrono livracha, which may be translated as "his/her memory for a blessing." It is commonplace in modern Judaism, when mentioning in writing the name of someone who has passed away, to add z"l after the person's name.

Zechut (Hebrew)—"Reward."

Zion—From the Hebrew word tsiyuwn, meaning "marker," "guidepost," or "sign."

Zionism—In the strictest sense a movement seeking to firmly reestablish the nation of Israel.

Zionism, Cultural—Focuses more on preserving the cultural aspects of ancient Jewish life rather than on establishing a particular nation-state.

Zionism, Christian—Christians who distinctly ascribe to, and passionately support, the existence of Israel as a nation. Many Christians see the term Zion as a euphemism for the Church, as well as for heaven, the dwelling place of the Lord. The term Zion is expressed as Sion in older English translations of the New Testament, such as the King James Version.

Zohar—The foundational mystical work in the literature of Kabbalah. Apparently Rabbi Kaduri was extremely familiar with and often quoted from this work. Zohar is a Hebrew word meaning "Radiance" or "Splendor." The Zohar is actually a collection of books that includes commentaries on the mystical aspects of the Torah. The collection incorporates various esoteric scriptural interpretations as well as additional material dealing with mysticism, mythical cosmology, and mystical psychology.

INDEX

SCRIPTURE INDEX

ABOUT THE AUTHOR

Carl Gallups is a bestselling author, evangelist, conference speaker, longtime conservative radio talk show host, and pastor. Carl has been the senior pastor of Hickory Hammock Baptist Church since 1987. Since that time, he has preached to tens of thousands of people on three continents.

He is a graduate of the Florida Police Academy, Florida State University (B.S.), and the New Orleans Baptist Theological Seminary (M.Div.), and served for many years as a member of the Board of Regents for the University of Mobile at Mobile, Alabama.

Before being called by the Lord into full-time ministry, Carl had a ten-year career in law enforcement, serving with the Florida Department of Corrections as an officer, and eventually as an administrator in Central Office. Carl also was a deputy sheriff with two different Florida sheriff's offices.

As a pastor, he has been the special guest speaker in the chapel services of the Southern Baptist Convention's Sunday School Board, New Orleans Baptist Theological Seminary, and the University of Mobile. Carl served for ten years as a national youth evangelist. By special invitation, Carl was also a featured speaker, along with Dr. Josh McDowell, at a "Right from Wrong" conference at the Ridgecrest Conference Center in Black Mountain, North Carolina.

Carl has been a talk radio host since 2002. He currently hosts the highly popular *Freedom Friday with Carl Gallups Show*, heard on 1330 WEBY AM out of Milton, Florida. The program broadcasts to four states along the Gulf Coast and has a large national and international audience by live stream on the Internet and in podcasts.

Carl is a popular guest commentator for radio interviews from coast to coast. He consistently appears in hundreds of markets through syndicated program interviews. Carl has appeared in several television interviews as well, including TBN, Atlanta Live, Christ in Prophecy TV, Creation Today TV, Coast Up Close TV, Dove TV, and the Richard Syrett Show out of Toronto, Canada.

An article about Carl and his Amazon.com (Science and Religion) bestselling book *The Magic Man in the Sky: Effectively Defending the Christian Faith*, (WND Books) appeared in a column in the *Washington Times*. The piece was written by columnist Jeff Kuhner who is also the host of the *Kuhner Report* on WRKO radio in Boston, Massachusetts.

Carl also produces contract videos and voice-over materials for several well-known online news sources. He is a published columnist for the PPSIMMONS syndicated Internet Blogspot, *The Santa Rosa Press Gazette*, and occasionally at WND.com. Millions around the world know his voice, commentary, and opinions.

Carl has been married to his wife, Pam, since 1973. They have a son, daughter-in-law, and grandson: Brandon, Hannah, and Parker.

CONTACT CARL GALLUPS ONLINE AT: WWW.CARLGALLUPS.COM

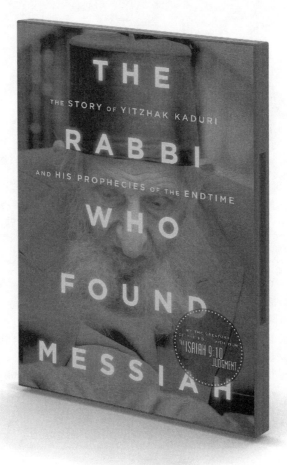

PRESENTS

WND FILMS TEACHING SERIES   VOLUME I

Cahn

BY THE CREATORS
OF THE NO. 1 FAITH FILM
THE ISAIAH 9:10
JUDGMENT.

RABBI JONATHAN CAHN

NEW YORK TIMES BESTSELLING AUTHOR OF *THE HARBINGER*

IN PARTNERSHIP WITH WND FILMS, MESSIANIC RABBI JONATHAN
CAHN IS RELEASING SOME OF HIS FINEST TEACHINGS,
DELIVERED AT CONFERENCES AND AT HIS OWN NEW JERSEY
CONGREGATION, THE BETH ISRAEL WORSHIP CENTER.

THREE DVD SET

PRESENTS

AMAZON'S NO. 1 FAITH MOVIE SINCE APRIL 2012

In this stunning documentary *The Isaiah 9:10 Judgment*, Rabbi Jonathan Cahn unravels the mystery behind this seemingly innocuous Biblical verse, and shows that ancient harbingers of judgment are now manifesting in America, just as they once did in Israel. This fascinating new DVD asks the question, "Is God sending America a prophetic message of what will soon be?" and Cahn provides the answers through mounting evidence that the answer is 'yes.'